TRANSitions.
Transdisciplinary, Transmedial and Transnational
Cultural Studies
Transdisziplinäre, transmediale und transnationale
Studien zur Kultur

Volume / Band 5

Edited by / Herausgegeben von
Renata Dampc-Jarosz and / und Jadwiga Kita-Huber

Advisory Board / Wissenschaftlicher Beirat:
Lorella Bosco (University of Bari, Italy), Leszek Drong (University of Silesia, Poland), Elizabeth Duclos-Orsello (Salem State University, USA), Frank Ferguson (University of Ulster, Ireland), Odile Richard-Pauchet (University of Limoges, France), Monika Schmitz-Emans (University of Bochum, Germany), Władysław Witalisz (Jagiellonian University in Kraków, Poland)

The volumes of this series are peer-reviewed.
Die Bände dieser Reihe sind peer-reviewed.

Ryszard Bartnik / Leszek Drong /
Liliana Sikorska (eds.)

Reimagined Communities

Rewriting Nationalisms in
European Literary Discourses

With one figure

V&R unipress

Bibliographic information published by the Deutsche Nationalbibliothek
The Deutsche Nationalbibliothek lists this publication in the Deutsche Nationalbibliografie; detailed bibliographic data are available online: https://dnb.de.

The publication is co-financed by University of Silesia in Katowice and Adam Mickiewicz University in Poznań.

© 2023 by Brill | V&R unipress, Robert-Bosch-Breite 10, 37079 Göttingen, Germany,
an imprint of the Brill-Group
(Koninklijke Brill NV, Leiden, The Netherlands; Brill USA Inc., Boston MA, USA; Brill Asia Pte Ltd, Singapore; Brill Deutschland GmbH, Paderborn, Germany; Brill Österreich GmbH, Vienna, Austria)
Koninklijke Brill NV incorporates the imprints Brill, Brill Nijhoff, Brill Schöningh, Brill Fink, Brill mentis, Brill Wageningen Academic, Vandenhoeck & Ruprecht, Böhlau and V&R unipress.
All rights reserved. No part of this work may be reproduced or utilized in any form or by any means, electronic or mechanical, including photocopying, recording, or any information storage and retrieval system, without prior written permission from the publisher.

Cover image: iStock, ID:165623873, chuwy.
Printed and bound by CPI books GmbH, Birkstraße 10, 25917 Leck, Germany
Printed in the EU.

Vandenhoeck & Ruprecht Verlage | www.vandenhoeck-ruprecht-verlage.com

ISSN 2751-8345
ISBN 978-3-8471-1657-8

Contents

Ryszard Bartnik / Liliana Sikorska / Leszek Drong
Introduction: Nationalisms as Cultural Artefacts 7

Michael McAteer
From Protestant Ireland to Revolutionary Hungary: Nationalism and
Transnationalism in Samuel Ferguson 21

Paweł Meus
German nationalism in the interwar period from a borderland
perspective: Alfred Hein and his interpretation of the national
question 45

Leszek Drong
Denationalizing Upper Silesia in Szczepan Twardoch's Fiction 61

Richard Jorge
Questioning Identities in the Postmodern Nation: Memory, Past and
the Self in Claire Keegan's 'The Night of the Quicken Trees' 81

Frank Ferguson
Writing Around the State: Memory Cultures in Contemporary
Northern Irish Writing 103

Michaela Marková
The Battles we refuse to fight today become the hardships our children
must endure tomorrow: The ethno-political conflict and its legacy in
selected contemporary Northern Irish novels for children and YA 119

Thierry Robin
Borderline Troubles in *Resurrection Man* and *Breakfast on Pluto:*
Remembering Northern Ireland before the GFA 137

Liliana Sikorska
Vanquishing mirages: nations and nationalisms in Barry Unsworth's
The Rage of the Vulture and Orhan Pamuk's *Silent House* 163

Ryszard Bartnik
'A writer beyond borders on gross ethics-related negligence':
J. M. Coetzee, life-writing and a moral railing against the modern world's
maladies 193

Bio Notes 215

Ryszard Bartnik / Liliana Sikorska / Leszek Drong

Introduction: Nationalisms as Cultural Artefacts

The beginning of the 21st century has been described, over the last few years, as characterized by "an explosion of 'new nationalisms'" (Wertsch 2022, p. 454; see also Wertsch 2021, p. ix). For James Wertsch, memory and narrative are crucial elements in the construction of national myths and foundations of "imagined political communities" (Anderson 2006 [1983], p. 6). Benedict Anderson, in *Imagined communities*, his seminal work concerned directly with the origins of nationalism, identifies nationality and nationalism as "cultural artefacts of a particular kind" (2006, p. 4). Following in Anderson's footsteps and taking his notion of 'imagined communities' as a guiding light, the present volume is meant, in the first place, to explore the confluence of politics and imagination. By placing not only well known but also emerging socio-political concepts in a variety of literary contexts, we want to tease out the intricate interplay of literary imagination and the European political realities shaped by nationalism as an evolving concept which informs many basic assumptions about group identity, inclusivity, boundaries and state borders in the old continent.

European nationalism is a complex phenomenon with far-reaching effects on the continent's history, culture, and politics. Its offshoots include nationalist discourses used to create a unified sense of identity and to promote the economic interests of a particular nation-state. While this book and this introduction do not focus on the historical development of nationalism, two contextual frameworks should nonetheless be remarked on to illustrate its dichotomous nature. Simply put, the roots of European nationalism can be found in the era of the French Revolution, which "excited successive ethnic groups", driven by the desire for liberation, self-determination, the need for national unity, "aspir[ing] to become independent nations" (Smith 2008, p. 2); unfortunately, all of the above was also accompanied by an advancing sense of the superiority of one nation over another. This tendency was further strengthened in the nineteenth century, when nationalist discourses of the time were used to justify imperial expansion and the oppression of 'peripheral' populations.¹

In contrast, the authors of this book offer an alternate view, where neither national self-determination nor imperial expansionism matter as much as deconstructing the ways these discourses operate to enhance a sense of collective identity and national pride, particularly among people of entrenched mindsets. By promoting a sentiment of separateness, such discourses help to forge a unified front of national identity while legitimizing the exclusion of *the other* from the confines of a given collectivity. As Giorgio Agamben wrote, it is in this approach that the life of *any groups* defined outside community frames is eventually deemed "politically irrelevant" and, as such, within the structures of *one* state or nation, becomes "freely" disposable, "may be arrested, imprisoned, [...] placed outside the law" (1998, p. 123, 139). Given the above, a critical analysis of similar narratives seems of utmost importance.

There is no denying that the logic of nationalism carries significant threats, traces of which are not difficult to find in European history over the last hundred years. The question we must ask ourselves is whether we are currently seeing a return to such fundamentalist – and thus quintessentially negative – thinking? If so, what is our attitude towards it? Furthermore, it is essential to inquire whether, at the beginning of the twenty-first century, there is any sense of a larger community whatsoever that is both premised on and indicative of European values? Most evidently, the onus lies on both writers and academics to understand the concept of Europeanness; to determine which European contexts they deem to be valid for debate; to contemplate the adjective 'European' in terms of whether it should be interpreted more broadly, so as not to limit Europeanness to a strictly geographic region, thus be able to evaluate the matter of shared values with reference to a global framework. Consequently, we assign those writers whom we wish to associate with the correspondingly construed European perspective an exceptional responsibility for accurately delineating potential restrictions associated with various applications of the logic of nationalism.

When Tony Judt asked in 1996 "how many Europes are there?" (2011, p. 45), he was not so much suggesting as stating that the division into the West, as more embedded in European values, and this *other* Europe, as permanently marked by the robustness of authoritarianism, was in fact undeniable and permanent.² On

---

1 Anthony Smith underscores the "assertion of the modernity of the nation [...] which rules out any rival definition of the nation, outside of modernity and the West" (2008, p. 14). According to Craig Calhoun, the processes of colonization had their own great dynamics; still, while consolidating new territories, Europeans had no intention of giving up on familiar national blueprints, as they required no further invention (1997, p. 23).
2 Judt hedges his bets against potential criticism by stating all sides have a "legitimate claim to the title [Europe], none with a monopoly." Yet, in the very next sentence, he concedes that

this conviction, he built his skepticism about the legitimacy of the enlargement of the European Union to the countries east of the river Elbe. It is not our aim to decide whether his diagnosis was correct, but it is worth noting that Judt drew a line of Europeanness, which he based on a binary opposition that precluded *the others* from reaching beyond the point of demarcation. In contrast to his assertions, Ann Rigney, in 2012, positioned herself differently, describing "Europe" as a "fascinating" concept, "an actual and imagined frame that occupies an intermediary position between the regional and the world", the essence of which is its "polyvalence" (2012, p. 610, 619). According to Rigney, the narrative of contemporary Europe is complex and multi-threaded, shaped by such motives as "resistance to fascism", "rejection of racism", or defense of democracy and "democratic principles" (2012, p. 612). Interestingly, writing almost two decades after Judt, she does not mention the negative divisions[3] which Judt had outlined so compellingly.

On the other hand, one should not be naively optimistic about the lack of divisions in the European realm. In recent years, it has been hard not to notice that the implementation of the motto of the European Union – "United in diversity", about which Solà and McMartin write in their article – has been subjected to a difficult test.[4] As can be observed, upholding shared values often turns out to be an abstract concept, and cultivating a democratic accord, as Anne Applebaum argues, gives way to attempts to silence *others*. According to her, "democracy itself has always been loud and raucous, but when its rules are followed, it eventually creates consensus." Unfortunately, as Applebaum adds, "the modern debate [...] inspires in some people the desire to forcibly silence *the rest*" (2020, p. 117) [emphasis added]. From here, it is only a step to sacrificing Europeanness and European values on the altar of a poorly-defined national (re)integration. John Clarke draws attention to the increasingly resonant tendency among various European populations to appeal to closed national make-ups in order to ensure, "in nationalist terms", development and "welfare [...] for 'our people'" (2021, p. 99). In such a space, the key, and perhaps the only

---

there are those "countries [...] that have for a long time been Europe", and there are *the other* lands, which are "in the implied process of becoming" (2011, p. 60).

3 The above statements of Rigney also have an impact on the literary field, if compared with the comments contained in the article 'The European Union Prize for Literature: Disseminating European values through translation and supranational consecration' by Núria Codina Solà and Jack McMartin. They emphasize the fact that "the linguistic and geographic borders of European literature have expanded to accommodate Europe's less dominant literary traditions, including those of nations situated at the periphery of the EU" (2022, p. 343).

4 In their article (Solà / McMartin 2022), we will find a reference to the official EU website, where we can read that the aforementioned motto means, inter alia, "being enriched by the continent's many diverse cultures, traditions, and languages" (https://european-union.europa.eu/principles-countries-history/symbols/eu-motto_en, date of access: 20.04.2023).

question, to ask, as phrased by Neil Young, concerns "whose nation" one has in mind. As he underlines, to reveal "the hypocrisies and double standards of 'state speak'" needs to be done "not least in the interests of pluralism" (2020, p. 279). Otherwise, selling a unitary national representation that does not allow for *other* people or groups to be included is the only option, leaving no room for diversity.

Nationalist discourse cannot be left unanalyzed, lest – perhaps unexpectedly for many Europeans – it should break out onto the stage more forcefully to become a basic tool for shaping public opinion. As noted by Eric Kaufmann, nationalist frames can be delineated not only vertically,[5] but also horizontally. In the latter case, the point of reference is not the pre-imposed, elitist legal definition of what is considered national, but rather the so-called "wisdom of crowds" weighed in by the populace. Nationalisms, in this case, are to be practiced from below, as if from various sources, "emerging from the interaction of individuals, groups and institutions." Kaufmann particularly underlines the individual dynamic in this regard, calling it "personal nationalism", which can also be reflected in literary productions (2017, p. 7, 19). When under its spell, literary discourse might, inadvertently, gear towards a "myopic"[6] sense of national integrity, with more walls being erected in the hope that this will allow representatives of a given nation to protect themselves against any external threats.

In this volume, scholars, as if guided by Orwell's principle of "unbiased criticism",[7] attempt to deconstruct some of the basic assumptions of the national perspective as outlined above. Their goal is to take a critical look at selected authors who understand the paradigm adopted by Hannah Arendt, emphasizing the personal, though often "vicarious", "responsibility" of being part of a larger community, which goes beyond the narrow limits of nationhood and implies that "we live our lives not by ourselves but among our fellow men" (2003, p. 158). As Timothy Snyder rightly points out, the consequences of one's actions or omissions are the result of "the minor choices [one] make[s]" as they "are themselves a kind of vote [...]. In the politics of the everyday, our words and gestures, or their absence, count very much" (2017, p. 33). Such minor choices often manifest in ill-defined language, whereby statements that are seemingly aimed at strengthening community, e.g., the European one, actually contribute to strengthening centrifugal tendencies. An interesting example, albeit from a different register, is

---

5 If constituted vertically, "nations' symbolic corpus can be read off elite documents and pronouncements" (Kaufman 2017, p. 7).
6 This is the term proposed by Bruce Johansen. In his article, he refers to the words of Pope Francis, who spoke of the rise of "myopic, aggressive nationalism" (2021, p. ix).
7 Although in a different context, Orwell's words about putting oneself in a position "when one considers the difficulty of writing honest, unbiased criticism in a time like ours" still hold their weight (2020, p. 13).

provided by Ewa Kozerska, who, in her article 'Pope Francis on Europe', emphasized European diversity by invoking the Pope's words about "the correct [sic!] formula of Europe [as] 'the family of nations'" (2022, p. 253). By resorting to this type of wording, which validates national separateness, one (un)intentionally suggests the opposite of what was intended.[8] In this regard, it is worth counterbalancing it with an opinion of Glenn Paterson, who, in one of his essays on contemporary Northern Ireland, points to the instrumentalization of the very term 'community.' In his view, the more often this word is in use,[9] the more it denotes divisions along ethnic, religious, or national lines. Therefore, if we want to find a framework that binds together all the texts and analyses contained in this volume, it can be outlined by Young's understanding of "transnational experience", which implicates the validity of discourse beyond any "deployments of national or sectional tribalism" (2020, p. 266).

Referring to Rigney's formulation (2012, p. 614), this volume presents, in a sense, a "European metanarrative" which, in various approaches, attaches importance to non-tribal and non-sectarian communal mindsets based on shared (European) values. In the whole range of concepts, as key to the above context, a significant place then will be occupied by such fundamental notions as dignity, diversity, democracy, freedom, personal integrity, and morality.[10] According to Young, individuals/groups/communities/populations that do not isolate themselves from, and are willing to affirm these values become more important than homogenized nations,[11] and hence their perspective evolves towards "post-nationalist" positions. This does not mean that the national paradigm is negated, but rather that a new momentum is built when "the intersectionality of nations, suppressed in nationalist forms of nationhood, becomes undeniably visible" (Cörüt / Jorgenden 2021, p. xiii) and, as such, is highlighted as a more constructive approach.

With the adoption of common European values as our point of departure, it is clear that certain patterns of thought that contradict these values will be highlighted and subjected to critical judgment. It is impossible to define them within a

---

8 In this configuration, it is difficult to talk about consolidating the European project and strengthening European values; rather, as Kaufmann points out, we should speak of a "new nationalism" and "[t]he rise of the populist right in the West [...] emerging as [its] most discussed manifestation" (2019, p. 446).
9 On the one hand, as Patterson indicates, the "C-word" signifies "aggregation"; on the other hand, because of conflict-ridden narratives, "communities is a word that, rather than multiplying, as most plurals do, actually divides" (2015, p. 50).
10 Solà and McMartin are in agreement when stating that the above category of shared values "include human dignity, the right to life, the right to the integrity of a person and the right to liberty" (2022, p. 347).
11 This tendency towards uniformity of a given national group is often marked, as Young claims, by a peculiar "obsession with (fixed) identity" (2020, p. 272).

closed catalogue; yet we can concentrate on the more characteristic ones. Jade McGlynn, for example, draws attention to the negative sides of "hyper-exploitation" of national glorious pasts, which results in the falsification of one's own history, collective narcissism,[12] and ultimately hostility towards *other* communities. Johansen, quoting Pope Francis, echoes in turn the destructive effect of "aggressive, [self-centered] nationalism" (2021, p. ix) on democracy. This kind of inward-looking protectionism obviously has an impact on the structures of (collective) memory. In the context of possible confabulations of national identity, it is worth mentioning Orwell's observation. According to him (Orwell 2020 [1942], p. 33), in the case of narrative formations of nationhood, "truth[s]" are invariably accompanied by adjectives, the function of which is to be supportive in constructing a set of myths and symbols.[13] According to Appelbaum, this kind of myth-making practice, without "a nuanced past", becomes the basis of "nationalist political projects" (2020, p. 74). Young makes no bones about his conviction that, in such cases, we should not remain neutral and instead expose "pathological mythmaking and nationalism [as] counterposed to [...] a European narrative" (2020, p. 287).

There are alternative projects, to be sure, but it must be acknowledged that most of those receive their impetus from a critical thrust directed at sundry embodiments of the national(ist) paradigm. Thereby, such concepts as "countermemory" (Foucault 1980, p. 139), "subversive micronarratives" (Appadurai 1996, p. 10) or various versions of minority politics and regional identity projects continue feeding on the underlying notion that they seek to contest. This has led to the preponderance of what Kevin Robins calls "methodological nationalism" (2006, p. 260; see also Rigney 2022, p. 164), that is, a national lens through which we perceive groups, ethnicities, communities and their collective memories. What looks quite promising, instead, is a recent focus on 'regions of memory', particularly in a European context. Simon Lewis and Joanna Wawrzyniak, in their introduction to *Regions of Memory*, explain that the notion used in the title of their book is meant "to challenge further the dichotomy of national and cosmopolitan memory" (2022, p. 1). They also mention a transcultural dimension to recent research on regions of memory, involving regions as "conceptual spaces united by particular histories and cultures as well as by geo-

---

12 To illustrate the above words, McGlynn refers to an interesting, timely example of the Russian practice of 'strengthening' nationalistic feelings through "the state's visible involvement in 'love-for-the-country' activities, accompanied by the widespread depiction of images that appear to show ordinary people performing unextraordinary, everyday patriotic actions" (2022, p. 222).
13 As more than an astute writer, Orwell, already in the 1940s, heralded the danger of falsifying (national) discourse: "This prospect frightens me much more than bombs – and [...] that is not a frivolous statement" (2020, p. 34).

graphical elements" (p. 2). Rigney, in the same volume, insists that regional memory should be seen as a "multi-scalar and multi-sited process operating on uneven topographies" (2022, p. 164) which means, among other things, that it should be redescribed in "postnationalist terms" (p. 164). If we can envisage regions of memory as sites for the production of new cultural discourses that can shake off the shadows of national and nation-binding myths or, at the very least, rewrite them along significantly decentralized lines, there is considerable likelihood that regional foci may resurface, as an alternative to national ones, in critical debates all across Europe.[14]

The creation of national myths, as highlighted by Hayden White (1981), corresponds to a highly subjective, often politicized, if not downright negative narrativization of history. Rigney underlines that Europe is continuously narrativized. As she argues, when the tensions described above begin to resonate, it is impossible to count on the aforementioned transnational experience, where "fellow Europeans are 'others' as well as 'one of us', [...] both domestic and foreign, in an extension of identity frames that can be seen as enriching" rather than menacing. The problem is, as Rigney claims, that "various neonationalist movements illustrate [and] experience [such frames] as a threat" (2012, p. 609). And this is where literary discourse comes into play, to shed light on and – as underlined by Daniel Syrovy – be "read [...] along various power structures" (2021, p. 3). In other words, when dealing with the issues of nation and identity, literature should be more interested in informing than in experimenting. Hence, the selection of writers who understand perfectly well how destructive "self-serving ideologies", such as expansive nationalism, can be for "the guardrails of democracy" (Johansen 2021, p. viii). Theirs is a commitment to European values; and they are vigilant against any discourse, especially when overshadowed by nationalist rhetoric, containing keywords that suggest restrictions on the individual or the collective. In this role, a set of authors have been cast here as adherents to Arendt's words of warning (2003, p. 160) against false authorities who produce "stock phrases, clichés", and – by and large – thought-defying language, which becomes an instrument for distorting reality.

As has been argued before, nationalist sentiments are nurtured by the stories members of ethnic and religious communities recount to themselves. Richard Kearney's solution to the on-going disagreements between countries and nations could have been alleviated "[i]f warring nations were able to acknowledge their own and the other's narrative identities" so as to "be able to reimagine themselves

---

14 The final decades of the twentieth century and the first decade of the twenty-first century already saw a growing popularity of the idea of "a Europe of the regions" and "new regionalism" (Keating 2008, p. 630) but the process of overcoming nationalisms within the European Union was markedly decelerated in the second decade of the twenty-first century.

in new ways" (2002, p. 82). Fueled by supranational interests, the great nineteenth and twentieth-century movements such as Romanticism, The Spring of Nations and The Celtic Twilight gathered speed aided by the literature written during the said periods. Poets and writers alongside politicians assumed the positions of leaders, their words expressing the anxieties of subdued nations. Their voices became those of national consciences, guiding, or better inciting, their co-nationalists to strive for statehood. Even though the nineteenth and early twentieth century poets, dramatists and novelists frequently used distancing factors, anchoring their works in fictional, rather than non-fictional contexts, their patriotic endeavors, and brave evaluations of the political situations in the countries such as Ireland and Poland, became an integral part of the new approaches to nationalism. By analogy, for Kearney, the recounting of national myths is always connected with "the rectification that contemporary historians bring to bear on the historical accounts of their predecessors" (2002, p. 79). It is not coincidental that the fascination with one's cultural past fostered the new perception of national and individual identity. Literature offers us also a different kind of freedom, as Orhan Pamuk in *Other colours. Writing on life, art, books and cities*, explains, "[t]he history of the novel is a history of human liberation: By putting themselves in another's shoes, by using our imaginations to shed our identities, we are able to set ourselves free" (2008, p. 228f). Yet, as the writer further maintains, "[…] with the waning of the nineteenth-century novel, the world lost its unity and its meaning. As we set out to write novels today, all we have are fragments and more fragments" (2008, p. 288).

Be it the world as a whole, or the world in pieces, the importance of literary works in conjunction with cultural texts is pivotal in our reconsideration of the question of nationalism within the framework of 'imagined communities.' The nationalist narratives of common cultures bound by language and shared history have always been juxtaposed by the divisionary power of religious and cultural differences. What the beginning of the twenty-first century envisioned as cosmopolitanism, twenty years later was undermined by Brexit and the economic and nationalistic goals of other countries. Once again, a dream of inclusive pan-European nationalism was curtailed by the needs and rights of the member countries, and Turkey, which was knocking on Europe's doors since the end of the nineteenth century, was left out.[15] The processes of inclusion and exclusion play into the never-ending needs to re-imagine communities in order to understand the mechanisms governing their creation, maintenance and dis-

---

15 The whole quotation reads: "My novels are made from these dark materials, from this shame, this pride, this anger, and this sense of defeat. Because I come from a nation knocking on Europe's door, I am only too well aware of how easily these emotions of fragility can, from time to time, take flame and rage unchecked" (Pamuk 2008, p. 231).

solution. The present volume, therefore, responds to the on-going need to examine the revisions of history and its literary renditions, not only in the form of (political) novels but also poetry and non-fiction.

As it transpires, the nineteenth century poets were the beacons of freedom and national culture; their enthusiasm, however, was certainly not uncritical. To that effect, Michael McAteer's 'From Protestant Ireland to revolutionary Hungary: Nationalism and transnationalism in Samuel Ferguson' analyzes two works by the Irish poet and scholar Samuel Ferguson (1810–1886): 'A Dialogue between the Head and Heart of an Irish Protestant' (1833) and the poem 'Hungary' (1849), which appeared in 1833 and 1849, respectively. McAteer reads 'A Dialogue' in the context of the British legislative reforms of the late 1820s–early 1830s that strengthened the position of Catholicism in Ireland, arguing that 'Hungary' should be seen in the light of transnational features present in 'A Dialogue'. Even though 'Hungary' is clearly based on "poetic truth", by writing about Hungarian patriotism, Ferguson, an Ulster Protestant, succeeded in distancing himself from pro-independence discourses in 1840s Ireland. The chapter, tackling the issues of transnationalism, analyzes the manifold expressions of nationalism in nineteenth-century Ireland.

Paweł Meus's 'German nationalism in the interwar period from a borderland perspective: Alfred Hein and his interpretation of the national question' examines the trajectories of the nascent movements towards autonomy in ethnic communities. At first glance, the signing of the Treaty of Versailles in 1918 promised the establishment of a new order in the context of theories of nationhood, based on the definition of a nation's right to self-determination. Meus pinpoints, however, the problems connected with such a definition as present in the works of Alfred Hein (1894–1945) that offer an insightful interpretation of the national question.

Similar preoccupations make their appearance in the chapter by Leszek Drong, who, in his 'Denationalizing Upper Silesia in Szczepan Twardoch's fiction' analyzes the writer's Silesian novels: *Drach* (2014) *Pokora* (2020) and *Chołod* (2022). The hard-won independence and the establishment of the Second Polish Republic in 1918, the People's Republic of Poland in 1945 and the Republic of Poland in 1989, nonetheless left the borderline ethnic group of Silesians without the recognition of their minority status. Following the ruling of the Supreme Court in 2013, stating that Silesians do not hold an autonomous nationality notwithstanding their cultural and linguistic distinctiveness, Twardoch engaged in the discussion concerning nationalism. Drong's reading of Twardoch's Silesian novels in the context of the writer's scrutiny of the current ideas on the minorities' self-definition in Poland, brings to focus the discourses of nationalism and regionalism of Upper Silesia, ever present in the writer's works.

Frank Ferguson's 'Writing around the state: Memory cultures in contemporary Northern Irish writing' reads the poetry of the Northern Irish poet Gerald Dawe alongside Ulster Scottish poets, Steve Dornan and Al Millar, all growing up during the Troubles like Ferguson himself. Ferguson demonstrates how in their poetry, they repeatedly make an effort to move beyond the linguistic, political and cultural discourses of the state of Northern Ireland. All of them acknowledge the impact of religion on Irish writing, but instead of antagonizing the representatives of different religions and nationalist sentiments, they create a literature of inclusion.

Michaela Marková's chapter entitled 'The Battles we refuse to fight today become the hardships our children must endure tomorrow: The ethno-political conflict and its legacy in contemporary Northern Irish writing for/about children and YA' looks at the current state of a policy, which, following the Good Friday Agreement, was to if not annihilate, then at least to attenuate, the conflicts and divisions in Northern Ireland. Using the recent Ulster University report on the current state of the educational system in Northern Ireland, Marková analyzes Young Adult's fiction, such as Garreth Carr's *Lost dogs* (2010) and *The dadness of Ballydogs* (2010) as well as Sue Divin's debut novel *Guard your heart* (2020), alongside the collection of Lyra McKee's journalistic writing, *Lost, found, remembered* (2020). Analysing the politics and poetics of the narratives, all of the aforementioned texts reflect the unresolved issues of ideology, slogans and the language used in describing past conflicts and possible futures of the post-Brexit Northern Ireland.

Richard Jorge's 'Questioning identities in the postmodern nation: Memory, past and the self in Claire Keegan's 'The night of the quicken trees" analyzes the short story, published originally as the final story in the collection *Walk the blue fields* (2007). The narrative is unlike the other ones, as it is grounded in fairy tales and Irish lore. While Keegan shifts the boundaries between fact and legend, the realistic and the supernatural mode of storytelling, she integrates the story into the collection through the use of the stereotypical, albeit individualized characters of the fallen priest, the lonely woman who bore his child, who died of SIDS, the disconcerted farmer, and the gossipy villagers. Presenting the west of Ireland as the symbolic and pastoral space offering escape from existing problems, Keegan exposes such typecasts, while the ostensible (post)modernity of the story is strengthened by the suggested supernatural elements as a means to probe the individual and collective memory. It would appear that Keegan's approach to nationalist attitudes is in line with Orhan Pamuk's denunciation of the political novel, which, as Pamuk holds, "is a limited genre because politics entails a determination not to understand those who are different from us, while the art of the novelist entails a determination to understand those who are different from us" (2016, p. 145). For him, "[t]he most political novel is the novel that has no political themes or motives but that tries to see everything and understand everyone, to construct the largest whole. Thus, the novel that manages to accomplish this impossible task has the deepest center" (2016, p. 145).

Thierry Robin's 'Borderline *Troubles* in *Resurrection man* and *Breakfast on Pluto*. Remembering Northern Ireland before the GFA'[16] is a comparative approach to the fashioning of boundaries on land, paper and screen. The chapter looks at the adaptations of two seminal novels depicting the Troubles in Northern Ireland: Patrick McCabe's *Breakfast on Pluto* (1998) and Eoin McNamee's *Resurrection Man* (1994), which were adapted for the screen by Neil Jordan in 2005 and Marc Evans in 1998, respectively. The claims that the language of identification lies with the Republican or Loyalist groups purports the sectarian representations of reality. In the author's view, despite the shared language and the common past, the divisions and conflicts are deployed so as to stress differences rather than underscore the similarities.

Liliana Sikorska's 'Vanquishing mirages: nations and nationalisms in Barry Unsworth's *The rage of the vulture* and Orhan Pamuk's *Silent house*', takes us back to the early 20th century, which witnesses the dissolution of one of the greatest and most lasting multi-ethnic empires, that of the Ottomans. Investigating these works, the author shows how the novels depicting Turkey and Europe in times of change discuss the incidents precipitating the abdication of Abdul Hamid and the creation of the modern Turkish Republic. Unsworth shows the events from the perspective of a British man who, because of his betrothal to an Armenian, becomes entangled in the Armenian cause, but offers also the point of view of the Sultan Abdul Hamid II.[17] Pamuk narrates the transformation of Turkey after the takeover by Mustafa Kemal Atatürk through the memories of an old woman and the experiences of her grandchildren. Despite the slightly ironic pronouncement of Pamuk, who maintains that "[l]iterary novels persuade us to take life seriously by showing that we in fact have the power to influence events and that our personal decisions shape our lives" (2016, p. 59), both novels reassess the issues of national, ethnic and religious identities. Indirectly, they also signpost imperial battles against minorities such as the Armenians and Kurds in Turkey, and the struggles between dissimilar versions of secular and religious allegiances demonstrating the thin line between theocracy and autocracy in the twentieth century Turkish politics.

Last but not least, in 'A writer beyond borders on gross ethics-related negligence: J. M. Coetzee, rails against the modern world's maladies' Ryszard Bartnik links the writings of the Nobel Prize winner from the turn of the centuries with the

---

16 GFA refers to the Good Friday Agreement, the power-sharing deal struck between Loyalists and Republicans which officially put an end to the Troubles after it was signed by both sides in Belfast on 10 April 1998.
17 Out of respect for the position of the Turkish ruler, we are using the capital letter. The quotations are faithful to Unsworth's spelling.

more current discussions on the Russian-Ukrainian conflict as being an example of an imaginary collectivity. Despite Coetzee's problematic ethnic identifications manifested against the divisions of the Afrikaaner and the English, his writings frequently challenge the established ideas of linguistic and cultural domination. Bartnik's reading of J. M. Coetzee's 'autobiographical' fictions emphasizes the enduring significance of both fiction and non-fiction in the ongoing debates on moral integrity that transcends national boundaries.

Nationalist discourses have been instrumental in undercutting European imperialism, identifying its role in the formation and deconstruction of collective identities. Holding a rather precarious position, nationalism in present-day reality is seen both in terms of the preservation of national cultural roots and as a bar to a more, irreligious, albeit multiethnic, society. Both modes are hampered by misconceptions concerning the mechanisms of inclusion and exclusion. The writers, whose works are analyzed in the present volume, show acute awareness of the vicissitudes of nationalism, leaving the readers with singular perspectives on re-imagined communities.[18]

Bibliography

Agamben, Giorgio: *Homo Sacer. Sovereign Power and Bare Life.* Stanford 2010.
Anderson, Benedict: *Imagined Communities: Reflections on the Origin and Spread of Nationalism*, Revised Edition. London and New York 2006 [1983].
Appadurai, Arjun: *Modernity at large: Cultural Dimensions of Globalization.* Minneapolis 1996.
Applebaum, Anne: *Twilight of Democracy. The Seductive Lure of Authoritarianism.* New York 2020.
Arendt, Hannah: *Responsibility and Judgement.* New York 2003.
Calhoun, Craig: *Nationalism.* Minneapolis 1997.
Clarke, John: 'Which Nation Is This? Brexit and the Not-so-United Kingdom', in: Cörüt, Ilker / Jongerden, Joost (eds.): *Beyond Nationalism and the Nation-state. Radical Approaches to Nation.* London 2021, p. 98–116.
Cörüt, Ilker / Jongerden, Joost: 'Radical Approaches to Nation: An Introduction', in: Cörüt, Ilker / Jongerden, Joost (eds.): *Beyond Nationalism and the Nation-state. Radical Approaches to Nation.* London 2021, p. ix–xxii.
Foucault, Michel: *Language, Counter-memory, Practice: Selected Essays and Interviews.* Ithaca and New York 1980.
Johansen, Bruce: 'Introduction', in: Johansen, Bruce / Akande, Adebowale (eds.): *Nationalism: Past as Prologue.* New York 2021, p. vii–xiv.
Judt, Tony: *A Grand Illusion? An Essay on Europe.* New York and London 1996.

---

18 In the words of Orhan Pamuk "The writer's signature is the unique way in which the writer renders the world" (2016, p. 44).

Kaufmann, Eric: 'Complexity and Nationalism', in: NATIONS AND NATIONALISM 2017/ 23:1, p. 6–25.
Kaufmann, Eric: 'Ethno-traditional Nationalism and the Challenge of Immigration', in: NATIONS AND NATIONALISM 2019/25:2, p. 435–448.
Kearney, Richard: *On Stories*. London 2002.
Keating, Michael: 'A Quarter Century of the Europe of the Regions', in: REGIONAL AND FEDERAL STUDIES 2008/18:5, p. 629–635.
Kozierska, Ewa: 'Pope Francis on Europe', in: Sondel-Cedarmas, Joanna / Berti, Francesco (eds.): *The Right-wing Critique of Europe: Nationalist, Sovereigntist and Right-wing Populist Attitudes to the EU*. London 2022, p. 245–260.
Lewis, Simon / Wawrzyniak, Joanna: 'Introduction: Regions of Memory in Theory', in: Lewis, Simon / Olick, Jeffrey /Wawrzyniak, Joanna / Pakier, Małgorzata (eds.): *Regions of Memory: Transnational Formations*. Cham 2022, p. 1–16.
McGlynn, Jade / Thaidigsmann, Karoline / Friess, Nina: 'Promoting Patriotism, Suppressing Dissent Views: The Making of Historical Narratives and National Identity in Russia and Poland', in: Krawatzek, Félix / Friess, Nina (eds.): *Youth and Memory in Europe: Defining the Past, Shaping the Future*. Berlin 2022, p. 221–229.
Orwell, George: *Fascism and Democracy*. London 2020.
Pamuk, Orhan: *Other Colors. Writings on Life, Art, Books and Cities* [Translated by Maureen Freely]. London 2008 [2007].
Pamuk, Orhan: *The Naïve and the Sentimental Novelist. The Charles Eliot Norton Lectures, 2009* [Translated by Nazim Dikbaş]. London 2016 [2010].
Patterson, Glenn: *Here's Me, Here. Further Reflections of a Lapsed Protestant*. Dublin 2015.
Rigney, Ann: 'Transforming Memory and the European Project', in: NEW LITERARY HISTORY 2012/43:4, p. 607–628.
Rigney, Ann: 'Articulations of Memory: Mediation and the Making of Mnemo-regions', in: Lewis, Simon / Olick, Jeffrey /Wawrzyniak, Joanna / Pakier, Małgorzata (eds.): *Regions of Memory: Transnational Formations*. Cham 2022, p. 163–184.
Robins Kevin: *The Challenge of Transcultural Diversities: Transversal Study on the Theme of Cultural Policy and Cultural Diversity*. Council of Europe Publishing 2006.
Solà, Nuria Codina / McMartin, Jack: 'The European Union Prize for Literature: Disseminating European Values through Translation and Supranational Consecration', in: Carb-Catalan, Elisabet / Roig Sanz, Diana (eds.): *Culture as Soft Power: Bridging Cultural Relations, Intellectual Cooperation, and Cultural Diplomacy*. Berlin 2022, p. 343–371.
Smith, Anthony D: *The Cultural Foundations of Nations. Hierarchy, Covenant, and Republic*. Malden and Oxford 2008.
Snyder, Timothy: *On Tyranny. Twenty Lessons from the Twentieth Century*. London 2017.
Syrovy, Daniel: 'Introduction', in: Syrovy, Daniel (ed.): *Discourses on Nations and Identities*. Berlin 2021, p. 1–14.
Wertsch, James V.: *How Nations Remember: A Narrative Approach*. New York 2021.
Wertsch, James V.: 'The Narrative Tools of National Memory', in: Roediger III, Henry L. / Wertsch, James V. (eds.): *National Memories: Constructing Identities in Populist Times*. New York 2022, p. 454–471.
Young, Nigel: *Postnational Memory, Peace and War. Making Past beyond Borders*. London 2021.

Michael McAteer

From Protestant Ireland to Revolutionary Hungary: Nationalism and Transnationalism in Samuel Ferguson

Introduction

This chapter considers nationalism in light of the critical theory of transnationalism that has emerged within the Humanities and Social Sciences over the past thirty years, drawing attention to aspects of contemporary human social life that challenge or weaken the power of nationalism in its nation-state form. Akira Iriye sees the frequency with which the terms 'global' and 'transnational' appear in book and journal article titles since the 1990s as evidence of the emergence of this new critical discourse within historiography towards the end of the twentieth century (Iriye 2013, p. 2). Arjun Appadurai considers mass media and mass migration as distinctive features of contemporary social experience that compel forms of imagination not bound "within local, national, or regional spaces" (Appadurai 1996, p. 4). Thomas Faist argues that contemporary patterns of immigration and assimilation are qualitatively different from those of the early-twentieth century, upon which notions of assimilation and ethnic pluralism within nation-states have been modelled, Faist observing "a more perpetual pattern of immigration on the horizon" (Faist 2000, p. 243f, 246). William Robinson protests that research into transnationalism "unfolds within the straightjacket of a nation-state framework" (Robinson 1998, p. 562).

Keeping these and other ideas in mind concerning the phenomenon of transnationalism, I consider certain aspects of nationalism that appear in the writing of the nineteenth-century Irish poet and scholar, Samuel Ferguson, aspects that can be characterized as transnational. My approach to transnationalism in the case of Ferguson is not to see nationhood as either inadequate to transnational experiences or perspectives, nor as a constituent feature of that "straightjacket" of the nation-state against which Robinson protests. On the contrary, I take on board Faist's disclosure that there is little empirical evidence to support the view that, even in the contemporary phase of globalization, the more transnational ties immigrants carry, the weaker their adherence to the norms and culture of the nation-state in which they settle (Faist 2000, p. 242).

Walker Connor's valuable assessment of modern ethnic nationalism grants further cogency to Faist's elaboration of the durability of nation-state formations in a transnational age, Connor's study gaining renewed pertinence in the context of the outbreak of large-scale military conflict in Eastern Europe in 2022. Connor states that if processes of modernization have led to a weakening of ethnic consciousness, it would be reasonable to expect that ethnic disharmony would be on the decline. He observes, however, that either in spite of or because of hyper-modernization, "a global survey illustrates that ethnic consciousness is definitely in the ascendancy as a political force, and that state borders, as presently delimited, are being increasingly challenged by this trend" (Connor 1994, p. 35). Connor's perspective astutely recognizes an important distinction between state and nation within nation-state political institutions. This factor is significant for understanding the relation between nationalism and transnationalism that emerges in Samuel Ferguson's poem on the Hungarian Revolution of 1848–49, when 'Hungary' is assessed through the lens of his first significant publication, 'A Dialogue Between the Head and Heart of an Irish Protestant', published in 1833.

Samuel Ferguson was born in Belfast in 1810, publishing poems in *Blackwood's Magazine* in Edinburgh during the 1830s. He was Ireland's most prominent living poet from the 1850s to the 1880s, by which time Thomas Moore's *Irish Melodies* had passed their peak, two other major figures in nineteenth century Irish poetry, Thomas Davis and James Clarence Mangan, were dead, and W. B. Yeats had not yet begun publishing. Much of Ferguson's poetry drew from Irish legend and antiquity, working on manuscript materials held at the Royal Irish Academy with the assistance of John O'Donovan, an Irish-language scholar who became Professor of Celtic Languages at Queen's University Belfast. Ferguson has three major achievements in Irish poetry of the nineteenth century. The first is *Lays of the Western Gael* of 1864, a collection of poems published across various journals over the preceding decades. The second is *Lays of the Red Branch*, a collection of poems published posthumously for Gavan Duffy's New Irish Library series in 1897. The poems in *Lays of the Red Branch* are based on the knowledge that Ferguson had acquired from antiquarian sources of the Ulster cycle of legends, the most renowned story of which is the *Táin Bó Cuailgne* or the War of the Bull of Cooley, involving Ireland's most celebrated mythical warrior, Cuchulain. The volume also includes Ferguson's verse drama on the Irish legend of Deirdre and the sons of Usnach. Ferguson's third achievement is his long epic poem *Congal*, first published in 1872: a tale of battle arising from the clash between paganism and Christianity at the beginning of the Christian era in Ireland.

Ferguson's 'A Dialogue'

Coming from the Protestant community in Ulster, Ferguson's conflicted relation to the Gaelic Irish tradition appears in a dialogue essay that he published in 1833 in the newly-founded journal, the *Dublin University Magazine*, under the title 'A Dialogue Between the Head and Heart of an Irish Protestant'. This essay gives public airing to anxieties within the Protestant population of Ireland that arose from reforms that the British Government had introduced concerning political and religious affairs between 1829 and 1833. Malcolm Brown describes 'A Dialogue' as "unrivalled for the lucidity with which it placed on display the conflicts of the Anglo-Irish mind" (Brown 1972, p. 39). Peter Denman considers 'A Dialogue' as a commentary on public affairs rather than a personal manifesto, published in response to three British legislative changes that modified the position of Protestantism as the religion of government in Irish society: the Catholic Emancipation of 1829, the Reform Act of 1832 and the Church Temporalities Act (Ireland) of 1833 (Denman 1990, p. 2). The last of these saw the repeal or part-repeal of a wide range of Acts that had become law in Ireland since the reign of King Henry VIII to secure Protestant authority in Ireland. In the process, the number of Anglican-affiliated Church of Ireland bishoprics was reduced significantly and the payment of Church rates by Irish tenant farmers (predominantly Catholic) or landowners to the Church of Ireland clergy was eliminated.

In 'A Dialogue', the voice of 'Heart' laments the fact that, despite having suppressed three rebellions in Ireland against British rule over the course of the previous 250 years, the 'controllers of Popery' had been betrayed by the British Liberal (Whig) Government in their legislative concessions to Irish Catholicism (Ferguson 1833, p. 586). 'Heart' regards with disgust ("manhood prostrated") what the voice of 'Head' sees as the 'tranquillity' that those recent legislative changes have brought to Ireland (Ferguson 1833, p. 586). Identifying Protestantism with liberty and Roman Catholicism with tyranny, 'Heart' regards the Government reforms as particularly galling in coming from the English Liberal Party, comparing the Church Temporalities Act to a Russian "ukase", or an edict from the Russian Tsar that automatically carried the authority of a law (Ferguson 1833, p. 587). This side-comment is telling in disclosing an aspect that critical commentaries on 'A Dialogue' overlook: its international dimension. It is significant to Ferguson's poem on the Hungarian Revolution that he published sixteen years later in 1849, a poem in which he refers to Russia's role in suppressing the Revolution. The passing allusion to Russia in 'A Dialogue' questions the movement that Akira Iriye sees emerging in historical studies during the 1990s. This trend concerns his idea that "global history" develops as an alternative to national history in the work of historians, with "transnational history" appearing as a new sub-field (Iriye 11). Rather than simply alluding to Russia as a point of contrast that lay beyond the custody of the British state in Ireland in the early nineteenth century, Ferguson incorporates this perspective into the issues of nationhood and state governance that he addresses in 'A Dialogue'. His work speaks to the pattern that Iriye observes in historical studies from the late twentieth century, but not in terms of nationality and transnationality at odds with each other.

Rome is much more significant than Russia as an international feature of 'A Dialogue', however. 'Head' fears not Irish patriotism, but Irish Catholicism. This point is critical. 'Head' draws the attention of 'Heart' to the fact that Irish Protestant Members of Parliament in London voted in favor of the Liberal Government's Reform Bills in the conviction that, without such reforms, large-scale rebellion would break out in Ireland. 'Head' regards the Repeal of the Act of Union and the establishment of the Roman Catholic Church as the inevitable outcomes of such a rebellion (Ferguson 1833, p. 588). Faced with this prospect, Protestant 'Heart' becomes despondent, confronted as it is with the need to swallow the bitter pill of concessions to the Irish Catholic majority. 'Head' sees this medicine as a necessity for the Union with Britain to survive, a survival upon which Protestant security in nineteenth-century Ireland depends – a matter that is not in dispute between 'Head' and 'Heart.' In this sense, Catholicism was as much an international threat to the domestic nation-state formation of Ireland in its constitutional relation to Britain, as it was an internal threat to that relation. Rather than an exclusively local issue, the long sectarian conflict in Ireland originated not only out of the universal appeal of core Christian teachings that assisted its transition across the territories of the Roman Empire. It also developed from its transcultural character, as Mark Juergensmeyer observes. Within the first one hundred years of its existence, Christianity became the religion of a multicultural population, absorbing doctrines from Gnosticism, Zoroastrianism, Judaism and Roman Emperor worship (Juergensmeyer 2003, p. 9). These extra-Christian influences residually informed the contest over Christian legitimacy in Ireland during the post-Reformation era and toleration of different claims for the true nature of Christian experience. One can see, for example, how certain strands of Protestantism saw 'Popery' as a continuation of the worship of the Roman Emperor, while Catholicism may well have considered Puritanism in the seventeenth century as a species of Gnosticism.

The admission of Irish Catholics into public life and constitutional politics through Catholic emancipation in the early-nineteenth century raised the threat of Catholic nationalism marginalizing, if not eventually obliterating, the land-owning Protestant minority in Ireland, particularly in the Catholic-dominated rural regions of the west and south. Yet the British Government's reforms, F. S. L. Lyons has argued, did not affect the material circumstances of the large Irish peasant population nor those of the Anglo-Irish gentry in any significant way.

Lyons even doubts whether the followers of Irish patriot Daniel O'Connell, who led the drive for Catholic emancipation, were its beneficiaries, "moving anxiously and amateurishly between English parties at Westminster" (Lyons 1973, p. 19). Lyons judges the Catholic Church itself as the one institution in Ireland that advanced significantly in consequence of emancipation, an institution that obviously had a long history in Ireland but one that was international with regard to its teachings, policies and practices (Lyons 1973, p. 19). R. F. Foster does not distinguish so categorically between the interest of the Catholic Church and the circumstances of the Irish Catholic population in consequence of the legislative change of 1829. Although in agreement with Lyons as to how little Irish life changed politically in the immediate aftermath of 1829, Foster still considers Catholic emancipation as "a constitutional social revolution," one that gave an emerging Catholic middle-class "a vital psychological boost" (Foster 1988, p. 302). James Murphy points to the irony that if British legislative moves towards emancipation and reform between 1829 and 1833 secularized relations between Church and State in Britain, they entrenched religious difference in Irish politics (Murphy 2001, p. 11–12). Likewise, Emer Nolan reflects this state of affairs by approaching Catholic literature in Ireland after emancipation in a sociological and political rather than a denominational sense (Nolan 2007, p. xii). This critical stance is reflective of the entrenchment that Murphy describes, but it also stands somewhat at variance with Lyons's observation that Catholic ecclesiastical interest in Ireland was by no means equitable with Irish ethnic nationalism.

Thus arises the question of whether Catholicism in Ireland after Catholic emancipation served to develop and consolidate the religious practices, beliefs and attitudes of the majority of its population, or whether it developed as a marker of Irish ethnic identity in the direction of constitutional or revolutionary political independence. Ferguson's 'A Dialogue' repudiates the idea of Catholicism in Ireland as the mark of genuine Irishness in two ways. First, 'Head' disparages the feeling in 'Heart' that Catholics in Ireland have a greater claim on Irish nationhood than Protestants because of their religious affiliation. 'Head' rejects the suggestion of 'Heart' that Protestants are, compared to Catholics, "strangers" in Ireland. He asserts that even Protestants from the last major wave of plantation in seventeenth-century Ireland had as much entitlement to consider themselves Irish by race as those Norman invaders had to call themselves English by the time of the reigns of Kings Edward I, II and III from the late-thirteenth century to the early-fourteenth century. He reinforces the point by declaring that the blood of 'Heart' is likely "drawn from a source as purely Irish as that of O'Connor or O'Brien" (Ferguson 1833, p. 589). The source of violent conflict in Ireland is not ethnic in the eyes of 'Head', but religious. In that sense, the terms of the conflict lie beyond Ireland, arising from the Protestant Reformation and the Catholic Counter-Reformation in Europe.

Second, 'Head' introduces the somewhat bizarre argument that the ultimate objective of the Catholics in Ireland was to influence England in the direction of French-style radical republicanism, thus prompting an English invasion of Ireland to coerce the country into its new liberal dispensation. Contending that the revolutionizing of England would weaken the British Empire and the home nation materially, 'Head' envisages a scenario in which Irish Catholics and Protestants combine to defeat the invading English. Such an Irish victory would leave Irish Protestants exposed as never before (Ferguson 1833, p. 590–91). The entire narrative of 'Head' in this aspect of 'A Dialogue' seems fanciful, ignoring the fact that the Catholic Church in France was one of the foremost targets of the *sans-culotte* revolutionaries during the creation of the French Republic. Its importance, however, lies in 'Head' resorting to the spectre of international revolutionary politics, taking hold in England, as a means of frightening 'Heart' into agreement with the pragmatism of 'Head' concerning the position of Protestants in Ireland. The threat to Protestant security arose not from the Gaelic Catholic majority native to Ireland as 'Head' sees matters. Rather it emerged from institutions and ideas beyond Ireland that influenced the Irish majority: the doctrines of the Counter-Reformation Roman Catholic Church and the political ideals of French and American Republicanism. Transnational institutions and universalist political thought shaped the terms of national conflict within the Ireland of Ferguson's youth.

Peter Denman and Eve Patten propose that Ferguson's 'Dialogue' is largely a staged affair, not to be taken at face value. Denman argues that the author absents himself from the extremes of sympathy and hostility towards Irish Catholics that the Protestant voice articulates, though Denman also identifies the rationality of 'Head' as far closer to Ferguson's outlook than the passion of 'Heart' (Denman 1990, p. 3–4). Noting that Ferguson was a trainee barrister at the time of publication of 'A Dialogue', Patten regards it as "a highly formulaic eighteenth-century debate between reason and passion, suggesting precedents drawn from David Hume and Adam Ferguson" (Patten 2004, p. 64). In her conviction that Ferguson was "rehearsing an argument from the sidelines" in 'A Dialogue', Patten takes issue with David Lloyd's view that it was Ferguson's open signal for Protestants to start a culture war with Irish Catholics following emancipation (Patten 2004, p. 64; Lloyd 1985–86, p. 155). This battle would take the form of Ferguson's challenge to the Catholic claim to an exclusive, authentic access to indigenous Irish civilization. It was a battle that he began soon after 'A Dialogue' in the 1834 issues of the *Dublin University Magazine*. In April, August, October and November of that year, the magazine published Ferguson's extended critique of English translations of Irish-language poems that the County Galway librarian and native Irish speaker, James Hardiman, published in two volumes in 1831 under the title, *Irish Minstrelsy* (Ferguson 1834).

Colin Graham approaches 'A Dialogue' from the perspective of Mikhail Bakhtin's theory of monologism and dialogism as applied to a postcolonial interpretation of Irish cultural and historical conditions. Pointing out that 'Head' and 'Heart' represent reason and feeling in "the loosest of formulations" only, Graham diverges from the assumption of Denman, Patten and Lloyd that 'A Dialogue' maintains a balance between reason and emotion (Graham 1998, p. 83). Graham is quite right on this matter. 'Heart' suggests that the condition of Irish Protestants in the aftermath of British Government reforms is the miserable one of an in-between state: one in which they are "neither English nor Irish, fish nor flesh, but a peddling colony, a forlorn advanced guard that must conform to every mutinous movement of the pretorian rabble" (Ferguson 1833, p. 591). From the perspective of some among the trader or landowning Protestant class in nineteenth-century Ireland, this description of 'Heart' might indeed seem to be an accurate one. Certainly when contrasted against the wild speculation of 'Head' concerning Catholic intrigue to push England in the direction of radical republicanism, the voice of 'Heart' appears the more sober one in this instance. In postcolonial theoretical terms, however, 'Heart' is also lamenting a state of existence, the inherent ambivalence of which he ought to tolerate at least, if not accept as a sign of positive distinction. 'Heart' attributes, after all, a hybrid nature to Irish Protestantism following Catholic emancipation, deconstructing the binary opposition of Irishness and Englishness. The "miserable [...] in-between state" of Irish Protestants that 'Heart' laments is, from a contemporary transnational perspective, an enriching dialogical alternative to the essentially monologic nature of nationalism as Graham sees it, drawing upon the thought of Bakhtin (Graham 1998, p. 84).

In the ease with which critics read 'A Dialogue' in response to Catholic emancipation and the Whig Reform Acts of the early 1830s, little consideration has been given to the possibility that Ferguson's early work is, in fact, a nationalist document. Nor have critics commented on the transnational aspect of the essay, with the notable exception of Graham's attention to its implications for Ireland's standing, not only within the United Kingdom but also within the British Empire. The voice that begins 'A Dialogue' with an outburst of invective against the Whig Government reforms is also the voice that speaks most sentimentally of a love of homeland. 'Heart' declares that "I love this land better than any other" and that "I love the people in it, in spite of themselves, and cannot feel towards them as enemies" (Ferguson 1833, p. 591). That qualifying clause, "in spite of themselves," expresses the revulsion that 'Heart' feels towards the superstition, casuistry and doctrinal error that Protestantism in Britain and Ireland identified historically with the Church of Rome. The entire dialogue takes this sectarian rift for granted. As Patricia Craig has pointed out, in his wish for a wholescale conversion of the Irish population to the Protestant faith, 'Heart' simply ignores the widespread reprobation of Catholic converts to Protestantism as 'turncoats' among Catholics in Ireland who remained faithful to Catholic religious practices and beliefs (Craig 2009, p. 85). This sense of betrayal would have been especially sharp through the century of legislative suppression of Catholicism in Ireland following the decisive victory of Protestantism against the Catholic challenge of James II in 1690.

If critics accept the inevitable Protestant bias of 'A Dialogue' – whether it be staged or sincere – they should equally acknowledge the role of Irish national identity. 'Heart' makes this sentiment obvious when declaring that he feels and knows that he is "the heart of an Irishman" (Ferguson 1833, p. 589). In contrast to other occasions when 'Head' admonishes 'Heart' for allowing emotion to govern practicality, 'Head' commends 'Heart' in this instance, reinforcing rather than dismissing his patriotic sentiment. 'Head' takes recourse to one of the most influential medieval pseudo-histories of Ireland, *Lebor Gabála Érenn* (*Book of Invasions*) to lend that feeling justification. This work was a source with which Ferguson was familiar through his friendship with the Irish antiquarian John O'Donovan. The rhetoric that 'Head' employs in support of 'Heart' is interesting in affirming the ethnic Irish nationalism of 'Heart' while simultaneously presenting nationalism as a force that incorporates different ethnicities:

> The Celt may have been expelled by the Nemedian, the Nemedian by the Fir Bolg, the Fir Bolg by the Tuatha De Danaan, the Tuatha De Danaan by the Scot, the Scot by the Anglo-Norman–but what of that? *They were all Irishmen in turn, and* WE *are Irishmen now* (Ferguson 1833, p. 589).

This flourish is an instance in which 'Head', as a voice of practical reason, simply disappears in 'A Dialogue', conflating ethnic groups and semi-mythical clans together in one overarching panoply of Irishness. There is more to the declaration than this inconsistency, however. It carries a creative tension between ethnicity and nationhood, one that pivots on a distinction between exclusivity and assimilation. Each tribe that 'Head' lists has 'expelled' its predecessor, suggesting that ethnic conquest has always been part of Irish history. Yet all of these tribes count as Irish, meaning that each of them has been absorbed into a larger idea of Irishness. It would be a mistake to regard the assimilationist notion of Irishness along the lines of "flexible citizenship" that Aihwa Ong proposes for transnational ethnicities such as those of contemporary China (Ong 1999, p. 1 ff). Irishness functions as a meta-ethnicity that emerges over a monumental timespan, absorbing layers of tribes from within or from afar. The medieval *Book of Invasions*, for example, traces Nemed genealogically to Noah from the Book of Genesis, while the Nemedian tribe was originally an equestrian nomadic people from Iran. However far removed the idea of Irish nationhood to which 'Head' appeals is to notions of flexible citizenship and transnational mobility in the contemporary era of globalization, it is still significant that migratory, transnational patterns are woven into its ancient fabric.

Having convinced 'Heart' of the integrity of his Protestant Irishness, 'Head' subsequently refutes the doubt of 'Heart' that Catholics lay a greater claim to national identity than Protestants, because of the centuries of English misgovernance of Ireland that Irish Catholics experienced. This argument of 'Head' is somewhat convoluted and tendentious when addressing the matter. First insisting that 'Heart' has every right to consider himself a true Irishman, 'Head' goes on to state that if the Irish people had the qualities necessary to constitute a true nation, they would have been able to resist English conquest, if not even become the dominant of the two nations. The latter claim is a very large one, considering how, through the British Empire, England became the most powerful nation on earth by the early nineteenth century. The truth as 'Head' sees it, is that Irish society up to the age of Queen Elizabeth I comprised of clans continually at war with one another. Whatever elements of nationhood developed in the country subsequent to the Elizabethan age, they came through English Protestant laws and institutions taking root (Ferguson 1833, p. 592). 'Head' thus moves deftly from endorsing ethnic nationalism to championing civic nationalism instead, the latter only developed under the influence of Ireland's neighbor, England. Thus, Ferguson's 'Head' proposes the development of Irish nationalism as part of the United Kingdom, not in opposition to it.

This perspective of Irish nationalism lies open to the objection that 'Head' makes unsubstantiated claims concerning the nature of pre-Elizabethan Irish society and that he assumes Protestantism as the only means through which civic society could evolve, thus ignoring the catastrophic impact of Puritanism in Cromwell's Irish campaign of the mid-seventeenth century. Before dismissing the turn of 'Head' to civic nationalism on these grounds, however, readers should remind themselves that 'Head' never advocates a repeal of the Catholic Emancipation (Roman Catholic Relief) Act of 1829 or the other Reform Acts of the early 1830s. On the contrary, he lauds the good sense of parliamentary Irish Protestants in facilitating these reforms despite their deep misgivings, thus avoiding the turbulence and destruction of full-scale rebellion in Ireland. The task facing Irish Protestants is two-fold as 'Head' perceives it: to consolidate a sense of Irish identity throughout the Protestant population of Ireland: to win as many Catholics as possible over to Protestantism, no longer through coercion but exclusively through force of argument. The significance of this conclusion derives not from its tenability or otherwise for the conditions that obtained in Ireland following Catholic emancipation. It is rather in the transnational dimension of nationalism, as it appears in 'A Dialogue', that the essay continues to hold relevance. Ferguson puts forward the idea that, as a nation, Ireland could achieve stability and security through an institutional framework of the United

Kingdom of Great Britain and Ireland. By this logic, to be a nationalist is, ironically, to be a unionist. Religion introduces another transnational aspect, since 'Head' considers Protestantism as a governing influence in consolidating Ireland into a progressive nation. When he thinks of Protestantism, 'Head' moves beyond Ireland and Britain. The figures he invokes are the Prussian Luther and the Swiss Calvin speaking against the Papacy in Rome (Ferguson 1833, p. 593). Indeed, by framing the Irish question so categorically in religious terms, 'A Dialogue' opens it up to the international character of Catholicism as a religious institution and the equally international character of the Reformation, expanding beyond Europe through the growth of Britain's Imperial territories during the eighteenth and nineteenth centuries.

Ferguson's 'Hungary'

Considering political and religious issues beyond Ireland as determining political and religious circumstances within Ireland, 'A Dialogue' shows Ferguson's transnational perspective at the start of his life as a writer. This aspect is most striking in the lament of 'Heart' that, despite his feeling of belonging to Ireland, the Irish Protestant is "neither Irish nor English," inhabiting a hybrid state that extends beyond both Irish and English geographical territories. It is also evident in the contention of 'Head' that Irish society from the earliest times absorbed diverse ethnic groups, tribes that had come from nearby or from afar, into a single meta-ethnic identity of Irishness. More contentious is the political claim of 'Head' that Irish nationhood emerged only through institutions and practices that the English Crown or English Government established. Finally, the transnational aspect of 'A Dialogue' appears in the argument that what divides the Irish people most seriously is not the hostility of some and the attachment of others to England. It is rather the fidelity of the majority to the Papacy and the teachings of the Catholic Church, and the commitment of the minority to the religious principles of the Protestant Reformation, religious loyalties of a most intimate nature that yet connect Irish people to places and peoples far beyond Ireland.

These aspects of 'A Dialogue' demonstrate how the transnational character of a poem published almost sixteen years later in the *Dublin University Magazine*, 'Hungary,' was not a new departure for Ferguson. Much had changed in Ireland in the period between the dialogue essay and the poem. Thomas Davis had appeared on the scene as a highly influential figure, co-founding *The Nation* newspaper in 1842 with the aim of supporting the repeal of the Act of Union of Great Britain and Ireland that had become law in 1801. Educated at Trinity College Dublin, Davis supported the Republican objectives of the United Irishmen who had staged an insurrection against British rule in Ireland in 1798. Ferguson admired Davis as essayist and balladeer, and while he remained adamantly opposed to the case for an independent Irish Republic, he changed his views concerning repeal of the Act of Union. This development is evident in Ferguson's participation in the Protestant Repeal Association, a specifically Protestant branch of the Repeal Association that Daniel O'Connell had founded the previous year, as leader of the Catholic emancipation movement in Ireland of the late 1820s. A May 1848 issue of *The Nation* reported the objectives of the Protestant Repeal Association. It was created not to underscore sectarian difference in Ireland but rather to demonstrate that the majority of middle class Irish Protestants wished for Irish legislative independence from Westminster as much as Roman Catholics. The Association saw the force of public opinion as the only means to achieve this end, thereby maintaining its distance from the long history of Irish rebellion against British rule. It also committed itself to "unimpaired loyalty to the Queen," upheld the rights of private property and was "utterly opposed to Republican principles" ('Protestant' May 1848, p. 1). The July 1, 1848 issue of *The Nation* records Ferguson as one of the participants at the inaugural meeting of the Association in Dublin ('Protestant' July 1848, p. 422). Ferguson's willingness to countenance an Irish parliament in Dublin, long after 'Head' had so stridently denounced a repeal of the Act of Union in 'A Dialogue' of 1833, is a measure of the impact that Davis had on him, made even more poignant by Davis's death from scarlet fever at the age of 30. It is also testimony to the catastrophe that befell Ireland through the years 1845–1848, when potato blight destroyed the staple diet of a huge portion of Ireland's agrarian population, leading to mass starvation, widespread death from cholera and mass emigration on a scale not witnessed before.[1]

Ferguson's 'Hungary' first appears in the *Dublin University Magazine* in September 1849. It was composed in response to news of final defeat of the Hungarian Revolution that had broken out in Budapest (then named Pesth-Buda) in March 1848. The Revolution was decidedly transnational in nature, involving Hungary, Austria, Transylvania, Russia, Poland, Croatia, Serbia and Turkey at various points. Not only was it part of the widespread series of uprisings that took place across Europe in 1848, it was a momentous development in its own right, the repercussions of which reverberated for a long time after.[2] One of

---

[1] The Great Famine is too vast a topic to address in the present context, attracting an enormous body of academic research over the past fifty years. For major scholarship on the Famine over the past ten years, see the large edited volume, *The History of the Irish Famine* (Kinealy 2018), Edna Delany's *The Great Famine: A History in Four Lives* (Delaney 2014) and the monumental *Atlas of the Great Irish Famine* (Crowley 2012).

[2] Istvan Deak's *The Lawful Revolution* is the major English-language account of the Hungarian Revolution (Deak 1979). See also *A Concise History of Hungary* (Molnár 2001, p. 183 ff); 'Na-

the issues to distinguish the Hungarian Revolution from the revolts that broke out in Paris, Berlin, Vienna, Milan and elsewhere in Europe was its ambiguous relation to the French Revolution of 1789-91, the undoubted source of inspiration for the anti-monarchist character of the revolutionary upsurge of 1848. Rather than attempting to institute an entirely new political regime based exclusively on the French Revolution's principles of liberty, equality and fraternity, the parliamentary supporters of the Hungarian Revolution founded their demands on an appeal to the old constitution of Hungary. The terms of this constitution involved the recognition of the Habsburg Emperor in Vienna as both the Imperial Sovereign and King of Hungary. He represented the Sovereignty of the Hungarian Diet and was legally forbidden from interfering with the authority of that Diet to exercise political rule over Hungarian territory. During an era of social and cultural reform in Hungary from the mid-1820s to the 1840s, known simply as 'the Reform Era', some Hungarian political figures took the view that the Habsburg Dynasty had reneged on that original acknowledgment of Hungarian legislative autonomy. They felt that Hapsburg rule over Hungary had gradually become absolutist rather than constitutional in nature. Hungarian patriots and Lajos Kossuth's Opposition Party in the Hungarian Diet demanded various reforms in 1848. These reforms amounted to a new Hungarian constitution, but one that received the agreement of the Austrian King Ferdinand I (or, as King of Hungary and other territories under Habsburg rule, Emperor Ferdinand V) in April 1848. On this basis, Istvan Deak describes the "bloodless Revolution" that later turned into a war as "a lawful revolution" (Deak 1979).

Ferguson's interest in Hungary suggests his familiarity with three widely read travel books on Hungary by English authors of the early-nineteenth century. The first of these was Richard Bright's *Travels from Vienna through Lower Hungary*, based on travels during the year of the Congress of Vienna in 1814. The second was John Paget's *Hungary and Transylvania*, published in two volumes in 1839. The third was a three-volume work by Julia Pardoe, *The City of the Magyar, or Hungary and Her Institutions in 1839-40*, published in 1840.[3] Awareness of the Hungarian Revolution was prominent in the Irish nationalist press, *The Nation* running an article vindicating the Hungarian cause in the same month that the *Dublin University Magazine* published Ferguson's poem on the same subject ('The Hungarian' Sept. 1, 1849, p. 2). Ferguson included 'Hungary' in *Lays of the Western Gael*, one of the few poems in that collection to address contemporary matters, as Peter Denman notes (Denman 1990, p. 99). The poem is a nationalist

---

tional Modernisation through the Constitutional Revolution of 1848 in Hungary' (Képessy 2019, p. 51 ff). For a recent Hungarian-language assessment of the Revolution, see András Gergely, 'A Forradalom és az Önvédelmi Háború ['The Revolution and the War of Self-Defence [own translation]] (1848–1849)' (Gergely 2019, p. 236 ff).

3 My thanks to Márta Pellérdi for drawing my attention to these works.

work with a decidedly transnational aspect. There are some aspects of 'Hungary' that reflect Ferguson's poems on Irish myth and legend. Conveying a sense of the contemporary Hungarian Revolution through the same imagery and tone that he often employs in his poems on Irish mythology, Ferguson surreptitiously betrays some empathy for the heroic ideals of Thomas Davis and the Young Ireland movement. This was a movement that, led by William Smith O'Brien, also rose up in rebellion in July 1848, albeit on a miniature scale and in a farcically disorganized fashion. Yet if this link between modern Hungary and ancient Ireland brings to surface the nationalist sentiment of 'A Dialogue,' the direction of this sentiment towards a distant Hungary rather than Ferguson's contemporary Ireland also illustrates the continuance of the transnational aspect to his work that first appears in 'A Dialogue.'

'Hungary' is composed of fourteen quatrains, each containing two rhyming couplets of even length. It introduces the Magyar people with a giant image, one that occurs in Ferguson's most popular verse, 'The Forging of the Anchor,' a poem that also appears in *Lays of the Western Gael*. Ferguson employs images of giants and the gigantic in his Irish mythological poetic drama *Deirdre*, some poems that he based on the Ulster cycle of legends, and most emphatically in his epic poem 'Congal.' 'Hungary' begins with the speaker warning away anyone who would dare to seek out the "host-rolling plain of the mighty Magyar" (Ferguson 1849, p. 292). Though he sharply observes the same "blustering energy" of 'The Forging of the Anchor' in 'Hungary', Denman mistakenly considers the first half of the poem as relishing the prospect of war between Hungary and Russia: the opening lines warn *against* those who would "own the dread rapture of war" (Denman 1990, p. 99). Indeed, there is no reference to Russia until the eighth verse of this fourteen-verse poem. The appearance of that reference recalls the comparison that 'Heart' makes between British Government reforms and a Russian ukase in 'A Dialogue', raising the question as to whether or not the poem regards the Russian defeat of the Hungarian Revolution as tyrannical. This matter is significant to any transnational reading of 'Hungary' in relation to circumstances in Ireland that Ferguson first addresses in 'A Dialogue.'

Through that grandiose scale with which he imagines the Hungarian plains in the opening verse, Ferguson captures the same sense of magnitude as 'The Forging of the Anchor':

Where the giants of yore from their mansion come down,
O'er the ocean-wide floor play the game of renown (Ferguson 1849, p. 292)

This image is almost exactly that which readers encounter in 'The Forging of the Anchor' when the poet exults "the broad-arm'd fisher of the Deep" whose "delight" and "glory" it is to sail by night and day, "[t]hrough sable sea and breaker white the giant game to play" (Ferguson 1865, p. 124). Ferguson also includes a giant as a simile in his version of the tragedy of Deirdre and the sons of Usnach, as they arrive back to the North of Ireland from Scotland. One of the sons describes the hill of Lurgeden, sloping towards the Ulster sea-shore, as "browed like frowning giant" (Ferguson 1880, p. 118). In his long poem 'Conary', one of the spies of the British pirate Ingcel describes hearing the striking of steel at a kindling fire in a vast hall at Bru'n-Da-Derga as if the strokes were those of a giant (Ferguson 1880, p. 68). In another poem based on tales from the Ulster cycle, 'The Tain-Quest,' the bard Sanchan speaks in the Castle of King Guaire of his attempts to recover the lost poem of the Táin (War) of the Bull of Cooley. Sanchan calls upon a witness to his efforts through "spell and spirit-struggle" to conjure access to the original verse. The witness in question is "Giant Bouchaill, herdsman of the mountain drove" (Graves 1916, p. 228). The most pronounced image of the giant in Ferguson's poetry appears in Book III of his epic work, 'Congal,' where a giant walks among the hills of Ulster close to where Congal and his fellow warriors are encamped. With the flapping of his great cloak, this giant takes flight into the air when confronted by Congal at night. The bard Ardan tells the King that the giant was "a mighty demon of old time: Manannan Mor Mac Lir, Son of the Sea" (Graves 1916, p. 288 ff).

Ferguson's image of Hungary as an ancient land of the giants stands in line with the grandiose manner through which he relates tales from Irish mythology in his poetry, especially those of the Ulster cycle. The word "host" for example, that he employs at the beginning of 'Hungary' in "the host-rolling plains," is one that proliferates throughout Ferguson's poetry. He uses it primarily in reference to a large gathering of warriors ready for battle in any of the many conflicts recorded in Irish legend or early Irish history upon which he bases many of his poems. His description of the Hungarian fighters charging into battle with "a thunder" of wheels is one that he also uses elsewhere on several occasions. In his posthumously published 'Lament for Thomas Davis', Ferguson writes of the salmon around Ireland's shores "thunder on their rocks and foam" (Graves 1916, p. xxvii). In 'The Downfall of the Gael' the speakers talks of "the hoarse thunder" of tumbling waves (Graves 1916, 38). In 'The Naming of Cuchullin', the warrior speaks of "the coming thunder of invasion" (Graves 1916, p. 113). The "rattle and the crash of circling thunder" is heard in 'Conary' and again at the end of 'The Tain-Quest' (Graves 1916, p. 210, 226). The sound of thunder also peals on several occasions throughout 'Congal.' This proximity of imagery and tone in 'Hungary' to poems based on Irish mythology reveal how Ferguson imagines the Hungarian Revolution in nationalist terms, implicitly relating Hungary's struggle for freedom to Ireland's ancient wars.

Ferguson's use of thunder as a verb in the fourth verse of 'Hungary' is a rare instance in his poetry of his drawing an explicit relation between freedom and song: "Freedom thunders her hymn in the battery's voice" (Ferguson 1849,

p. 292). This line carries a contemporary political significance that is missing from Ferguson's poems on Irish mythology, in which Irish wars are those of a long-gone age, of a purely mythical time in many cases. This absence shows Ferguson's concern to avoid the overtly republican sentiment of such ballad poems as Thomas Davis's 'The West's Asleep', one in which "the crashing wave and lashing sea" demand 'Freedom and Nationhood' for Ireland (Rolleston 1914, p. 349). Ferguson's line from 'Hungary' would sit very well in such a fervently patriotic poem as 'The West's Asleep', suggesting that 'Hungary' may be Ferguson's way of expressing his patriotic feelings for Ireland without identifying with the militancy of the Young Ireland Movement of the 1840s that Davis had inspired. In this respect, 'Hungary' repeats some of the ambivalences around nationalism that Ferguson first betrays in 'A Dialogue'. As discussed already, 'Heart' expresses his love of Ireland and 'Head' insists on the right of Protestants of settler ancestry to consider themselves Irish. Yet both 'Heart' and 'Head' are opposed in 'A Dialogue' to a form of nationalism that would sever ties with England completely. The Davis-like imagery through which Ferguson evokes the Hungarian Revolution echo the patriotic sentiments of 'Heart' and 'Head' in 'A Dialogue'. The attribution of this imagery to the cause of Hungary rather than that of Ireland distances Ferguson from the patriots of Young Ireland, however; just as 'Heart' and 'Head' distance themselves from Repeal of the Act of Union and full Irish independence from England. 'Hungary' thus acts as a means of intimating yet suppressing Irish nationalist feeling, demonstrating how the transnational character of this poem signifies his ambivalence towards Irish nationalism.

Ferguson's evocation of freedom thundering "her hymn in the battery's voice" in 'Hungary' is not only political but also religious. As with many of the *Irish Melodies* of Thomas Moore, the ballads of Thomas Davis are 'songs' of liberty. Ferguson's line is a 'hymn' of freedom, one that connects specifically to the bible in the phrase that immediately precedes it, calling on "the Lord Sabaoth to rejoice, now that battle is underway" (Ferguson 1849, p. 292). The term 'Sabaoth' is the Hebrew word for 'host' that appears regularly in the Old Testament, primarily in connection with armies gathered for battle. One of the most striking examples of its occurrence is in the refrain for Psalm 46. The *New Jerusalem Bible* retains the original Hebrew word:

> Yahweh Sabaoth is with us,
> Our citadel, the God of Jacob (Wansbrough 1985, p. 860).

The *King James Bible* opts instead for the English word with the phrase 'Lord of hosts' in the refrain, while the *Evangelical Heritage* version chooses a more contemporary militant phrasing:

> The Lord of Armies is with us,
> The God of Jacob is a fortress for us (*Holy Bible* 2019)

Ferguson's 'Lord Sabaoth' links back to "the host-rolling plains" in the second line of 'Hungary' in such a way as to characterize the Hungarian Revolution as akin to a holy war, reminiscent of the many battles described in the Old Testament. The quest for freedom is to be heard in "the soaring hurrah" and "blood-stifled moan" of battle, sounds that form the hymn of praise that freedom sends to "the foot of thy throne" (Ferguson 1849, p. 292).

Ferguson sustains this biblical language in the third and fourth verses of the poem to a point where Hungary's battle for freedom becomes comparable to that of the Israelites in the Old Testament. The third verse begins with a call on God to hear the appeal of his people, a call to a "God of freedom" (Ferguson 1849, p. 292). As noted earlier, Irish Catholics identified the notion of religious freedom in the mid-nineteenth century with Catholic Emancipation Act of 1829 that Daniel O'Connell had brought about. It is possible that Ferguson implicitly acknowledges the emotional power of Catholic emancipation in 'Hungary' – especially in the aftermath of the Great Famine – when we recall the recognition by 'Heart' of the sacrifices that Catholics in Ireland had made through the centuries for their religious faith. Any such acknowledgement is implicit only, however, given that the subject of the poem is Hungary, not Ireland. Furthermore, the strongest sense of religious identity in 'Hungary' is that of biblical Protestantism, particularly since the religious imagery in the poem draws from the Old Testament primarily. This bears testimony to Ferguson's Ulster Protestant heritage and to the belief expressed in 'A Dialogue' that Catholic domination of a future Ireland, grown more independent from England, threatened Irish Protestants with 'tyranny'. Thus, transnationalism in a religious sense in 'Hungary' accentuates the complex relationship between nationality and religion, when observing discreet identifications with Irish religious history in Ferguson's poem. There is an almost Cromwellian zeal in the speakers call to God for "the edges of slaughter" to be sharp on the fighters' swords and for their bullets to bring swift deaths to those upon whom they fire. The fourth verse of 'Hungary' maintains this tone, with the biblical image of the God of wrath bringing plagues on his enemies. The speaker calls upon "Holy Nature" to arise and wrathfully "shake pestilence" on the path of the enemy, so that the tyrannical invaders may find themselves on the same path as "Sennacherib invading the city of God!" (Ferguson 1849, p. 292). The second Book of Kings records that Yahweh sent an angel to destroy the army of the Assyrian king Sennacherib as they travelled to take the city of Jerusalem (2 Kings, 19:35–36). This biblical event was the subject of an 1815 poem by Lord Byron, 'The Destruction of Sennacherib.'

The seventh verse of 'Hungary' draws again on the Old Testament when the speaker calls for "the moon-melted masses" to decay in silence like "the snail of the Psalmist consuming away" (Ferguson 1849, p. 292). Psalm 58 is the source for this image, during which the writer prays that the wicked may wither away "like the slug that melts as it moves" (Psalm 58: 8). Thus the speaker in 'Hungary' imagines that the only sign that the enemy had been there would be the stench left in the air. Significantly, Ferguson describes the rotten corpses of the defeated enemy of the Magyar as those of the Scythian. The most widely known source of information on the Scythian people in Ferguson's lifetime was to be found in ancient Greek historian Herodotus's *History of the Persian Wars*, an annotated edition of which was published in 1848, the year before the appearance of Ferguson's 'Hungary' (Stocker 1848). Antiquarians speculated that the Scythians originated in Persia, a people who migrated to Southern Russia and Ukraine to establish a powerful empire in the eighth and seventh centuries BCE, centred on Crimea. Particularly in light of Stocker's recent edition of Herodotus's work, it would have been easy for Ferguson to equate the Russian invaders of the Hungarian plain with the Scythian people, a race that had acquired a reputation for prowess in war and horsemanship in ancient times.

Scythian carries two associations that complicate Ferguson's use of the term in 'Hungary.' Firstly, the native Irish custom of 'boolies' in Edmund Spenser's *A View of the State of Ireland*, first published in 1633, is identified with the practices of Scythian people. The term 'boolies' in Spenser's work describes groups of people in Ireland who lived with their cattle on hills and mountains, moving to new areas once those which they had inhabited had ceased to be suitable for cattle grazing. In dialogue with Eudoxus, Ireneaus asserts that this same practice occurred among "all the Tartarians and the people about the Caspian Sea, which are naturally Scythians" (Spenser 1997, p. 55). Within a few years of the publication of *A View of the State of Ireland*, Geofrey Keating completed his pseudo-historical book, *Foras Feasa ar Éireann* (*The History of Ireland*) (Comyn 1902, p. xi). Keating's work draws upon the compilation of manuscripts dating back to the seventh century AD that are known collectively as *Lebor Gabála Érenn* (*Book of Invasions*). From this tradition, Keating claims a Scythian ancestry for the early inhabitants of Ireland through the arrival of Neimheadh in Ireland, coming from Scythia into Europe through the Baltic Sea (Comyn 1902, p. 175). Keating's book records Neimheadh as a descendent Japheth, one of the three sons of Noah named in the Book of Genesis. An antiquarian scholar, Ferguson was certainly familiar with both Spenser's *A View of the State of Ireland* and Keating's *Foras Feasa ar Éireann*, such that he would have been aware of the connection that had been made, however speculatively, between the early inhabitants of Ireland and the Scythian people. Keating's work carries another aspect that is intriguing for Ferguson's use of the term "Scythian" in 'Hungary'. Not only does he record an ancestral link between the Irish and the Scythians, he also claims that the Hungarians descended originally from the Scythians, along with the Huns, the Lombards and the Goths (Comyn 1902, p. 227).

It is unlikely that Ferguson had taken note of Keating's speculative claim concerning the Scythian origin of the Hungarians when composing 'Hungary,' though he would have been aware of the widely known and widely disputed claim for a connection of Ireland's early inhabitants to the Scythian people. This knowledge casts a certain element of doubt over how readers of the late 1840s might have interpreted the couplet that concludes the seventh verse of 'Hungary':

> Till the track of corruption alone in the air
> Shall tell sicken'd Europe the Scythian was there! (Ferguson 1849, p. 292).

A straight reading of these lines is that the stench of the bodies of those killed in battle is not just the trace of deaths caused by war. This odour of slaughter is also a sign of the corrupting influence of Tsarist Russia that "sickens" Europe when its forces intervene to put down the Hungarian fight for freedom. Yet the couplet is open to another interpretation. The phrase, "the Scythian was there," may also refer to the Scythian peoples who were said to have come into Europe in ancient times and who had settled in Ireland. This reading generates ambiguity as to what exactly Ferguson is expressing: perhaps sending the message that Europe is sickened in his own time by sudden recognition that the Scythian people had once inhabited the continent, a recognition that is particularly troubling for Ferguson in the case of Ireland, his native country. Once more, rather than effacing nationalism, the transnational character of 'Hungary' complicates it, especially through the poem's discreet relation to history, politics and religion in Ireland.

The ambiguity surrounding the term "Scythian" in 'Hungary' signals a transition in the tone and sentiment of the poem in its final five verses. The speaker warns against the danger of sympathy for "humanity's cause" risking the 'inhumanity' of hatred towards the Russian people, a hatred that would loosen the connection of the Hungarian struggle to "the ties of Christ's brotherhood" (Ferguson 1849, p. 292). Ferguson makes two important moves in this respect. He grants the particular Hungarian struggle a universal significance: a struggle for a people to live freely as one in which the cause of humanity is at stake. At the same time, he uses this universal perspective to argue for empathy between the warring factions, imagining Christ as the figure of universal fraternity. In one sense, this attitude repeats the articulation of a desire for unity that appears under two aspects in Ferguson's 'A Dialogue.' The first of these aspects is the empathy that Protestant 'Heart' feels for Catholics in Ireland on the grounds of their common identity as Irish people. The second is the more practical insistence of 'Head' that Protestants maintain the union of Ireland with England in order that Ireland avoids the bloodshed and sectarian violence that rebellion would unleash. In another sense, however, the change in tone verse nine of 'Hungary' indicates how much Ferguson's outlook has altered since the publication of 'A Dialogue' almost sixteen years earlier. Whereas then his characters gave voice to Irish Protestant determination to resist the rise of Catholic influence in Ireland, now, with Catholic emancipation having bedded down and with the country having undergone the horror of the Great Famine, Ferguson turns to Christ as the figure to whom all differing Christian denominations declare their fidelity. Whether the speaker's appeal to Christian fraternity in 'Hungary' carries an echo of 'A Dialogue' or shows how far Ferguson has left it behind, however, the question remains at the level of discreet implication. This appeal arises in consideration of Hungary at war with Russia, not Ireland at war with England nor Irish Protestants at war with Irish Catholics. The transnational aspect of nationhood in this instance lies in Ferguson's recourse to an image of Christ as a figure who binds all nations together. Ferguson accentuates this transcendence of national boundaries in verse ten. The speaker asks the rhetorical question as to whether mothers in Moscow have the same hearts as mothers in Budapest, when they breastfeed their children left without fathers, who have been killed in battle ('A Dialogue' 292). In verse eleven, he calls on the pity of the "God of Russian and Magyar" for the "war-wearied nations" (Ferguson 1849, p. 292).

The tenth, concluding verse of 'Hungary' introduces a final reversal of tone into the poem. This is one of shock at news of the defeat of the Hungarian Revolution, setting the heart of the speaker racing once more:

> What! Görgey surrendered! What! Bem's battles o'er!
> What! Haynau victorious! (Ferguson 1849, p. 292).

These are the only lines in the poem in which the speaker names men who were involved in the events. In the summer of 1849, General Artúr Görgey ordered the Hungarian forces to lay down their arms rather than enter battle with the Russian army of Tsar Nicholas I, a move that Lajos Kossuth regarded as a betrayal. Józef Bem was the leader of Hungarian armed forces who had retreated to Transylvania in the summer of 1849, where he fought numerous battles, suffering final defeat in July 1849 at the battle of Segesvár. General Julius von Haynau was the leader of the Austrian forces who imposed a violent crackdown in the aftermath of the Revolution, including the execution of many of its leaders. Ferguson's references to Görgey, Bem and Haynau not only illustrate how informed he was when composing 'Hungary'. They also make it impossible for him to end the poem on a note of Christian reconciliation. Instead, he leaves the reader with a poignant reflection on the incomprehensible mystery of God, one that leaves the believer with no choice but to accept God's will, however harsh and unjust it may appear:

> –Inscrutable God!
> We must wonder, and worship, and bow to thy rod! (Ferguson 1849, p. 292).

The rhyming of 'God' and 'rod' returns readers to the earlier part of poem, which invokes the Old Testament God of war. Now, however, it is not a God who grants victory but one who imposes defeat on the Hungarian people. The imperative is for people to maintain their faith in God in times of defeat as much as in times of victory.

There is no doubting the nationalist aspect of the speaker's shock in this final verse of 'Hungary' at news of the Hungarian surrender to the Russian Army and the retribution of the Austrian Army under General von Haynau. The conclusion leaves it unclear, however, as to how readers of *The Dublin University Magazine* were to regard this nationalism in September 1849. One response may have been that Ferguson's nationalism in this instance had nothing whatever to do with Ireland: that he was simply lamenting the defeat suffered by a relatively small nation at the hands of Tsarist Russia, a country that receives mention in 'A Dialogue' only in relation to tyranny. Another may have been that it had everything to do with Ireland: that, unwilling or unable to express his admiration openly in a Protestant Unionist magazine for the gallantry of the exiled leaders of the Young Ireland rebellion of 1848, Ferguson did so in a coded manner. This interpretation would read Artúr Görgey and Józef Bem as a Hungarian William Smith O'Brien and a Hungarian Thomas Meagher. One final line of interpretation may be the most accurate. In urging the Hungarian people to accept their final defeat as the will of God, the speaker in 'Hungary' is also implying that the Irish people must accept the catastrophe of the Great Famine as the will of that same "inscrutable" God. Oliver P. Rafferty illustrates the extent of this providentialist attitude during the time in which *The Dublin University Magazine* first published Ferguson's poem. It was an attitude held not exclusively by Irish Protestants, but one that was characteristic of the Protestant response to the widespread starvation, disease and emigration that wiped out approximately one-fifth of the Irish rural population in the late 1840s (*Violence*, 70–86).

Conclusion: Nationalism/Transnationalism

In his introduction to the edited volume, *Transnational Perspectives on Modern Irish History*, Niall Whelehan describes the transnational approach as follows: "Transnational history is a means to challenge impressions of national uniqueness and exceptionalism, to transcend the borders of the nation-state and trace connections and parallel developments between multiple territories" (Whelehan 2015, p. 1). Aspects of Samuel Ferguson's writing that I have discussed in this essay suggest that this transnational perspective is already embedded within the history of Irish nationalism. The voices of 'A Dialogue between the Heart and Head of an Irish Protestant' show the continual involvement of Irish nationalist discourse in disputes concerning its nature with respect to ethnicity, religion and constitutionality. 'A Dialogue' raises the question not only of what an Irish nation means, but also of its relation to the state. Arguing against repeal of the Act of Union between Britain and Ireland, 'Head' moves in a direction opposite to that of many Irish nationalists in claiming that Ireland takes its nationhood from institutions founded by the British monarchy and English Government in the country. 'Head' thereby extends the borders of the Irish state beyond the territory of the Irish nation, conceiving of Irish statehood as inextricably bound to English political institutions. In this radical digression from the orthodoxies of Irish republicanism and later forms of Irish nationalism, 'A Dialogue' testifies to the discrepancies between ethnic consciousness and state borders that Walker Connor considers to be increasing rather than abating with the progressive modernization of human societies (Connor 1994, 35). Framing Irish politics in religious terms following Catholic emancipation in 1829, 'A Dialogue' also positions it in relation to international institutions and historical movements: those of the Catholic Church, the Protestant Reformed Churches and secular liberal republicanism. Readers thereby see that the issues at stake concerning Protestantism in Ireland, following English legislative reforms of the late 1820s–early 1830s, transcend conditions specific to Ireland. Indeed, they situate the Irish experience into the most transnational of contexts, given the implications that British Government religious reforms of the period carried for Britain's governance of its colonial territories across the world.

The transnational features of 'A Dialogue' act as a useful guide to understanding Ferguson's poem that was written in response to news of the final defeat of Hungary by Austrian and Russian forces in 1849, bringing to an end the Hungarian Revolution that began in the Spring of 1848. Just as the international dimensions of 'A Dialogue' complicate its significance as a nationalist essay, so Ferguson's turn to Hungary in 1849 complicates whatever connection his poem, 'Hungary,' may have to Irish nationalism of the period. The nationalist character of the poem is not in dispute, appearing in the use that Ferguson makes of the same imagery and tone that he employs in his narrative poems of Irish mythology. Nor is there any disputing the fact that, under the influence of the Young Ireland ballad poet and essayist, Thomas Davis, and in the aftermath of the Great Famine of 1845-1848, Ferguson's nationalist sympathies had deepened. By 1848, he was prepared to countenance the Repeal of the Act of Union and the restoration of an Irish parliament in Dublin. These factors suggest that 'Hungary' identifies the cause of Hungary with that of Ireland, thereby illustrating how a transnational perspective may serve to strengthen rather than weaken nationalist sentiment. As I have argued, however, two considerations complicate this assessment. The first is the fact that Ferguson's turn to the situation in Hungary is also a turn away from Ireland towards a distant land, at a time when Ireland was struggling to come to terms with the calamity of widespread famine and emigration that befell the country from 1845. The attention in 'Hungary' is away from a country that, by the nineteenth century, was ethnically a loose combination of Gaelic, Ulster-Scottish and Anglo-Irish. Instead, the poem addresses a Central European conflict that involved several different ethnicities: Magyar, Austrian, Croatian, Serbian, Polish, Russian, and, in the immediate Post-War phase, Turkish. The second consideration is Ferguson's use of biblical language and imagery that reveals the influence of his Ulster Protestant upbringing, at a time when Catholicism was beginning to challenge the authority of Protestantism as the religion of governance in Irish political life. This aspect of 'Hungary' links the poem back to the Protestantism of 'A Dialogue' and to the argument entertained therein: the legislative changes introduced by the British Government, most especially the Church Temporalities (Ireland) Act of 1833, violated the British Constitution and were therefore tyrannical. If the Russian suppression of the Hungarian Revolution was equally tyrannical, as Ferguson's poem suggests, then 'Hungary' may well imply not a fate shared in common by Ireland and Hungary, but rather the common predicament of post-Catholic emancipation Irish Protestants and the Magyar people. Read together therefore, 'A Dialogue of the Head and Heart of an Irish Protestant' from 1833 and 'Hungary' from 1849, illustrate crucial transnational aspects in Ferguson's writing, aspects that bring the complexity of his nationalist thought into the public arena.

Bibliography

Appadurai, Arjun: *Modernity at Large: Cultural Dimensions of Globalization*. Minnesota MN 1996.
Bright, Richard: *Travels from Vienna through Lower Hungary*. Edinburgh 1818.
Brown, Malcolm: *Sir Samuel Ferguson*. Lewisburg PA 1972.
Connor, Walker: *Ethnonationalism: the Quest for Understanding*. Princeton NJ 1994.
Comyn, David (trans.): *The History of Ireland by Geoffrey Keating*. Vol. 1. London 1902.
Craig, Patricia: 'In the Long Run (on Samuel Ferguson)', in: IRISH PAGES 2009/6 (1), p. 81–91.
Crowley, John / Smyth, William J. / Murphy, Mike (eds.): *Atlas of the Great Irish Famine*. New York 2012.
Deak, Istvan: *The Lawful Revolution: Louis Kossuth and the Hungarians, 1848–49*. New York 1979.
Delaney, Enda: *The Great Irish Famine: A History in Four Lives*. Dublin 2014.
Denman, Peter: *Samuel Ferguson: the Literary Achievement*. Washington DC 1990.

Holy Bible: Evangelical Revised Version, 2019, available at https://www.biblegateway.com/ [29 Dec. 2022].

Faist, Thomas: *The Volume and Dynamics of International Migration and Transnational Social Spaces*. Oxford 2000.

Ferguson, S.: 'A Dialogue between the Head and Heart of an Irish Protestant', in: DUBLIN UNIVERSITY MAGAZINE Nov. 1833/II (XI), p. 586–93.

Ferguson, S.: 'Hardiman's Irish Minstrelsy.–No. 1', in: DUBLIN UNIVERSITY MAGAZINE April 1834/III (XVI), p. 465–78; 'Hardiman's Irish Minstrelsy.–No. 2', in: DUBLIN UNIVERSITY MAGAZINE August 1834/IV (XX), p. 152–67; 'Hardiman's Irish Minstrelsy.–No. 3', in: DUBLIN UNIVERSITY MAGAZINE Oct. 1834/IV (XXII), p. 444–67; 'Hardiman's Irish Minstrelsy.–No. 4', in: DUBLIN UNIVERSITY MAGAZINE Nov. 1834/IV (XXIII), p. 514–42.

Ferguson, S.: 'Hungary', in: DUBLIN UNIVERSITY MAGAZINE Sept. 1849/XXXIV (CCI), p. 292.

Ferguson, Samuel. *Lays of the Western Gael*. London 1865.

Ferguson, Sir Samuel. *Poems*. Dublin 1880.

Gergely, A.: 'A Forradalom és az Önvédelmi Háború ['The Revolution and the War of Self-Defence' [own translation]] (1848–1849)', in: Gergely, András (ed.): *Magyarország törénete a 19. Században* [*The History of Hungary in the Nineteenth Century*]. Budapest 2019, p. 236–278.

Graham, Colin: *Ideologies of Epic: Nation, empire and Victorian epic poetry*. Manchester 1998.

Graves, Alfred Perceval, introd.: *Poems of Sir Samuel Ferguson*. Dublin 1916.

Iriye, Akira: *Global and Transnational History: The Past, The Present, and Future*. Houndmills Basingstoke 2013.

Juergensmeyer, Mark (ed.): *Global Religions: An Introduction*. Oxford 2003.

Képessy, Imre: 'National Modernisation through the Constitutional Revolution of 1848 in Hungary: Pretext and Context', in: Gałędek, Michał / Klimaszewska, Anna (eds.): *Modernisation, National Identity and Legal Instrumentalism*, vol. II: *Public Law*. Amsterdam 2019, p. 51–68.

Kinealy, Christine / King, Jason / Moran, Gerard (eds.): *The History of the Irish Famine*. New York 2018.

Lloyd, D.: 'Arnold, Ferguson, Schiller and the Politics of Aesthetics', in: CULTURAL CRITIQUE Winter 1985/86:2, p. 137–69.

Lyons, F. S. L.: *Ireland Since the Famine*. 2nd ed. London 1973.

Molnár, Miklós: *A Concise History of Hungary*. Cambridge 2001.

Murphy, James H.: *Abject Loyalty: Nationalism and Monarchy in Ireland During the Reign of Queen Victoria*. Cork 2001.

Nolan, Emer: *Catholic Emancipations: Irish Fiction from Thomas Moore to James Joyce*. New York 2007.

Ong, Aihwa: *Flexible Citizenship: The Cultural Logics of Transnationality*. Durham NC 1999.

Pardoe, Julia: *The City of the Magyar or Hungary and her Institutions, 1839–40*. Three vols. London 1840.

Patten, Eve: *Samuel Ferguson and the Culture of Nineteenth-Century Ireland*. Dublin 2004.

'Protestant Repeal Association', in: THE NATION May 6, 1848, p. 1.

'Protestant Repeal Association', in: THE NATION July 1, 1848, p. 422.
Rafferty, Olivier J.: *Violence, Politics and Catholicism in Ireland.* Dublin 2016.
Robinson, W. J.: 'Beyond Nation-State Paradigms: Globalization, Sociology, and the Challenge of Transnational Studies', in: SOCIOLOGICAL FORUM 1998/13.4, p. 561–593.
Rolleston, T. W. (ed.): *Thomas Davis: Selections from his Prose and Poetry.* Dublin: London 1914.
Spenser, Edmund: *A View of the State of Ireland* (1633). Andrew Hadfield / Willy Maley (eds.). Oxford 1997.
Stocker, Charles William: *The History of the Persian Wars, from Herodotus.* Vol. 1. 2nd ed. London 1848.
Tedeschi, M. / Vorobeva, E. / Juahiainen, J.: 'Transnationalism: current debates and new perspectives', in: GEOJOURNAL 2022/87, p. 603–19.
'The Hungarian Struggle', in: THE NATION Sept. 1, 1849, p. 2.
Wallerstein, Immanuel: 'The Construction of Peoplehood: Racism, Nationalism, Ethnicity', in: Balibar, Etienne / Wallertstein, Immanuel (eds.): *Race, Nation, Class: Ambiguous Identities.* London 1991, p. 71–85.
Wansbrough, Henry (gen. ed.): *The New Jerusalem Bible.* London 1985.
Whelehan, Niall (ed.): *Transnational Perspectives on Modern Irish History.* New York 2015.

Paweł Meus

German nationalism in the interwar period from a borderland perspective: Alfred Hein and his interpretation of the national question

The end of the First World War brought new geopolitical reality in Europe, which, for some nations, represented the beginning of state independence, while for others, drew up a difficult balance sheet of losses. In order to calm mounting tensions in European society after the grueling battle and, to strengthen the just-restored but very fragile peace, the victorious powers had to organize an order that would not only satisfy their interests as victors, but also avoid providing pretexts for future conflicts. Central and Eastern Europe was a particularly sensitive area of the emerging structure where hitherto multi-ethnic communities united in heterogeneous powers under the domination of a single nation were claiming the right to their own statehood. The architects of the new order were able to overcome this difficult task by using a universal criterion – the nation. This was pointed out even before the end of the war by American President Thomas Woodrow Wilson, who based his fourteen-point speech on the right of nations to self-determination. In fact, this is still an important foundation of the democratic Western world today (Geiss 2017, p. 152). Although, as Jörg Fisch indicates, it is difficult to establish a clear definition of a nation and to determine who exactly has the right of self-determination, this rather general principle seems to be the fairest possible solution (Fisch 2010, p. 40).

Despite its inevitable imperfections, the right of people to self-determination became the main determinant of the Treaty of Versailles, which defined the new state order and guaranteed its permanence. That solution was difficult to accept for the previous hegemons who had lost the war, as the new states were created on lands separated from their territories. Germany, which was blamed for the war, was severely affected by the treaty arrangements. They were also deprived of large areas of land, including those inhabited in large parts by the German population, thereby undermining as a punishment the nation's right to self-determination (Geiss 2017, p. 156). This inequality became one of the main arguments raised by Germans dissatisfied with the post-war settlement, who turned their resentment primarily against Poland. Indeed, the newly formed Polish state comprised the largest part of the territories lost by Germany. The losses suffered struck at the dignity of the German nation, in which a new kind of nationalism naturally took shape, directed against the Treaty of Versailles and against its beneficiary, Poland. The irresolvable conflict of interests between the two countries marked their relations of the inter-war period, and the question of a peaceful change of borders was one of the most important foreign policy problems of the Weimar Republic (Lawaty 1993, p. 21). Despite his conciliatory policy with regard to territorial losses in the west, the German Foreign Minister Gustav Stresemann, a man of merit for peace and the improvement of relations with other European states, constantly opted for a diplomatic revision of the Polish-German border (Piper 2021, p. 54). The thorn in Germany's flesh was constantly the so-called Polish Corridor, i. e. the area of Second Republic of Poland that provided it with the access to the Baltic Sea that was guaranteed in the Treaty of Versailles, but which also separated East Prussia from the rest of the German state. This was the symbolic area where all Germany's resentments related to the course of the entire border with Poland accumulated, i.e. first and foremost the aforementioned tearing apart of the coherent territory of the state and depriving Germany of the highly industrialized part of Upper Silesia, as well as the question of Danzig, which became a free city, and in the longer term also depriving Germany of Greater Poland (Tebinka 2020, p. 32, 42 ff).

The starting point for German anti-Polish revisionist policy, however, was the period just after the signing of the Treaty of Versailles, when the borders took their long-established shape and plebiscites were held in ethnically ambiguous areas – in Upper Silesia and, according to Polish nomenclature, in Warmia, Masuria and Powisle, and, according to German nomenclature, in West and East Prussia. The fierce language of the propaganda campaign and the nationalist prejudices formed at the time remained present for years in the discourse on the border. Mutual aversion was based on differences resulting from the political, social, cultural and 'national-psychological' development of the two states; and the German narrative eagerly referred to stereotypes from the imperial period that had taken root for generations in the German consciousness (Lawaty 1993, p. 22 f.). In the forefront, the Germans emphasized the cultural gap between the West as represented by Germany and the East as embodied by Poland. According to Germany, the natural role of the German nation as 'culture disseminators' (German: *Kulturträger*) in the East, which had been providing nations such as Poland with economic, technical, social or cultural innovations for centuries, arose of that difference (Lawaty 1993, p. 22 f). Strong negative emotions were an integral part of the propaganda on the German-Polish border, with what an atmosphere of insecurity was fostered, especially among the population living in the border areas, and mutual injustices were remembered. The uncertainty resulting from such a strategy intensified mutual antipathies and preserved nationalist thinking.

That tendency is particularly evident in the case of East Prussia, which presents itself as a mutilated and lonely island (Hartmann 2007, p. 218).[1] And its intensification outside the plebiscite period comes in the late 1920s and early 1930s, when the problems of economic crisis and unemployment create fertile ground for nationalist inclinations which were weakened at an earlier time (Hofmeister 2010, p. 450). Propaganda publications are produced on this wave, drawing form and content from established and verified methods. These are usually novels of a popular science nature based on a compilation of official documents and individual recollections from the First World War or plebiscites. Regina Hartmann reports that the most important representatives of this trend were the brothers Fritz and Richard Skowronnek, as well as Hans Martin. These publications are intended to show the difficult events from a German perspective, in which Germans are portrayed as peaceful and virtuous victims of devious enemies (Hartmann 2007, p. 218f). In the trend of those publications is Alfred Hein's book *Über zertrümmerte Brücken – vorwärts!* (1933), in which the author presents the recent history of East Prussia and emphasizes its important role for Germany. Starting from, in the author's opinion, the unjust settlement of the First World War and the new territorial division of Europe, this book brings together arguments to show that East Prussia is an example of a region in Europe which developed through German culture and is exclusively German territory. Furthermore, the author of this book attempted to prove that Poland has no right to claim this territory, even though a part of the native population living in this region exhibits Polish cultural characteristics. This text seems even more interesting in the context of the apotheosis of one's own nation, as it was probably written under the influence of the author's activity in an institution dealing with pro-German propaganda. The second text in the current of nationalist propaganda in literature is the short story *Verratene Zuflucht*. It shows the relationship between a Pole, who is portrayed as a traitor and a greedy person, and a German, who is depicted as a victim of the division of Silesia after the First World War. This story is even more remarkable as it relates to the author's home region and contains a heavy load of subjective opinion.

A close look at the biography of the author, who initially grew up and worked in the eastern borderlands of Germany, is intended to show the factors influencing his creative stance and the position he takes in his works. However, this biography is only intended to complement the attempt at a synthetic presentation of Alfred Hein's work, which focuses on the relationship between Germans and Poles after the First World War and has a nationalistic orientation. This

---

1 It should be noted that the presentation of Polish-German relations from the Polish side is based on emphasizing the harm done to the Polish population under the sovereignty of the German state. Gustaw Morcinek's *Wyrąbany chodnik* can serve as an example.

attempt is based on a general discussion of the content of the short story *Verratene Zuflucht* and Hein's book *Über zertrümmerte Brücken – vorwärts!*, as well as a more in-depth characterization of selected passages and quotations from the latter work. The above-mentioned intentions do not claim to be a comprehensive analysis but aim to bring the forgotten viewpoint of the Germans, especially after the drama of the Second World War, and their claims to the question of the nation and its rights, closer to the reader. The second important task of this chapter is to assess the impact of the arguments used by Alfred Hein on the audience and to define them against the background of the pro-German propaganda narrative of the interwar period.

Alfred Hein's biography and works perfectly reflect the German view of the border issue, as he was associated with both plebiscite areas and devoted considerable space to them in his works. A biographical sketch of the author should provide the best justification for this claim and, moreover, bring the forgotten artist closer to the public. Alfred Hein was born on 7th October 1894 in Beuthen (now Bytom) in Upper Silesia into the family of a teacher and researcher of local culture. At home, alongside his upbringing in respect for the German state, he encountered the customs of the Silesian people, which are reflected in his numerous works. While still at school, he made his debut by publishing his poems in, among others, the literary magazines *Die Bergstadt* and *Die Lese. Literarische Zeitung für das deutsche Volk* (Meus 2022, 108). In 1914, he volunteered for service in the First World War and was sent to the Western Front where he served as a messenger. The harsh realities of war gradually revised his idealistic patriotism but in the meantime he wrote numerous poems and sketches dedicated to the soldier's everyday life which were published in frontline newspapers. One of his poems, 'Eine Kompagnie Soldaten,' brought him wider recognition as it became a popular and award-winning march after the war. Hein's first poetry cycles, *Sammelnde Trommel* (1917) and *Terzinen an die tote Isot* (1918), are still marked by the young man's confrontation with war, while his next cycles, *Die Lieder vom Frieden* (1919), *Der Unerlöste* (1919) and *Der Lindenfrieden* (1920) have pacifist overtones (Dampc-Jarosz / Meus 2019, p. 108 ff).

After his military service, Alfred Hein settled in Königsberg (now Kaliningrad), where he married the daughter of a local banker, Helena Laue, with whom he had two daughters. The couple took a honeymoon trip to Frombork, during which the writer was able to discover the landscapes and traditions of East Prussia. The result of the trip was Alfred Hein's first praise of nature and the German culture and customs of the region in the novella *Die Frauenburger Reise* (1921). At the same time, he became involved in the cultural life of Königsberg where he was active in the local branch of the Goethe-Bund, an association of intellectuals and artists striving for freedom of art and science. In addition, from 1918 to 1923 he worked as an editor and theatre critic for the *Königsberger*

Hartungsche Zeitung (Meus 2022, p. 109). This was an opinion-forming newspaper with a long-standing liberal tradition strongly linked to the German Democratic Party (Deutsche Demokratische Partei) where the long-time provincial mayor and anti-Polish supporter Ernst Stiehr was an activist (Fiedor 1970, p. 434). The fact of working in the editorial office during the plebiscite in the area could certainly not have left a trace in Hein's consciousness, but he was committed to Germanness during the plebiscite in his native Upper Silesia. He was to be specially awarded a local decoration for this activity.[2] Hein's stance towards the Poles in Upper Silesia is contained in the short story *Verratene Zuflucht* (Hein 1968, p. 126 ff), which at the same time exemplifies his work on this subject. The story depicts the fate of a friendship between a Pole and a German, which ends after the division of Silesia. The exact content of the story will be explored and commented on later in the chapter.

From 1923 Alfred Hein had been the director of the Reich Agency for Homeland Service (Reichszentrale für Heimatsdienst) in East Prussia before being transferred in 1929 to the Central German branch in Halle (Saale), where he worked until 1931 (Meus 2022, p. 109f). The writer's new workplace naturally focused his attention on the promotion of Germanness and thus made his work more strongly marked by it. The Reich Agency for Homeland Service existed from 1919 to 1933, and its main task was to awaken and sustain a nationwide political consciousness among Germans. In its first period of activity, this propaganda institution dealt with issues related to the Treaty of Versailles, i.e. combating the thesis of Germany's war guilt, the issue of reparations and the fight over the course of the borders. Later on, its activities continued to focus on providing information on the effects of the Treaty of Versailles, in addition to familiarizing citizens with the constitution and providing orientation on the economic position of the state and the most important social policy issues (Richter 1963, p. 39 ff, 50). While working at the Reich Agency for Homeland Service, he gave many lectures on the culture and heritage of the German people and took part in conferences organized by this institution. During one of them, he befriended Max Worgitzki – the director of the Allenstein (now Olsztyn) branch of the Heimatbund (Knauer 1983, p. 111) organization and one of the leading opponents of Polishness in Warmia and Masuria (Fiedor 1970, p. 430). This paramilitary organisation was supposed to defend Germany against Bolshevik and Polish influences (Jendrzejewski 2012, p. 271 ff), and played an important propaganda role during the plebiscite (Fiedor 1970, p. 430). The writer's friendly acquaintance with the local activist could not fail to influence his al-

---

2 Annke-Margarethe Knauer (1901–1987) – a long-time co-worker and life companion of the writer in her memoirs about him – mentions the Silesian Eagle medal of the second class. Cf. Knauer 1983, p. 25.

ready strong patriotic views. This period was not limited to activity within his tenure but also brought new works. In 1926, Alfred Hein published, together with Wilhelm Müller-Rüdersdorf, a volume on regional themes entitled *Oberschlesien*, which consisted of poems, stories and descriptions depicting the culture, history, landscape, folk customs and industrial character of Upper Silesia. The volume was published as part of the *Brandstetters Heimatbücher Deutscher Landschaften* series at the Friedrich Brandstetter publishing house in Leipzig, which was dedicated to individual regions of Germany. In the same year he published the novella *Delta des Lebens*, in which he depicted the grandeur of the Giant Mountains against the backdrop of a love story and, at the same time, questioned industrialisation and modern metropolitan life. Alfred Hein's most important work, the novel *Eine Kompagnie Soldaten. In der Hölle von Verdun*, was published in 1929. In this book the author depicted the life of soldiers at the front of the First World War based on his own experiences. Its English translation *In the Hell of Verdun* by F. H. Lyon was published in London in 1930.

From the 1930s onwards, Hein was active as a freelance writer. In addition to novels, novellas and short stories, he mainly produced press texts with a focus on history, culture and nature (Meus 2022, p. 110). In 1931, he wrote the children's book *Annke – Kriegsschicksale eines ostpreußischen Mädchens (1915–1918)*, in which he depicted the abduction of East Prussians to Russia during the First World War and their return to their homeland as seen through the eyes of a child. In his novel *Sturmtrupp Brooks* (1933), he depicted the story of a former captain from East Prussia who is dissatisfied with the post-war order prevailing in Germany. The following books by Alfred Hein were published in the series *Aus deutschem Schrifttum und deutscher Kultur: Die Erstürmung des "Toten Manns" am 20. Mai 1916* (1932) – an account of a day's fighting on the Western Front of the First World War, *Der Alte vom Preußenwald. Hindenburgs sieghaftes Leben* (1933) – a biography of Paul von Hindenburg, *Über zertrümmerte Brücken – vorwärts!* (1933) – an expression of dissatisfaction with the separation of East Prussia from the rest of German territory under the Treaty of Versailles and *Gloria! Victoria!* (1934) – a depiction of the 1914 Battle of Tannenberg from the East Prussian perspective. The works published in this series have a strong national character and place Hein on the borderline between patriotism and nationalism. The timing of their publication, i.e., the period of the Nazi takeover, provides the basis for accusations against the writer of supporting the Third Reich (Kunicki 2006, p. 437). However, one must be careful with such judgements, as Alfred Hein, regardless of the political mood in Germany, represented extreme right-wing views still rooted in the imperial period. Although in many places the ideology of the Nazi regime overlaps with the writer's views and his position is difficult to assess clearly, in his defense it should be pointed out that he was unable to accept the unification of literature by party injunctions and focused primarily on children's and youth literature as less restricted by the regime, as he wrote to his friend Max Worgitzki in a letter in 1937 (Hein 1937, letter). In *Greift an, Grenadiere!* (1939) Hein made the events unfolding on the Western Front the subject of a children's story. A year later, the children's book *Beates Vater* (1940) was published, in which the artistic development of the young illustrator was shown. He took up the Silesian theme anew in the novella *Verliebte Ferienreise* (1941), which is an affirmation of the uncomplicated and tradition-oriented life in the Giant Mountains and, at the same time, a rejection of the big-city rush. In the novel *Du selber bist Musik* (1942), Hein described the difficult choice of a music student who has to choose between art and starting a family. Similar accusations to the books published as a part of the *Aus deutschem Schrifttum und deutscher Kultur* series can be levied against notebooks for young people, as they praise German imperialism alongside biographies of famous figures from German history and contain aggressive propaganda against everything that is not German. Alfred Hein's writing activities were finally interrupted by being called up to the army in 1944. He stationed in Silesia until the entry of the Red Army, where he was taken into Soviet captivity on 8th May 1945. With a blood infection, he was transported to Halle (Saale), where he died on 30th December 1945 and was buried (Pioskowik 2015, p. 3f). Alfred Hein's biography testifies to the strong influence of historical events and the places where he lived on his literary work and the world created in them. The main themes are the First World War, the nature, history and tradition of Silesia and East Prussia, and art as a universal value that brings happiness.

Similarly to the strictly literary works, Alfred Hein's propaganda activity also shows the close connection between his experiences and the views he proclaimed. The short story *Verratene Zuflucht*, already mentioned, which features two friends, the German Robert Dinklage and the Pole Kurt Ziaja is very personal. They both attended the same school and fought together for Germany in the First World War. However, their paths diverged when, as Hein states: "the revolution came and the Pole reached for Upper Silesia" (Hein 1968, p. 126). Hidden underneath this statement is the change in the previous political order and the division of Upper Silesian industry, which is supposed to have led to a great deal of misunderstanding and even hostility, as the hitherto functioning of regional enterprises was significantly affected by the unreasonably, from a German perspective, drawn national border. Hein puts the blame for this state of affairs on the Upper Silesians of Polish origin, who are represented by Ziaja. This one, despite his hitherto loyalty to the German state and friendship with Germans, suddenly breaks off all relations after the rebirth of the Polish state. The Pole becomes an insensitive industrialist who, out of fear for his factory, does not acknowledge his past. The German, whose family misfortunes have meanwhile driven him into poverty, was forced to abandon his studies and work hard. He crosses the border every day to earn a modest income in the Polish part of the divided region. There he is, however, subjected to harassment and taunts from bands of Polish troublemakers, who on one occasion want to beat him up. When seeking refuge with his old friend, he is not helped. Instead, he is handed over to his aggressive attackers.

In this story, Alfred Hein uses a very simple division between the good and the hard-working, who are severely tried by fate but do not give up, and the clever, who pay attention only to their own gain, even when they hurt others with their decisions, which is characteristic for this type of propaganda text. In German agitation, it is always the German who is the good hero, while the Pole makes up the latter group, as Hein's story strongly demonstrates. The author is unable to accept that Silesians who feel Polish want to serve their homeland and not a state that is hostile to it. Hein's rhetoric is very straightforward and harsh in its assessment, as he presents the world created in the story as black and white. There is no room for doubt. The Poles, in the author's view, must come across as negative characters characterized by insensitivity and ingratitude. The Germans, on the other hand, are shown as victims of Polish intrigues. This division of roles is typical for German propaganda during the struggle over the course of the Polish-German border. Its strong use should not come as a surprise. The author treats the issue emotionally because it stems from his Silesian background.

The prominent issue of the new geopolitical order after the First World War was also addressed by Alfred Hein in his book *Über zertrümmerte Brücken – vorwärts!* He wrote it on the basis of his experience at the Reich Agency for Homeland Service, and it is undoubtedly an example of an agitational struggle for German interests based on a multifaceted narrative. This incisive story presents the history and cultural role of East Prussia. At its center, there is the Treaty of Versailles, which the author regards as an unfounded dictate. Using East Prussia as an example, Hein depicts Germany's post-war fate as degrading. At the same time, he creates himself as an exponent of the opinion of the majority of Germans about the Treaty of Versailles when he deftly combines facts and emotions in a complaint about the crippling of German industry due to the confiscation of trains, aircraft and merchant fleets, and war reparations that violate international law and are unfulfillable. Furthermore, the treaty is intended to be French revenge for the German victory in 1870/71 and to humiliate Germany by drastically reducing its military strength and suffering significant territorial losses (Hein 1933, p. 8 ff). Hein undermines the victory of the Triple Entente states, led by France as Germany's eternal enemy, and thus the meaningfulness of the Treaty of Versailles. As a representative of the affected Germans, he writes:

So 'peace' is supposed to ensure victory on paper, which is never achieved on the battlefield.
The day of the Treaty of Versailles has arrived. They are disarming Germany. Already their army is diminished as if it were to defend a mere 'Brandenburg electorate.'
There must be no German soldiers on the Rhine, whose left bank is occupied by enemies.
The German fleet, which – for the first time in the history of the world – has defeated the English fleet at Skagerrak, considered invincible, is about to be spent. However, at Scapa Flow our sailors sink the German ships before the enemy can take them.
Rail wagons, aircraft, cannons and an entire merchant fleet, all this the enemy demanded for itself. And even much more: cows and livestock, horses, pigs and sheep in their hundreds of thousands – even medicines and dyes from our factories.
And money, money, money.
And 'fair borders'!
This is how the German east became a region that to this day has not experienced true peace. Poland and Lithuania are the pets of the haters. They got what they demanded on hypocritical grounds. 'Boche'[3] will pay everything, the slogan went (Hein 1933, p. 9f, own translation).

In the quotation, the settlements of the First World War, which Alfred Hein considers unfair regarding the situation at the front in the last days of the war and the potential of the German troops, are challenged. He thus refers both to all the soldiers who had to fight in the devastating war and to the families of the fallen. He subconsciously shows that the sacrifices made so far have been in vain. Hein also wants to make his compatriots aware of Germany's complete vulnerability as a punishment for the war, which Germany, in the author's opinion, was supposed to have unjustly lost. Here he introduces the camouflaged thesis that the other powers of the civilized world at the time had conspired against Germany and made it a 'scapegoat.'

According to Hein, who does not mention Germany's role in relation to the genesis of the war, the humiliation is disproportionate to the military defeat, as it covers many areas of state functioning. The first argument is the exaggerated reduction in the size of the military, which is supposed to result in complete dependence on other states. This is difficult to accept, as Germany has to go from being one of the superpowers to a 'second-class' state. This rationale is not only to make Germans fear for autonomy, but above all a sense of humiliation. Secondly, a sense of injustice and restriction and thus humiliation is to be associated with the surrender of all means of transport, which, according to the author, is to bring the economy to an abrupt halt and, in the long term, to regress. Thirdly, Germany is to be deprived of food and basic goods for health and security. Hein presents

---

3 'Boche' is a derisive term used by the Allies during World War I, often collectively ('the Boche' meaning 'the Germans').

the guidelines of the authors of the Treaty of Versailles very generally as demands and immediately labels them negative. By adding further points, he intensifies the fear and the feeling of growing injustice as he presents restrictions that are closer and closer to everyday life. The reader may thus get the impression that the entire world has formed an alliance against Germany, which has lost its subjectivity in all areas of state functioning. The punishment depicted in the above quotation and appropriately emotionally charged by the author seems at once disproportionate. This is a deliberate effort by Hein to be able to conclude the gradation of 'German misfortunes' with the strongest of the effects of the Treaty of Versailles – a change of borders involving territorial losses. In the Germans reading the text, who felt aggrieved by the course of affairs after the First World War, this last point must have aroused unequivocally negative emotions, led by indignation and hatred of the states to which the territories hitherto under German sovereignty had acceded. Hein refers to these states as 'pupils' of the authors of the Treaty of Versailles and thus the victors of the war. With this term alone, Hein shows great resentment towards these states and fuels resentment. In order to perpetuate all the negative emotions that have been stimulated, Hein writes that the slogan of Germany's opponents is a sentence containing a contemptuous term for the Germans and expressing the conviction that they must pay for everything possible. The accompanying quote, in which Alfred Hein summarizes the findings of the Treaty of Versailles, is thoroughly subjective and presents a nationalist view of the issue being described. Its purpose is to arouse resentment against the Treaty of Versailles and to prepare readers for arguments designed to prove the author's point.

Hein finds the new routing of the border between his homeland and Poland, reborn after more than 100 years of partitions, particularly painful. As a result, East Prussia was separated from the rest of the German state, and the author describes it as a 'torture wound in the East' (German: 'Folterwunden im Osten' – Hein 1933, p. 12). In order to demonstrate the Germanness of the region and thus undermine its separation from the rest of the German state, he invokes history from the Middle Ages onwards and writes about the colonial spirit that has marked it since the time of the Teutonic Order. Its German name 'der Deutsche Orden' (literally 'the German Order'), which is used by Hein, is a natural indication of the strong German culture that managed to create and maintain a prosperous economic system and space where newcomers from Franconia, Silesia, Saxony, the Rhineland or the Netherlands live in harmony. Hein compares the existing reality in East Prussia to the grand castles of the knights, which are supposed to be a testimony to the stability and strength and, above all, the high level of civilizational development of the region. According to the author, its flourishing is made possible by the enthusiasm of its inhabitants, which is based on diversity and a sense of duty. At this point, Hein refers to the Germans' pride in their nation intellectual and economic achievements, which previous generations had toiled to preserve and develop. In the author's opinion, the only threat that led, already in the Middle Ages, to a temporary weakening of the region's position were the Poles. Hein mentions that all the settlers "hastily came here as if to a paradise on earth, and it was only when this dreaming land under the protection of mighty fortresses and wise hands was continually invaded by Polish raiders that the defensive power of the knights ceased" (Hein 1933, p. 34). The mention of fortified castles can also be linked to the image of the homeland as a fortified stronghold that the enemy, that is, according to Hein, the Poles, cannot enter. Here, the author mobilizes the Germans to defend themselves against the Poles and once again arouses resentment towards them. In the context of the second issue, Hein cites Immanuel Kant, both as a prominent German thinker and as a celebrated representative of the region. At the same time, he emphasizes that difficult events in the history of East Prussia did not shake its economic and cultural development. One of these was to be the Battle of Grunwald[4] and the subsequent Peace of Torun, which could not stop the flourishing of German civilization. With this reference, Hein points to Poland as a danger to the established order in East Prussia (Hein 1933, p. 29 ff). He also sees the Russians, who abducted the local population during the First World War, as another threat. However, they did not give up during their captivity and, after returning to their homeland, they energetically set about rebuilding the region, with which they were to prove that only German culture and the German way of life would lead to prosperity and happiness (Hein 1933, p. 14 ff). By pointing to the Poles and Russians, Hein constructs two worlds in his message – a Germanic world and a Slavic world. The latter is intended by the author's narrative to be dangerous for the Germans and to cause them anxiety.

As a current threat to East Prussia, Alfred Hein presents the claims of the Polish state on territories partly inhabited by Polish people. Although he admits that Germany lost the Klaipėda Region after Lithuania took it over (Hein 1933, p. 47), it is Poland that is supposed to pose a threat, because, as the author states, it would 'insidiously' want to enlarge its territory. It thus instils fear in the honest and hardworking inhabitants of East Prussia. In order to emotionally emphasize the division into bad Poles and good Germans created in the book's narrative, Hein describes the attitudes adopted by the representatives of both nations during the plebiscite. He mentions the 'Warsaw instigators' (Hein 1933, p. 23), who were supposed to try to buy the votes of lazy and greedy people in favor of

---

4 In German historiography, two battles are referred to as the 'Schlacht bei Tannenberg' (English: Battle of Tannenberg). The first of these took place in 1410 and in Polish historiography it is called the 'Battle of Grunwald' (English: Battle of Grunwald). At that time, the Teutonic Order was defeated by the united Polish-Lithuanian army. And in the second battle called 'Schlacht bei Tannenberg,' the German army defeated the Russian army in 1914.

Poland. By doing so, he indirectly characterizes the Poles as dishonest and vanity-minded schemers who want to conquer an advanced civilized area. Hein, however, emphatically stresses that the majority of the local population values honesty and industriousness and therefore remains loyal to the Germans. The sensible ones include many Masurians and even quite a few of the population of Polish origin, who are convinced of better future prospects under German protection (Hein 1933, p. 23).

Another of the presented advantages of the Germans is their unity, even of those who no longer live in East Prussia, but believe that with their vote in the plebiscite they will save the existence of their homeland. To reinforce his thesis, Hein cites the fictional example of a Chicago millionaire who comes from a Masurian family.[5] Jim Schimanski came to Europe because he could not bear the thought that "Poland is stealing here in the east the eternal German cultural area, ten times the size of Alsace-Lorraine, tearing away from the middle of an organically knit national body" (Hein 1933, p. 24). The German apologist from overseas believes so strongly in the correctness of his convictions that he instructs the English soldiers overseeing the plebiscite that only a victory in favor of Germany would ensure the region's ultimate belonging to the motherland and thus the right prospects for the future. With his explanations to the English, Hein addresses the western world with the message that only a German presence in eastern Europe guarantees not only the development of the region, but also a more stable peace. An allusion to the English doubts of the 1920s about the demarcation of the German-Polish border and the division of the German state is apparent here (Tebinka 2020, p. 45).

The greatest resentment towards Poland is expressed in the section containing a description of the so-called Polish Corridor. Hein lamentably lists the numerous consequences of the separation of East Prussia from German territory, which include restricted access to the Vistula River, severed railway lines, broken bridges, difficult contact between citizens living in two separate parts of the state, and, above all, the so-called Polish Corridor itself. The author is convinced that the division of the hitherto homogeneous country is unwise, as it paralyses the export of goods from East Prussia and impedes passenger travel. Furthermore, he

---

5 Hein includes many stories about the fate of Germans connected to East Prussia, for whom the separation of East Prussia from the country as a whole is painful. These are always unambiguously positive characters, such as Theodor Jankowski – a pro-German Masurian and soldier who fought in the First World War, who had to leave his hometown after the area was annexed to Poland (Hein 1933, p. 14 ff); Christian Kötelhön – a factory owner living in Berlin, who, wanting to show his son his hometown, explains why they have to cross another country to get to Germany again (Hein 1933, p. 43 ff) or the starost from Marienwerder (now Kwidzyn), who shows a foreign professor the resulting damage to the local community from the demarcated border (Hein 1933, p. 52 ff).

accuses Poland of weakening the position of Danzig (now Gdańsk), which, as a typically German city, was separated from the state that formed its identity and made a free city that was losing its importance. Writing about the Germanness of Danzig, he points out that only the post office and the ammunition depot are Polish. The clandestine construction of a Polish port in Gdynia, which on the one hand economically harms the port of Danzig, on the other hand is supposed to additionally serve as a naval port, is supposed to be destructive to the centuries-old German tradition (Tebinka 2020, p. 45). Poland is again presented as a dangerous neighbor, who not only hinders the growth of centers developed thanks to German culture and work, but also arouses fear with its actions, assessed by the author as hostile.

In order to summarize his own subjective, though not unjustifiably emotional, German view of the issue of Polish-German relations in the interwar period, Alfred Hein deftly appeals to a seemingly objective authority. He quotes the words of Pierre Valmigère, a French writer and doctor of jurisprudence, who admonishes Poland as follows:

> You are heading for disaster and digging your own grave with your hands. What madness drives you? Why do you need to add to your already vast territories those few square kilometers occupied by a population hostile to you and which you are plunging into despair with your outdated polonization methods? This is not about justice, it is simply about cause and effect. Germany will never get over the fact that it is cut in two (Hein 1933, p. 60, own translation).

The above-mentioned words, as an opinion of an authority from one of the states that created the Treaty of Versailles, are meant to be impartial and thus convince readers that Hein's arguments in the book are also objective.

Alfred Hein's position on the question of the Polish-German border, presented in the form of the popular science book *Über zertrümmerte Brücken – vorwärts!* is undoubtedly a testimony to the German anti-Polish campaign, which, from the perspective of the 21st century, should be regarded as nationalist. It is based on the revisionist policy of the Weimar Republic, which cast doubt on the provisions of the Treaty of Versailles, especially its part concerning the new geopolitical order in Central and Eastern Europe (Kacprzak 2007, p. 148).

In the context of the publication date of the book – 1933 – it is important to mention the author's attitude towards the new government represented in the book. Although Hitler's policy on the border issue was intended to lull the Poles' vigilance, and its neutral tone only changed at the beginning of 1939 (Bednarz 2016, p. 136), Alfred Hein remains faithful to the rhetoric of the Weimar Republic in his text. This discrepancy is superficial, however, as Germany's foreign policy, and especially in its relations with Poland, always had similar aims (Lawaty 1993, p. 24f). The portrayal of German culture as superior to that of Poland, and the juxtaposition of hard-working and honest Germans with scheming and lazy Poles is convenient for every power in Germany. In the last chapter, Hein writes with hope for the future under National Socialist rule and believes that a good development of the region will ensure its proper development (Hein 1933, p. 75ff). It is difficult to assess clearly whether Hein, with the conclusion of his publication, deliberately advocates the regime that is forming in Germany or whether this is naivety. However, it undoubtedly works in favor of the Third Reich.

However, one cannot be surprised by the author's rhetoric when one considers his biography and the times in which he lived. German policy of the interwar period, irrespective of the ruling party and political system, was anti-Polish. Not even the apparent efforts of the National Socialists to improve relations with Poland shortly after their seizure of power changed this (Kacprzak 2007, p. 148). It was in Germany's interest to regain the territorial unity of the state and economically important territories such as Danzig or Upper Silesia. Hein, as a German from divided Upper Silesia who worked as director of a propaganda institution in East Prussia, which had been separated from the whole of the state, and spoke with approval of Sterssemann's (Knauer 1983, p. 79) policy naturally could not represent a different position. A similar statement can be applied to the majority of Germans at the time, who felt aggrieved. The works of Alfred Hein approached in this chapter – *Verratene Zuflucht* and *Über zertrümmerte Brücken – vorwärts!* – are thus an expression of the convictions of many Germans, and the arguments used in them show this nation as 'honest guardians of culture and civilization.' This picture, however, is incomplete and thus false, as it only highlights the good points of the Germans themselves and justifies their actions through the mechanisms inherent in nationalist propaganda – a sense of fear for their own freedom and a desire to make up for the injustices suffered. All of Germany's frustrations led it to cross a dangerous line, beyond which negative emotions begin to materialize and lead to disastrous consequences. In the case of Polish-German relations, the Second World War exposed the hatred of Germans towards Poles, stimulated by texts like Hein's book, which caused far more suffering and harm than the problems arising for Germans from the Treaty of Versailles.

Bibliography

Bednarz, Paweł: 'Polska i Polacy w świetle propagandy niemieckiej na przykładzie satyr w tygodniku "Kladderadatsch" w latach 1930–1939', in: Andrzej Adamski (ed.): *Kultura – media – teologia*. Warszawa 2016, p. 133–135.

Dampc-Jarosz, Renata / Meus, Paweł: 'Zwei Stimmen für ein "neues Zeitalter der ernsten Arbeit und des Fortschritts". Der Beitrag von Max Herrmann-Neiße und Alfred Hein zur Erziehung der deutschen Jugend nach dem Ersten Weltkrieg', in: Junk, Claudia / Schneider, Thomas F. (eds.): *Krieg in Comic, Graphic Novel und Literatur II*. Göttingen 2019, p. 101-113.

Fiedor, Karol: 'Znaczenie plebiscytu na Warmii, Mazurach i Powiślu dla formowania nacjonalistycznego frontu antypolskiego w Niemczech', in: KOMUNIKATY MAZURSKO-WARMIŃSKIE 1970/3, p. 427-447.

Fisch, Jörg: *Das Selbstbestimmungsrecht der Völker. Die Domestizierung einer Illusion*. München 2010.

Geiss, Peter: 'Das Selbstbestimmungsrecht der Völker und seine Grenzen. Konzeptsensibler Geschichtsunterricht am Beispiel der Pariser Friedensordnung von 1919/1920', in: Geiss, Peter / Heuser, Peter Arnold (eds.): *Friedensordnung in geschichtswissenschaftlicher und geschichtsdidaktischer Perspektive*. Göttingen 2017, p. 151-174.

Hartmann, Regina: 'Krieg regional: Ostpreußen in einem Kriegsroman – ein Fall von 'Information Warefare"', in: Glunz, Claudia / Pełka, Artur / Schneider, Thomas F. (eds.): *Information Warfare. Die Rolle der Medien (Literatur, Kunst, Photographie, Film, Fernsehen, Theater, Presse, Korrespondenz) bei der Kriegsdarstellung und -deutung*, Göttingen 2007, p. 217-229.

Hein, Alfred: *Über zertrümmerte Brücken – vorwärts! Ostpreußische Schicksalsbilder*. Langensalza 1933.

Hein, Alfred: 'Letter to Max Worgitzki from 1st January 1937, Berlin' (German Literature Archive in Marbach, box 1934).

Hein, Alfred: 'Verratene Zuflucht', in: Knauer, Annke-Margarethe (ed.): *Alfred Hein. Zuhausmusik. Geschichten, Betrachtungen, Briefe und Gedichte. Ein Kranz der Erinnerung an den Dichter und seine oberschlesische Heimat*. Augsburg 1968, p. 126-129.

Hofmeister, Björn: 'Kultur- und Sozialgeschichte der Politik in der Weimarer Republik 1918 bis 1933', in: *Archiv für Sozialgeschichte. Verwissenschaftlichung von Politik nach 1945*. Bonn 2010/50, p. 455-501.

Jendrzejewski, Artur: 'Niemieckie organizacje cywilno-wojskowe w Prusach Wschodnich w latach dwudziestych XX wieku: w świetle dokumentów gdańskiej ekspozytury polskiego wywiadu wojskowego', in: KOMUNIKATY MAZURSKO-WARMIŃSKIE 2012/2 (276), p. 269-287.

Kacprzak, Paweł: 'Niemiecka mniejszość narodowa w Polsce w latach 1919-1939', in: Kania, Leszek (ed.): *Studia Lubuskie. Prace Instytutu Prawa i Administracji Państwowej Wyższej Szkoły Zawodowej w Sulechowie*. Sulechów 2007, p. 145-158.

Knauer, Annke-Margarethe: Alfred Hein. Ein Lebensbild aus der Sicht von Annke-Margarethe Knauer. Berlin 1983 (Typescript in German Literature Archive in Marbach, box 1925).

Kunicki, Wojciech: '...*auf dem Weg in dieses Reich.' NS-Kulturpolitik und Literatur in Schlesien 1933 bis 1945*. Leipzig 2006.

Lawaty, Andreas: '1918. Das Ende des Ersten Weltkrieges. Deutschlands Zusammenbruch und die Wiederherstellung des polnischen Staates', in: *Nordost-Archiv. Zeitschrift für Regionalgeschichte. Wendepunkte der deutsch-polnischen Beziehungen im 20. Jahrhundert: 1918 – 1939 – 1945 – 1990* II/1993/1, p. 19-34.

Meus, Paweł: 'Alfred Hein', in: Rostropowicz, Joanna (ed.) *Schlesier von den frühesten Zeiten bis zur Gegenwart/Ślązacy od czasów najdawniejszych do współczesności*. Opole 2022, p. 108–111.

Pioskowik, Stefan: 'Mit musikalischer Sensibilität durchs Leben', in: OBERSCHLESISCHE STIMME 2015/2(315), p. 3–4.

Piper, Ernst: 'Gefährdete Stabilität. 1924–1929', in: INFORMATIONEN ZUR POLITISCHEN BILDUNG. WEIMARER REPUBLIK 2021/346:1, p. 42–59.

Richter, Johannes Karl: Die Reichszentrale für Heimatdienst. Geschichte der ersten politischen Bildungsstelle in Deutschland und Untersuchung ihrer Rolle in der Weimarer Republik. Berlin 1963.

Tebinka, Jacek: 'Polen und seine Verbündeten auf der neuen Landkarte Europas nach dem Ersten Weltkrieg', in: *Historie. Jahrbuch des Zentrums für Historische Forschung Berlin der Polnischen Akademie der Wissenschaften. Plebiszite, Selbstbestimmung, Minderheitsrechte* 2021/13, p. 30–46.

Leszek Drong

Denationalizing Upper Silesia in Szczepan Twardoch's Fiction

1. Szczepan Twardoch's Silesian Novels

Szczepan Twardoch's writings and other public articulations involve a plethora of critical remarks on, and references to, nationality and nationalism. Ever since 2013, when his vociferous outburst on FB concluded with "Pi...ol się, Polsko!" ["F*ck you, Poland!"] ('Pie...l się Polsko' 2014), he has courted controversy and polarized his readers. Many Silesian 'autochthons' (Kamusella 2016a, p. 196; for the significance of this designation, see section 4 of this chapter) take his side and see in him a spokesperson for regional autonomy and unique Upper Silesian identity. Others, mostly loyal Polish citizens who have little to do with Upper Silesia and its history, are poised to set fire to the patriotic stake with Twardoch's effigy or possibly even to his actual body, consecrating it to the eternal flames of a special hell for the worst sort of renegades. Condemnations are often accompanied by angry pronouncements and accusations of high treason ('Twardoch w prokuraturze' 2014; Świderska 2014). It is worth bearing in mind that Twardoch used the incriminating phrase to express his dissatisfaction with the Polish Supreme Court's ruling about the status of Silesian ethnicity; the Supreme Court decided that Upper Silesians do not constitute an autonomous nationality despite their ethnic (i.e., cultural and linguistic) distinctiveness ('Sąd Najwyższy' 2013). Thereby the Supreme Court refused to recognize an independent national minority in the south of Poland, justifying its ruling by the threat its recognition would pose to the unity and integrity of the Polish state.

Much of what Twardoch has written since 2013 may be interpreted as an artistic exploration of the key issues of nationality and nationalism raised in the public discussions that ensued from his FB outburst. The complexity of his novels directly concerned with Upper Silesia and national loyalties (or indifference) makes it necessary to establish a central concern that will organize my argument in this chapter. Once we acknowledge his characters' rejection of all sorts of nationalisms, the concern is best identified by an inquiry into Twardoch's literary alternatives to national(ist) sentiments in Upper Silesia in the aftermath of the

Great War. To make sense of how he envisages Upper Silesian distinctiveness, it is imperative, in the first place, to explore various conceptualizations of the basic sociological and political categories his writings address in light of recent research on nations and nationalism. By quarrying *Drach*, *Pokora* and *Chołod* for attitudes to and descriptions of nationalism and regionalism, further complicated by the notion of chthonism[1] with reference to Upper Silesia, I want to make the case for Twardoch's skepticism about nationalism as an ideology, amounting – especially in *Drach* and *Pokora* – to a uniquely Silesian mixture of neotribalism and transnationalism as an inclusive minority politics. I will be arguing that his outright rejection of Polish nationalism (or 'turbopatriotism' – see Napiórkowski 2019, p. 14) does not necessarily thrust Twardoch into the arms of Silesian, Czech or German nationalists: his novels offer glimpses and, not infrequently, sweeping visions of a historically unique chthonic community, infused with what Françoise Lionnet and Shu-mei Shih classify as a 'minor transnationalism' (2005, p. 10f; see also Verdery 1998, p. 291; Clavin 2005, p. 422f and Ernste, van Houtum and Zoomers 2009, p. 577) and transculturality (see Welsch 1999, p. 194). As a consequence, the chapter will also pursue the vectors of tension between denationalizing and transnationalizing impulses in Twardoch's recent works.

As well as a matter of politics, ideology and history, nationalism has been premised, at least since Ernest Renan's famous essay 'What Is a Nation?' published in 1882, on a notion of collective memory. It is highly significant that the Polish Supreme Court's ruling does not address a diachronic aspect of the Silesian claim to distinctiveness. Needless to say, that would have opened a veritable Pandora's box and further antagonize the parties involved in the debate. The fact remains that Polish nationalism is strategically blind to what we may describe as the uniquely Silesian experience in the 20th century. The experience is rather hermetic: besides articulations in German, mostly in writing, the languages of the Upper Silesian ethno-regional minority include Polish, Silesian (I will say more about its status soon) and, to a more limited extent, Czech. Simultaneously, the sheer range of those languages is testimony to Silesia's multiculturalism and multilingualism that, despite Chancellor Bismarck's *Kulturkampf* launched in 1871, flourished at the beginning of the 20th century. And yet there is no denying that the most commonly used languages to convey 20th-century Silesian traumas are hardly universal and easily accessible for readers outside of what James Björk identifies, somehow restrictively, as the Polish *Mitteleurope* (2001, p. 477). Twardoch's fiction has been widely translated into German (and even into Silesian) but there are no English translations available

---

[1] I discuss Twardoch's earth-oriented narratives in sections 3 and 4 of this chapter. The focus on the chthonic is not unique to his writings, however, and may be found in such seminal works concerned with Silesia as Henryk Waniek's *Finis Silesiae* (2021 [2003]).

(with the exception of *The King of Warsaw*, 2020), which is one of the most important reasons for making their themes and plots available to Anglophone audiences[2] at least in the form of a critical discussion that this chapter seeks to develop.

Twardoch's historical fiction set in, or related to, Upper Silesia seems to privilege the interwar period and the experience of both world wars in the first half of the 20th century. In *Drach*, *Król*, and *Chołod*, there are episodes concerned with more recent periods, or, like in *Chołod*, a frame narrative[3] set in the present and featuring Twardoch the writer (and explorer), but, on the whole, his interest is in the times when Upper Silesia underwent formative developments after becoming exposed to fierce Polish and German irredentisms in the aftermath of the Great War. That is particularly strongly accentuated in *Pokora*, a novel that Twardoch himself feels "intimately close to", to the extent that he admits identifying with its eponymous protagonist ('Szczepan Twardoch' 2022). Crucially, the historical focus on central Europe (including also Germany and, partly, Russia in *Chołod*) after the Great War is justified by its importance for understanding Upper Silesians' 'national indifference' (Polak-Springer 2012, p. 487; see also Brendan Karch 2016, p. 149; Böhler 2018, p. 114; Judson 2016, p. xiv, and Brian Porter-Szűcs 2014, p. 85). The years 1918–1922 constituted a turbulent political breaking point, when the fate of old and new states and nations was to be decided. For a brief historical moment, Upper Silesians could entertain dreams of their own free state (Bjork 2001, p. 489; Struve 2016, p. 219; Kamusella 2016a, p. 193; Böhler 2018, p. 115) while contested territories abounded in Europe (e.g., Ulster between Ireland and the UK, Alsace between France and Germany or East Prussia again between Poland and Germany; for examples of contested cities, see O'Dowd 2012, p. 158ff). Political violence against civilians was a common phenomenon in those areas where conflicts of national interest were instigated by the prolonged deliberations of the Versailles Peace Conference (for examples and discussions of violence in Upper Silesia and a comparison with Ulster and Ireland at large, see Wilson 2010; Eichenberg 2010, p. 231 and Gerwarth 2008, p. 179). Eichenberg puts emphasis on paramilitary violence that "served as a central element in the establishment of social identities that came to define the Irish and Polish nations" (2010, p. 232). In Upper Silesia, paramilitary violence

---

2 For articles in English that are at least partly concerned with Twardoch's writings, see Drong 2021 and Drong 2023.
3 The narrative structure and plurality of perspectives in *Chołod* constitute not only an intertextual reference to one of the most famous Polish works of fiction written by Jan Potocki (*The Manuscript Found in Saragossa*) but also a thematic and structural allusion to Mary Shelley's *Frankenstein*, a multivocal and multicultural narrative of, *inter alia*, sea voyage and arctic exploration.

amounted to a protracted civil war, instigated by two opposing nationalisms (Kornprobst 2008, p. 8ff; Polak-Springer 2015, p. 3).

Finally, Twardoch's recent writings may be construed as a literary response to what James Wertsch identifies as "an explosion of 'new nationalisms' at the beginning of the 21st century" (2022, p. 454; see also Wertsch 2021, p. ix). For Wertsch, memory and narrative are crucial elements in the construction of national myths and foundations of 'imagined political communities' (Anderson 2006 [1983], p. 6). In Twardoch's fiction, another aspect of early 20th-century existence in central Europe comes to the fore – proximity of borders and partitions. His novels offer rich and complex images of borderland predicaments and dilemmas which affect local characters' self-identifications. Silesian borderlands, "a border region par excellence" (Thum 2005, p. 229), emerge – especially in *Drach* and *Pokora* – as crucial "remembrance environments" (Zerubavel 1996, p. 284). They constitute a formative *topos* that Twardoch often relies on for representations of Upper Silesian ethno-linguistic community.

2. National and transnational memories in *Mitteleurope*

As a political and philosophical concept, nationalism emerged towards the end of the 18th century to be developed throughout the 19th century (Anderson 2006 [1983], p. 4; Smith 2008, p. 3). Modern reflection on the sources, unfolding and manifestations of nationalism, however, began with Ernest Renan's seminal essay 'What is a Nation?' published in 1882. Its publication coincided with the intensification of efforts on the part of many national movements and institutions to instill a national spirit into disparate citizens of frequently multiethnic and multicultural empires and already existing nation-states as well as several European stateless nations (Smith 2008, p. 27).[4] For example, in late 19th-century Prussia, the *Kulturkampf* was an attempt to create a linguistically and denominationally homogenous German nation out of the hodge-podge of Prussian peoples. In Ireland, 19th-century nationalism was a mode of contestatory politics intended to undermine the colonial rule of the British empire. In his essay, Renan, himself a 19th-century thinker, offers several penetrating insights into nationalism, many of which have retained their topicality till the present day. Far from assuming that religion, language, race or ethnicity could be a criterion for binding a nation together (Renan downplays those assumptions by relegating them to the sphere of "ethnographic politics" – 2018 [1882], p. 257), he accentuates the will of

---

4 Summing up the semantic duality of nationalism with reference to contemporary political contexts, Michael Billig observes that nationalism is "associated with those who struggle to create new states or with extreme right-wing politics" (1995, p. 5).

the citizens as a prerequisite in the formation of nationhood (2018 [1882], p. 257). His notion of the nation, though detached from religious commitments, involves "a spiritual principle" which, in turn, comprises "a possession in common of a rich legacy of memories" and "the desire to live together, the will to perpetuate the value of the heritage that one has received in an undivided form" (p. 261). Renan's focus on collective memory and common tradition is remarkable, inasmuch as he also realizes how much has to be forgotten for a large group of individuals to form a coherent national community (see p. 251).[5] The emphasis on memory and imagination (see Armbruster, Rollo and Meinhof 2003, p. 886) continues to inform critical inquiry into, and reflection on, nationalism towards the end of the 20th century and at the beginning of the 21st century.

Collective memory (involving such notions as tradition, commemoration, legacy or heritage as well as, perhaps less directly, the canon), as we shall see below, has been commonly conceptualized as 'national memory' in contemporary discussions of nationalism (see Wertsch 2021, p. xii). It is undoubtedly a crucial factor in the development of what I would call *a common political and cultural imaginary* which undergirds Renan's 'spiritual principle.' When, in his 1983 book, Ernest Gellner notes that nationalism has been often defined as "the striving to make culture and polity congruent, to endow a culture with its own roof, and not more than one roof at that" (1983, p. 43), his focus is primarily on a common, possibly homogenous culture that constitutes the foundations for the national edifice crowned by the roof of a specific form of political organization. At the same time, Gellner is well aware that nationalism is, in the first place, an ideology, rather than an architectural infrastructure in a literal sense (p. 45). Published in the same year as Gellner's seminal work, *Imagined Communities* by Benedict Anderson offers an inciting elaboration on nationality and nationalism as "cultural artefacts of a particular kind" (2006, p. 4). It is clear that, like Renan and Gellner, he also subscribes to the stipulation of "the cultural roots of nationalism" (p. 7). Unlike Renan, however, Anderson associates those roots with "religious imaginings" (p. 10) and claims that religious communities – alongside dynastic realms – underlie the emergence of modern nationalisms. Another less obvious though quite significant aspect of his discussion of nationalism is connected with Anderson's insistence that it is not just national communities that may be described as 'imagined': he notes that all communities rely on shared ideas and ideologies to communicate internally. Their members belong to a community because "in the minds of each lives the *image* of their communion" (p. 6 [own emphasis]). Anderson's idiom (i. e., 'communion') further emphasizes tight links between his notion of nationalism and religion.

---

5 In the context of Irish history, Guy Beiner develops one the most wide-ranging and thorough epistemologies and ontologies of forgetting in recent humanist research – see Beiner 2018.

The point that he makes about all kinds of communities being bound, in the first place, by a shared imaginary is worth noting at this juncture, as it will serve as a useful context for discussing Upper Silesia further on in this chapter. In the very first pages of his *opus magnum*, Anderson mentions "old nations" which may appear to be fully consolidated and yet they are often "challenged by 'sub'-nationalisms within their borders" (p. 3). Those sub-nationalisms, as he writes in his Introduction to the 1991 (second) edition of *Imagined Communities*, "dream of shedding their sub-ness one happy day" (p. 3). Anderson's acknowledgement is premised on an incontrovertible recognition of obvious tensions and agonisms within nation-states in modern Europe. It opens our eyes to the predicament and aspirations of national and ethnic minorities whose existence is threatened by the refusal, on the part of state actors or institutions, to recognize their autonomous traditions, languages, history and values. With no land of their own (and thus failing to meet one of the traditional criteria of modern nationhood), those marginalized communities are reduced to their own alternative imaginaries. They come to rely almost exclusively on their own collective memory that is different from, and not infrequently subversive of, a national memory; they become, as James Wertsch has it, strictly "mnemonic communities" (2021, p. 104).

Anthony Smith, discussing the cultural foundation of nations, makes note of the aspirations of the above-mentioned communities and identifies them as "nations without states" (2008, p. 27). This is an important step in the process of according recognition to such communities although Smith makes it crystal clear that their aspirations to territorial autonomy may never be fulfilled. Instead, he notes, "[t]heir drive for internal autonomy tends to focus on social, economic and cultural goals [...] without recourse to outright independence and sovereignty" (2008, p. 27). The inclusion of ethnic or regional communities in the general category of nations carries significant consequences in this context because of Smith's prior definition of the nation as a community entitled to several prerogatives. Those prerogatives involve the cultivation of "shared myths, memories, symbols, values, and traditions" as well as the possession of "a historic homeland" and "a distinctive public culture" (2008, p. 19). Smith mentions also "shared customs and common laws", which may or may not be part of a distinctive public culture. The question I want to address in further sections of this chapter concerns the relevance of this definition to two temporal contexts in Upper Silesia: 1) a hundred years ago, when Upper Silesia witnessed a plebiscite and then was partitioned, and 2) more recently, in a period following 1989 and involving geopolitical transformations in eastern and central Europe. Unquestionably, in recent years, Twardoch's novels have been affected by current political and cultural developments in Upper Silesia (and in Poland at large) and, simultaneously and reciprocally, his novels and other writings have affected the "collective cultural identity" (Smith 2008, p. 18; for how fictional narratives affect things in the real world, see Bruner 2003, p. 8 and Rigney 2022, p. 167 ff) of his own mnemonic community.

Also recently, some of the most interesting and illuminating conceptions related to the evolution of nationalism and its ties with religious sentiments have emerged from Rogers Brubaker's sociological writings, especially *Ethnicity without Groups* (2004) and *Grounds for Difference* (2015). It is my claim in this chapter that his ideas align with the ramifications of Twardoch's representations of Upper Silesian community, or, at the very least, that Brubaker's views constitute an illuminating context for making sense of Twardoch's attitudes to nationalism. In *Grounds for Difference*, Brubaker points out that religion is "a powerful framework for imagining community" (2015, p. 104). What religion has in common with nationalism is that both are modes of cultural and social identification (p. 104). In fact, when Brubaker writes about "the resurgence of public religion" (p. 4) in the 21st century, he registers a theme that has accompanied discussions of nationalism for many decades now. Renan, in his 1882 essay, insists that religion should not be a basis of modern nationality (2018, p. 258 f) and yet the very occurrence of a normative claim like that is testimony to the persistence of a historical covenant between the two. Also, as I have indicated earlier in this section, Renan's vocabulary used to describe the nation – 'spiritual principle', 'soul', 'shared moral consciousness' (p. 261 ff) – owes quite a lot to a religious idiom. Religion is endorsed as a significant factor that constitutes the cultural foundations of modern nationalisms by both Anderson (2006, p. 12) and Smith who notes "complex relations between religious and national symbols, memories, and traditions" (2008, p. 8). He also mentions 'covenantal' nationalism which encourages public worship of the nation (xv). For Twardoch, as we shall see in the following sections, that kind of attitude is anathema while his own Silesian gods are described, in *Drach*, as black, dragon-like chthonic monsters,[6] rather than traditional (usually anthropomorphized) Judeo-Christian deities.

There is another reason why Brubaker's (and, largely, also Smith's) notion of nationalism offers us convenient critical tools to approach the relation between religion and the nation. Crucially, Brubaker, clearly inspired by Anderson's notion of imagined communities, detaches nationalism and nations from biological realities of human existence and lets both concepts float freely as an ideological air we breathe in complex social contexts and environments. At the beginning of *Ethnicity without Groups*, Brubaker observes, with a clearly pronounced skepticism, "the tendency to represent the social and cultural world as a

---

6 Twardoch's novel, with all its mythic and chthonic undertones, draws some inspiration from the ur-narrative of 20th-century Upper Silesian experience, *Cholonek* (1970) by Janosch. The full title of that novel, originally written in German, reads: *Cholonek oder der liebe Gott aus Lehm* [*Cholonek or the Good Lord God from Clay*].

multichrome mosaic of monochromatic ethnic, racial, or cultural blocs" (2004, p. 8). Instead, he claims, ethnicity, as a manifestation of 'groupism', should be conceptualized along markedly different lines because yielding to the above-mentioned tendency – the groupism fallacy (see p. 2f) – is of very limited use as a methodological assumption. Ethnicity, on his view, emerges from "categories, schemas, encounters, identifications, languages, stories, institutions, organizations, networks, and events" (p. 4), and all those are subject to continuous fluctuations and evolutions in time. Far from subscribing to a constructivist agenda, which Brubaker identifies with individualism and the imperative to banish organized groups altogether, he pursues a balanced itinerary whose destination is an incisive critique of groupism as tendency to see solid substance where there are often only contingently clustered ideas.

Of course, Brubaker's purely ideological ontology of nationalism does not make it any less captivating and empowering in practice, and the empowerment may be a two-edged weapon because in most cases it materializes at the cost of someone else's (or some other community's) disenfranchisement. Smith conveniently captures the value and potential of nationalist ideology by describing it in terms of a resource. Nations, he says, consist in "sets of social and cultural resources on which the members can draw, and which, in varying degrees, enable them to express their interests, needs, and goals" (2008, p. 23). Literary narratives, especially those grounded in the past of a community, may aspire to the role of such cultural resources, with writers performing as "ethnopolitical entrepreneurs" (Brubaker 2004, p. 10) who build up and solidify the cultural capital of a given community. In my discussion of Twardoch's ethnopolitical aspirations, I will come back to the complexity of the process of empowering Upper Silesians by means of historical fiction published in Polish and thus made readily available to the Polish reader.

The use of plural forms in the above quotation excerpted from Smith's book on nationalism cannot and should not be brushed aside. His discussion of nations qua resources anticipates a penetrating study of national and state narcissism in which Roediger, Putnam and Yamashiro deflate the significance of a sense of group pride (2022, p. 210) that some people feel as members of a particular nation by emphasizing that "most people possess many intersecting social identities" (2022, p. 225). From an intersectional perspective, nationality is only one of many complex – and complexly intertwined – categories that underlie our self-understanding and self-identifications (see Hill Collins and Bilge 2020, p. 12 and p. 36f). Furthermore, positioning nationality alongside a number of aspects and social categories which characterize our 'groupness', or our sense of belonging, paves the way for the recognition of an increasingly popular perception of ethnic groups as "flexible entities that change over time and whose values, memories and symbols are continuously in flux" (Coman 2022, p. 404). That is truer than anywhere else in borderlands, or in "a borderland cultural region" (Dembinska 2013, p. 48), such as Upper Silesia, where, according to Patricia Clavin, transnationalist perspectives may shed "new, comparative light on the strengths and the fragilities of the nation-state" by accentuating "the ways in which local history can be understood in relation to world history" (2005, p. 438). She makes the case for transnationalism as an adequate and useful description of the social space inhabited by communities that, in their everyday existence, practice "transnational encounters" (p. 423) which she identifies with 'border-crossings' of various kinds and in varying dimensions. In Twardoch's fiction, border-crossings and transnational encounters constitute a crucial element of the cosmopolitan message embodied by his protagonists, including Josef Mangor, Alois Pokora and Konrad Widuch. However, a caveat is necessary here: a transnational and cosmopolitan reading of the characters that inhabit Twardoch's fictions set in the first half of the 20th century is possible from the present vantage point, when conceptualizations of nationality, nationalism and transnationalism have evolved to recognize the "fluidity of [such] categories" (Clavin 2005, p. 422) as national and ethnic identity, gender identification (think of Judith Butler's seminal works: *Gender Trouble* and *Bodies that Matter*), political affiliation and cultural attachments.

3. Silesian aspirations in *Drach* and *Pokora*

Two novels by Twardoch focus on the period following the Great War, when the fate of Upper Silesia was to be decided by the Versailles Peace Conference and then the League of Nations in Geneva. *Drach* and *Pokora* showcase the Silesian community as it was back at the beginning of the 20th century, the former offering a wide-ranging portrayal of Upper Silesia as a contested territory and the latter shadowing Alois Pokora in his peregrinations across *Mitteleurope*, with a substantial section of the novel set in Berlin. Although in *Pokora* the onus of the second person narration is on the individual, Alois is also implicated in many contexts relevant to geopolitical transformations of Upper Silesian territory in the early 1920s. *Drach*'s take on historical time is different in that respect, largely because its subplots unfold synchronically, various temporal planes dovetailing one another (Czyżak 2016, p. 38). That is possible due to the introduction of a non-human narrator, i.e., the Silesian land, represented symbolically by the eponymous 'drach.'[7] Josef Magnor enjoys a privileged access to the wisdom of the *drach*, mediated by old Pindur, who is a magus-like figure, responsible for

---

[7] "The land is a huge dragon" ["ziemia to jest srogi drach"], says Pindur, combining Polish and Silesian in a single sentence (Twardoch 2014, p. 360).

initiating the young protagonist into the ways of nature and the local land. Many significant conversations between the two are set in the woods, far away from any civilization. Out of all the novels by Twardoch, *Drach* in particular is concerned with problematizing human (and animal) attachment to the land, echoing, in this respect, *Hanyska* [*The Autochthon Woman*] (2008) by Halina Buchner. As a consequence, this quintessentially Silesian novel undoubtedly deserves the hallmark of chthonic fiction.

Identifying *Drach* as chthonic fiction, and detecting chthonic elements in other novels by Twardoch, has some far-reaching consequences for defining the ethnic community whose primary concern is a quasi-religious attachment to their territory and to their households (see Dembinska 2013, p. 60). Upper Silesians in Twardoch's novels often travel either across the land or, especially in the case of local coal miners, down into the body of the land. In a pivotal episode of *Drach*, Josef Magnor spends some time in a mine shaft, looked after and fed by his friends and co-workers, when he hides from the law as a consequence of his actions (i.e., committing murder) above ground. The Silesian land, penetrated and ruthlessly exploited by coalmining industry, becomes more than just his motherland (2014, p. 134) – its subterranean cave is like a forgiving mother's womb, always prepared to shelter the delinquent Silesian. Alois Pokora, in turn, comes back to his *heimat* from political and personal peregrinations imposed on him, rather than chosen willingly, by the demobilization of the Prussian army in the aftermath of the Great War. Upper Silesia is a destination that he opts for when he is disoriented and confused by the disintegration of hitherto familiar communities and nation-states. Its pull is stronger from the appeal of world solidarity that communism seems to promise while he is in Berlin. Even Konrad Widuch from *Chołod*, though physically dislocated from central Europe in the 1930s and the 1940s, is haunted by memories of Pilchowice/Pilchowitz, where he was born, and of the local people, including Father Scholtis (intertextually borrowed from Twardoch's prior novel), Alois Pokora's biological father.

Both Josef Magnor and Alois Pokora are presented against a carefully reconstructed backdrop of a geopolitical drama that unfolds in the years immediately following the Great War. Their homeland, so far almost unequivocally Prussian,[8] has become a bone of contention between the successor to the German Empire, unofficially known as the Weimar Republic, and the newly created Polish state (the Second Republic). Both states want Upper Silesia for economic reasons to do with its natural resources and highly developed heavy industry (Porter-

---

8 I am not discounting the existence of Polish nationalism that started developing in Silesia in the second half of the 19th century. Still, its scale and impact were, until the conclusion of the Great War, of little significance in comparison with the efforts made by the champions of the *Kulturkampf* (Davies 2005, p. 101; Karch 2016, p. 153).

Szűcs 2014, p. 33; Böhler 2018, p. 115). The flamboyant nationalist rhetoric paraded in the region in the years prior to the Plebiscite (and often in the years to follow) obscures the fact that Polish and German nationalisms with regard to Upper Silesia were at bottom irredentisms, i.e., territorial appetites, rather than movements to unite all the peoples of a given nation under one flag and name. The Upper Silesians – 'neither Germans nor Poles', to modify, slightly, a neat formula used in the title of James Björk's monograph from 2008 – on either side of the partition introduced in 1922 are simply a collateral benefit, useful inasmuch as they can be exploited in the coalmines and other workplaces in the Upper Silesian industrial basin in the absence of skilled workforce from other regions of Poland.[9] That sheds some light on the reasons why Alois Pokora protests vehemently at a certain point: "I don't want to be a Pole!" ["Nie chcę być Polakiem!"] (Twardoch 2020, p. 213).

Alois Pokora exclaims those words with no premeditation, almost instinctively disclaiming a national identification when asked about the Polish state that Piłsudski and Korfanty, two prominent Polish politicians, are in the process of establishing. At the beginning of the same conversation with Baronessa, a German transgender communist, Alois offers a positive identification that, significantly, he inflects in order to indicate his origins:

> He is an officer, Baronessa, says the twin with the blue tie.
> A German officer, says Baronessa, and then I suddenly realize that I have to raise a protest.
> I am from Upper Silesia, I say, and I can hear my voice tremble. My name is Alois Pokora.
> A Pole then, says Baronessa, suddenly appearing to be more interested, and I don't know what to tell her.
> No, I am simply from Upper Silesia, says Alois Pokora. (Twardoch 2020, p. 206 [own translation])

Here and elsewhere (see 2020, p. 110f), Pokora quite skillfully navigates the discourse of national identifications. He knows – or feels – that Upper Silesia, as a region and a territory, is not on a geopolitical par with already established nation-states but he is also clearly aware of the possibility of disentangling his allegiances from the two competing (German and Polish) nationalisms and offering those allegiances to what he perceives as his homeland. Towards the end of his narrative, when the die is already cast and the civil war in Upper Silesia is over, leaving in its trail a new border cutting the region in half, Pokora declares forcefully that he wants to take no sides (2020, p. 509). There are several turning points in his biography but the first and crucial one occurs when he leaves his

---

9 See Davies reporting on Lloyd George's memorable skepticism about giving Upper Silesia to Poland, which George compares to giving a clock to a monkey – 2005, p. 291.

home and family. It is described as an identity-transforming experience (p. 64); henceforth he will keep asking himself one basic question: "Who are you?" (p. 135). The 1922 partition of Upper Silesia does not furnish him with a satisfactory answer.

It is fair to describe what Alois Pokora and Josef Mangor (and many other Silesian characters in Twardoch's fiction) experience and articulate as a local or regional identification. Their sense of belonging is tied to a physically bounded territory, even if in *Drach* the land is represented in mythic terms. It has its own memory (and it remembers everything – 2014, p. 16), which amounts to the collective memory of the local community; moreover, it can speak in the name of the community because – by a masterful use of prosopopoeia – the ostensibly inanimate acquires the power of narrating the story on behalf of the autochthons. In *Pokora*, those chthonic aspects are less powerfully accentuated but the protagonist's refusal to aspire to a national identification brings his existence down to the ground level of the real, rather than the purely ideological. In fact, Alois Pokora registers, at several points in the novel, protean moments ("one world is dead; another one has not been born yet" – 2020, p. 347), when it seems that the prospect of a third way (see Bjork 2001, p. 489), i.e., an Upper Silesian statehood emerging from the ashes of the old-world order, is quite likely to materialize (2020, p. 279f). Crucially, Pokora envisages the Free Upper Silesian State in terms of "a realm of dignity" (2020, p. 467) for people like him.

4. Crossing boundaries – the chthonic and the transnational

The Plebiscite held on March 20, 1921 and, subsequently, the partition of Upper Silesia put an end to the aspirations of many Upper Silesians for their own free state. The leaders of the Union of Upper Silesians and the Silesian People's Party negotiated with Czechoslovakia, Germany and Poland and petitioned the Paris Peace Conference to amend Article 88 of the Versailles Treaty which eventually precluded the possibility of voting for an independent Upper Silesian state in the Plebiscite. The petition was opposed by the French, and Upper Silesians ended up voting for either Poland or Germany. There was no third option; no other geopolitical solutions were envisaged as a consequence of the ballot. Eventually, in 1922, the border between Poland and Germany cut Upper Silesia into two unequal parts. When Twardoch, in his novels, revisits Upper Silesia, and more specifically his native Pilchowice and other towns and villages on the German side of the 1922 border, his characters serve as a reminder that the lie of the Silesian land will never be defined by a line on a map. Two aspects of Twardoch's attitude to the land transpire from *Drach* and *Pokora*: one is connected with a programmatic transnationalism of his representations of local history and the other points clearly, especially in *Drach*, to 'a chthonic metaculture' of the Upper Silesian community.

By a chthonic metaculture, Edward A. Tiryakian means one of the three basic cultural formations which have persisted or reappeared intermittently from antiquity to modernity in various historical contexts and configurations. Interacting with Christian and Gnostic metacultures over the course of the history of Western civilization, the 'Chthonic' metaculture, which Tiryakian describes in terms of "a basic ontological affirmation of earth as the primordial locus of reality, and of the forces of life that have to be cultivated, enhanced or placated in order to insure the reproductive processes of survival" (1996, p. 105), is particularly relevant to Upper Silesia. Even though the word 'chthonic' is traditionally associated with ancient Greek gods of the underworld and the dead (Felton 2007, p. 91), it also applies to the earth in a more general sense of agricultural activities and their significance for survival (Scullion 1994, p. 93). Chthonic gods are also a major presence in Celtic mythology (Medyńska 2002, p. 135ff), which may be a more direct inspiration for Twardoch's vision of the cultural foundations of Upper Silesian community when he references "Celtic traces" (Twardoch 2014, p. 134; see also Drong 2023, p. 68) still to be found in the region. Chthonic elements abound in *Drach* and in *Chołod* (although, in the latter, Widuch's attachment to the land is of a different nature, possibly because he is physically detached from his homeplace) but they also appear in *Pokora*, especially in an episode with Alois's German comrades hunting and killing a deer. Alois experiences a communion with nature and its creatures by being encouraged to put his feet into the belly of a recently killed animal. He is frozen; his comrades suggest that he take advantage of the waning warmth of the deer's carcass (Twardoch 2020, p. 337f). Like Josef Mangor, deposited in the womb of his coal mine for safety and self-preservation, Alois taps into the chthonic resources of nature, rendering Twardoch's 'sustainable' vision of Upper Silesian existence sharp and explicit. Significantly, Alois feels closer to the dead animal than to his German companions.

Emphasis on the chthonic is closely related to a transnational approach to borders, boundaries and partitions (Ernste, van Houtum and Zoomers 2009, p. 579) clearly in evidence in Twardoch's fiction. The transnational manifests itself, among other things, in the refusal to recognize administrative impositions devised by political powers, usually on a state level. Representations of 'debordering', which Cathal McCall associates, in contemporary contexts, with "the process of Europeanization" (2012, p. 214), are on display in *Drach* and *Pokora*, exposing the nation-state as responsible for forging borders "in the national imagination through a history of war, political endeavour and cultural enterprise" (McCall 2012, p. 222). Transnationalism is about border-crossings in many different senses of the phrase; crucially, it permits "the study of encounters that both attract and repel, between people, institutions and artefacts of all kinds" (Clavin 2005, p. 423). Intense interest in transnationalism as a sociological and political concept is of relatively recent provenance (Verdery 1998, p. 291) and yet its latent presence in the Silesian meso-universe is indubitable when Alois wants to settle the nationalist conflict between Poland and Germany in the name of universal, transborder values of peace and quiet, hoping for the cessation of violence and hostilities (Twardoch 2020, p. 499f; see Kamusella 2016b, p. 19). He is prepared to accept a border as long as it brings about "a normal world in which [he] can go to work, come back home, drink a schnapps after dinner and light a cigarette, and drink a decent Silesian coffee" (2020, p. 500).

In *Drach*, once it materializes, the border between Poland and Germany is described as being both there and not there (See Twardoch 2014, p. 120f and p. 318). And then, after being abolished in 1939, it persists in cultural and political narratives and policies imposed on the local population (Kamusella 'Upper Silesia…' 2016, p. 13). The partition line, by introducing new distinctions (Green 2012, p. 577), soon becomes the sort of border that has the potential to generate new identities (Wilson and Donnan 2012, p. 18). The partition generates, too, new conflicts of interest and raises difficult questions about one's sense of belonging. Valeska, Josef's wife, is encouraged to move homes so that, as soon as the partition takes effect, she may end up on the Polish side of the border. Her neighbor, Czoik, tries to explain the problems that will arise unless she does so:

> 'You have to move out, and quickly so, before it is a shame [to live here]', Czoik adds in reply to Valeska's silence.
> 'Because the Reich is going to be here', Czoik says.
> Valeska shrugs her shoulders.
> 'But the Reich has always been here. I have never been anywhere else but in the Reich. I don't need Poland. I want to know where my man is. I am not moving anywhere, not to any Poland.'
> 'You don't have to go far from here. Just across the border.'
> 'And where is this border going to be?' (Twardoch 2014, p. 299 [own translation])

This conversation is conducted entirely in Silesian, a local lect syntactically similar to Polish, with some German loan words.[10] Significantly, in the conversation above, in an idiom which has no German loan words whatsoever besides the old name for the Prussian state (the Reich; 'Rajch' in the original), Valeska shows very little enthusiasm for the new Polish state, and yet, in the 1920s, the patterns of speech that she uses were commonly recognized, by Polish propaganda in Upper Silesia, as the Polish language. Ultimately, she refuses to leave her household behind and cross the border (which is not there yet) to settle

---

10 For an in-depth discussion of Silesian in the context of other minority and regional languages in Central Europe, see Kamusella 2021, p. 59ff.

down in a new home in Poland. In that respect, she has much in common with Agnes from Eva Tvrdá's *Dědictví* [*The Inheritance*] and Maria from Helena Buchner's *Hanyska* [*The Autochton Woman*].

Another prominent element of the conversation quoted above involves the frequent use of deictic pronouns with reference to the characters' current location. They use a variety of pronouns to describe 'here' and 'not-here', thus relativizing current and future administrative divisions of territory and introducing a simple binary distinction between their homeplace and the rest of the universe to stress their chthonic 'in-groupness' based on attachment to the local land. When Valeska mentions her disinclination to leave her place, she also uses negative forms to describe other locations (her potential destinations) – those words include 'nikaj' (nowhere) and 'nikaj indziyj' (nowhere else). By way of contrast, her own place is 'kajś' (somewhere), a pronoun reminiscent of the title of one the most interesting and popular recent narratives about Upper Silesia and its history (Rokita 2020). Valeska's sense of belonging and self-identification are defined by her own place on earth and the direct connection she has with it, rather than any bureaucratic dispensations with official determinations of her national identity.

5. Conclusion

Magdalena Dembinska, in her insightful study of contemporary Upper Silesians, identifies their community as "a European collectivity" (2013, p. 54), noting the effect of transnationalization on the process of their nation formation (p. 49). What Twardoch offers in his novels, however, is closer to regional, or perhaps even local (rather than pan-European), contestation of national categories and state borders. Huib Ernste, Hank van Houtum and Annelies Zoomers associate that sort of perspective with 'methodological transnationalism' (2009, p. 579) but their analysis is detached from the context of specific geopolitical transformations in central Europe in the 1920s. Twardoch's transnationalism is definitely local and bounded by the particularity of the historical experience of his own mnemonic community. His characters make no claims about nationalism in general; all they do is articulate their visceral disapproval of becoming someone else's human resources, of being *ennationalized* (Kamusella 2016a, p. 194) and *homogenized* (Polak-Springer 2012, p. 490) according to the fluctuating whims of current state policies. Dembinska emphasizes that Upper Silesians have developed "multidimensional, complementary identifications" which, in turn, underlie a common "borderland identity that attaches great importance to the local territory" (2013, p. 49). Inspired by such insights, Twardoch's fiction, set in the 1920s and in other periods of Silesian history, contributes to "the spectacularisation and memorialization of borders, borderlands and border-crossings" (Schimanski and Nyman 2021, p. 4) in his native region. It reifies Upper Silesian vernacular memory (Breuer 2014, p. 84) characteristic of the local chthonic community, with its own partisan history (Moses 2022, p. 106), and infuses subversive energy into the regional contestations of ethnic nationalism in central Europe, both in the immediate aftermath of the Great War and in the present.

Bibliography

Anderson, Benedict: *Imagined Communities: Reflections on the Origin and Spread of Nationalism*, Revised Edition. London and New York 2006.

Armbruster, Heidi / Rollo, Craig / Meinhof, Ulrike H.: 'Imagining Europe: everyday narratives in European border communities', in: JOURNAL OF ETHNIC AND MIGRATION STUDIES 2003/29:5, p. 885–899, doi: 10.1080/1369183032000149622.

Beiner, Guy: *Forgetful Remembrance: Social Forgetting and Vernacular Historiography of a Rebellion in Ulster.* Oxford 2018.

Billig, Michael: *Banal Nationalism.* London, Thousand Oaks and New Delhi 1995.

Björk, James: 'A Polish Mitteleuropa? Upper Silesia's Conciliationists and the Prospect of German Victory', in: NATIONALITIES PAPERS: THE JOURNAL OF NATIONALISM AND ETHNICITY 2001/29:3, p. 477–492, doi: 10.1080/00905990120073717.

Björk, James: *Neither German nor Pole: Catholicism and National Indifference in a Central European Borderland.* Ann Arbor 2008.

Böhler, Jochen: *Civil War in Central Europe, 1918–1921: The Reconstruction of Poland.* Oxford 2018.

Breuer, Lars: 'Europeanized Vernacular Memory: A Case Study from Germany and Poland', in: Lucy Bond, Lucy / Rapson, Jessica (eds.): *The Transcultural Turn: Interrogating Memory Between and Beyond Borders.* Berlin 2014, p. 83–102.

Brubaker, Rogers: *Ethnicity without Groups.* Cambridge, MA, 2004.

Brubaker, Rogers: *Grounds for Difference.* Cambridge, MA, 2015.

Bruner, Jerome: *Making Stories: Law, Literature, Life.* Cambridge, MA and London 2003.

Clavin, Patricia: 'Defining Transnationalism', in: CONTEMPORARY EUROPEAN HISTORY, Theme Issue: Transnational Communities in European History, 1920–1970, 2005/14:4, p. 421–439.

Coman, Alin: 'Toward a Dynamical – in the Field – Approach to Collective Memory', in: Roediger III, Henry L. / Wertsch, James V. (eds.): *National Memories: Constructing Identity in Populist Times.* New York 2022, p. 389–408.

Czyżak, Agnieszka: 'Śląskie lochy i smoki – wariacje historyczne Szczepana Twardocha', in: CZYTANIE LITERATURY. ŁÓDZKIE STUDIA LITERATUROZNAWCZE 2016/5, p. 37–45.

Davies, Norman: *God's Playground: A History of Poland in Two Volumes. Volume II: 1795 to the Present.* New York 2005.

Dembinska, Magdalena: 'Ethnopolitical Mobilization without Groups: Nation-Building in Upper Silesia', in: REGIONAL & FEDERAL STUDIES, 2013/23:1, p. 47–66.

Drong, Leszek: 'Borderland Anxieties: Brexit, Upper Silesia and Irish Partitions in Recent Novels by Glenn Patterson and Szczepan Twardoch', in: PORÓWNANIA 2021/30:3, p. 209-227, doi.org/10.14746/por.2021.3.14.

Drong, Leszek: 'Literary representations of borders and partitions in provincial memory cultures (Northern Ireland and Upper Silesia)', in: ORBIS LITTERARUM 2023/78:1, p. 59-71, doi.org/10.1111/oli.12370.

Eichenberg, Julia: 'The Dark Side of Independence: Paramilitary Violence in Ireland and Poland after the First World War', in: CONTEMPORARY EUROPEAN HISTORY 2010/ 19, p. 231-248, doi: 10.1017/S0960777310000147.

Ernste, Huib / van Houtum, Henk / Zoomers, Annelies: 'Trans-World: Debating the Place and Borders of Places in the Age of Transnationalism', in: TIJDSCHRIFT VOOR ECONOMISCHE EN SOCIALE GEOGRAFIE 2009/100:5, p. 577-586.

Felton, Debbie: 'The Dead', in: Ogden, David (ed.): *A Companion to Greek Religion*. Malden, Oxford, Carlton 2007.

Gellner, Ernest: *Nations and Nationalism*. Ithaca, NY 1983.

Gerwarth, Robert: 'The Central European Counter-Revolution: Paramilitary Violence in Germany, Austria and Hungary after the Great War', in: PAST & PRESENT 2008/ 200, p. 175-209.

Hill Collins, Patricia / Bilge, Sirma: *Intersectionality*. Cambridge 2020.

Judson, Pieter M.: 'Preface', in: Kamusella, Tomasz / Björk, James / Wilson, Tim / Novikov, Anna (eds.): *Creating Nationality in Central Europe, 1880-1950: Modernity, violence and (be)longing in Upper Silesia*. London and New York 2016, p. xiii-xvi.

Kamusella, Tomasz: 'The Changing Lattice of Languages, Borders, and Identities in Silesia', in: Kamusella, Tomasz / Nomachi, Motoki / Gibson, Catherine (eds.): *The Palgrave Handbook of Slavic Languages, Identities and Borders*. Basingstoke and New York 2016a, p. 185-205.

Kamusella, Tomasz: 'Upper Silesia in modern Central Europe: on the significance of the non-national/a-national in the age of nations', in: Kamusella, Tomasz / Björk, James / Wilson, Tim / Novikov, Anna (eds.): *Creating Nationality in Central Europe, 1880-1950: Modernity, violence and (be)longing in Upper Silesia*. London and New York 2016b, p. 8-52.

Kamusella, Tomasz: *Politics and the Slavic Languages*. London and New York 2021.

Karch, Brendan: *Nation and Loyalty in a German-Polish Borderland: Upper Silesia, 1848-1960*. Cambridge 2016.

Kornprobst, Markus: *Irredentism in European politics: Argumentation, compromise and norms*. Cambridge 2008.

Lionnet, Francoise / Shih, Shu-Mei: 'Introduction: Thinking through the Minor, Transnationally', in: Lionnet, Francoise / Shih, Shu-Mei (eds.): *Minor Transnationalism*. Durham and London 2005, p. 1-26.

McCall, Cathal: 'Debordering and Rebordering the United Kingdom', in: Wilson, Thomas M. / Donnan, Hastings (eds.): *A Companion to Border Studies*. Chichester 2012, p. 214-229.

Medyńska, Małgorzata: 'Dana, Éire, Cesair: The Fluctuating Identity of the Irish Chthonic Goddesses', in: Kalaga, Wojciech / Rachwał, Tadeusz (eds.): *(Trans)-Formations I. Identity and Property: Essays in Cultural Practice*. Katowice 2002, p. 137-152.

Moses, A. Dirk: 'Partisan History and the East European Region of Memory', in: Simon Lewis, Simon / Olick, Jeffrey / Wawrzyniak, Joanna / Pakier, Malgorzata (eds.): *Regions of Memory: Transnational Formations*. Cham 2022, p. 101-138.
Napiórkowski, Marcin. *Turbopatriotyzm*. Wołowiec 2019.
O'Dowd, Liam: 'Contested States, Frontiers and Cities', in: Wilson, Thomas M. / Donnan, Hastings (eds.): *A Companion to Border Studies*. Chichester 2012, p. 158-176.
Polak-Springer, Peter: 'Landscapes of Revanchism: Building and the Contestation of Space in an Industrial Polish-German Borderland, 1922-1945', in: CENTRAL EUROPEAN HISTORY 2012/45, p. 485-522.
Polak-Springer, Peter: 'The Nazi 'recovered territories' myth in the eastern Upper Silesian borderland, 1939-1945', in: Kamusella, Tomasz / Björk, James / Wilson, Tim / Novikov, Anna (eds.): *Creating Nationality in Central Europe, 1880-1950: Modernity, violence and (be)longing in Upper Silesia*. London and New York 2016, p. 170-184.
Porter-Szűcs, Brian: *Poland In The Modern World: Beyond Martyrdom*. Chichester 2014.
Renan, Ernest: *What Is A Nation? And Other Political Writings*. Translated and edited by M. F. N. Giglioli. New York 2018.
Rigney, Ann: 'Articulations of Memory: Mediation and the Making of Mnemo-Regions', in: Simon Lewis, Simon / Olick, Jeffrey / Wawrzyniak, Joanna / Pakier, Malgorzata (eds.): *Regions of Memory: Transnational Formations*. Cham 2022, p. 163-184.
Roediger III, Henry L. / Putnam, Adam L. / Yamashiro, Jeremy K.: 'National and State Narcissism as Reflected in Overclaiming of Responsibility', in: Roediger III, Henry L. / Wertsch, James V. (eds.): *National Memories: Constructing Identities in Populist Times*. New York 2022, p. 209-235.
Rokita, Zbigniew: *Kajś. Opowieść o Górnym Śląsku*. Wołowiec 2020.
Schimanski, Johan / Nyman, Jopi: 'Introduction: Images and Narratives on the Border', in: Schimanski, Johan / Nyman, Jopi (eds.): *Border images, border narratives: The political aesthetics of boundaries and crossings*. Manchester 2021, p. 1-22.
Scullion, Scott: 'Olympian and Chthonian', in: CLASSICAL ANTIQUITY 1994/13:1, p. 75-119.
Smith, Anthony D.: *The Cultural Foundations of Nations: Hierarchy, Covenant, and Republic*. Malden, MA; Carlton, and Oxford 2008.
Struve, Kai: 'Ascribing identity: public memory of the plebiscite and uprisings', in: Kamusella, Tomasz / Björk, James / Wilson, Tim / Novikov, Anna (eds.): *Creating Nationality in Central Europe, 1880-1950: Modernity, violence and (be)longing in Upper Silesia*. London and New York 2016, p. 210-229.
Thum, Gregor: 'Wrocław and the myth of the multicultural border city', in: EUROPEAN REVIEW, 2005/13:2, p. 227-235.
Tiryakian, Edward A.: 'Three Metacultures of Modernity: Christian, Gnostic, Chthonic', in: THEORY, CULTURE & SOCIETY 1996/13:1, p. 99-118.
Twardoch, Szczepan: *Drach*. Kraków 2014.
Twardoch, Szczepan: *Pokora*. Kraków 2020.
Twardoch, Szczepan: *Chołod*. Kraków 2022.
Verdery, Katherine: 'Transnationalism, nationalism, citizenship, and property: Eastern Europe since 1989', in: AMERICAN ETHNOLOGIST 1998/25:2, p. 291-306.
Waniek, Henryk: *Finis Silesiae: Görlitz-Gleiwitz, 23:55*. Kotórz Mały 2021.

Welsch, Wolfgang: 'Transculturality – the Puzzling Form of Cultures Today', in: Featherstone, Mike / Lash, Scott (eds.): *Spaces of Culture: City, Nation, World*. London 1999, p. 194–213.
Wertsch, James V.: *How nations remember: a narrative approach*. New York 2021.
Wertsch, James V.: 'The Narrative Tools of National Memory', in: Roediger III, Henry L. / Wertsch, James V. (eds.): *National Memories: Constructing Identities in Populist Times*. New York 2022, p. 454–471.
Wilson, Timothy: *Frontiers of Violence: Conflict and Identity in Ulster and Upper Silesia 1918-1922*. Oxford 2010.
Wilson, Thomas M. / Donnan, Hastings: 'Borders and Border Studies', in: Wilson, Thomas M. / Donnan, Hastings (eds.): *A Companion to Border Studies*. Chichester 2012, p. 1–26.
Zerubavel, Eviatar: 'Social memories: Steps to a sociology of the past', in: QUALITATIVE SOCIOLOGY 1996/19, p. 283–299, doi.org/10.1007/BF02393273.

Internet sources

"Pie…l się Polsko' – Twardoch do prokuratury', 2014, available at: https://lubimyczytac.pl/aktualnosci/3608/pie-l-sie-polsko---twardoch-do-prokuratury [Dec 15, 2022].
'Twardoch w prokuraturze za słowa: 'Pier*** się Polsko'. 2014, available at: https://dziennikzachodni.pl/twardoch-w-prokuraturze-za-slowa-pier-sie-polsko/ar/1088704 [Dec 15, 2022].
Świderska, Agnieszka: 'Pier…l się Polsko: Co dalej z doniesieniem na Szczepana Twardocha?'. 2014, available at: https://gloswielkopolski.pl/pierl-sie-polsko-co-dalej-z-doniesieniem-na-szczepana-twardocha/ar/1089400 [Dec 15, 2022].
'Sąd Najwyższy: Ślązacy nie są odrębnym narodem'. 2013, available at: https://dzieje.pl/aktualnosci/sad-najwyzszy-slazacy-nie-sa-odrebnym-narodem [Dec 15, 2022].
'Szczepan Twardoch: Plotę, co mi ślina na język przyniesie, i bywa, że mam ten język dość niewyparzony'. 2022, available at: https://weekend.gazeta.pl/weekend/7,150724,29167040,twardoch-gdy-czytalem-kolejne-zdanie-szesciokrotnie-zlozone.html [Dec 15, 2022].

Richard Jorge

Questioning Identities in the Postmodern Nation: Memory, Past and the Self in Claire Keegan's 'The Night of the Quicken Trees'

Since its appearance in the nineteenth century, nationalist discourses have conditioned the politics of Europe. Born as a response to dominant imperialism, these discourses arose to reassert collective identities in the face of a changing world beginning to be perceived as globalized, emphasizing "the importance of unity within, cleaving to one's own" (Boehmer 2005, p. 182). While such discourses have been useful in reinstating suppressed collectives and ensuring "silenced stories do not remain that way" (Gunning 2013, p. 175), they are based on a dichotomous, reductionist and exclusive opposition of the self versus the other which simplifies the sociocultural complexities of postcolonial nations. Paradoxically, in their decolonizing efforts, these have become "as exclusive and gendered in composition as the canonical historical paradigm [they] sought to refute in the first instance" (Connolly 2007, p. 197). Therefore, these discourses have produced "historically neglected social groups" (Hartnett 2011, p. 2) at the heart of the now-independent nations. Postcolonial discourses have examined the creation and destruction of collective identities, providing a voice for those whose identity was delegitimized under colonial rule, but also questioning the role of nationalist discourses in postcolonial nations in their attempt at "over-homogenizing, [eliding] the multiplicity of subaltern classes and groups" (Graham 1996, p. 365).

Even in postcolonial nations, where nationalist discourses are perceived as a necessary tool to articulate lost voices "to represent the most achieved form of self-realization for oppressed peoples" (Boehmer 2005, p. 176), such discourses are dangerous as they require a univocal, unifying voice "based [...] on the underpinnings of stereotype and essentialism" (Flannery 2001, p. 31). By implementing these univocal discourses, minority cultures are marginalized by those who were once colonized, suppressing divergent selves, "in quest of unity [which] tended [...] either to suppress or to mask internal differences" (Boehmer 2005, p. 182–3). Through a depiction of the character of Margaret, the appropriation of the folktale narrative, and her questioning of a church-dominated national discourse, Claire Keegan's 'The Night of the Quicken Trees' (2007) explores the marginalization of subcultures and minorities in a postcolonial, independent Ireland. Keegan's (2007) short story questions the univocal nationalist discourse present in the post-independence Irish State, which strongly identified with the local, rural, and, most remarkably, church-dominated community, in what has been defined as "the Catholic triumphalism of the new state" (Jackson 2010, p. 283). This paper analyses how Keegan's (2007) fiction utilizes narrative techniques to give voice to the subaltern, questioning imposed collective and invented memories over individual, diverging narratives. To do so, it explores three interconnected areas: Keegan's (2007) appropriation and adaptation of traditional folktale structures and narrative devices, the narrative opposition between superstitious beliefs and the established church as a univocal representative of the Irish State and the questioning of a Catholic-led, community-driven discourse.

The Irish folktale as a subverting narrative structure

Having been raised on a farm at the heart of rural Wicklow (Aosdána 2022), Claire Keegan's ease at depicting rural landscapes is hardly surprising. Indeed, the stories in *Walk the Blue Fields* (2007) are all set in rural Ireland, including the last story in the collection, 'The Night of the Quicken Trees'. The story narrates the arrival of Margaret in the Hill of Dunagore (Lisdoonvarna, Co. Clare), close to the Cliffs of Moher, on the west coast of Ireland. There she moves into the house of the recently deceased priest, her relative and, as the narrative unveils, her former lover. 'The Night of the Quicken Trees' (2007) relates Margaret's attempts to deal with her past and adapt to her new environment and community, with a great part of the narration being a mixture of present narrative action interspersed with past recalling. As the narrative unfolds, the reader is introduced to her odd neighbor, Stack, the gossips of the nearest town (Lisdoonvarna), and the harshness of landscape. After a visit to a fortune teller, Margaret becomes the town's healer, which prompts a momentary acceptance at the heart of the community. However, as time passes by and Margaret's willingness to exercise her healing powers wanes, she becomes the target of the town's anger. This reaction prompts Margaret to fulfil her early promise, "she decided she would stay in that house for as long as she could without harming anybody or letting anybody harm her. If either of these things happened, she would move on" (Keegan 2007, p. 127).

The story is interspersed with magic references and "extra-ordinary irruptions that recall a premodern rural oral folk culture" (Smith 2019, p. 195). Keegan (2007) could have opted for a different narrative approach to tell Margaret's story, which is, in the end, a story of failed acceptance. However, she decided to adopt and adapt the narrative frame of the Irish folktale to embed her story. Proof of this is that the narrative proper is preceded and followed by references to Irish folktales. Although these sections do not (arguably) belong to the narrative itself nor is there any intention that the reader takes them to be part of it, structurally, they do form part of the story, as they are located immediately after the title section. Indeed, the introductory part works as a conditioning device. This section, taken "from 'Feet Water', an Irish fairy tale" (Keegan 2007, p. 123), plays a twofold function. While it introduces one of the running themes in the story (that of superstition), it also conditions readers' perception of the narrative. Thus, even before the narrative proper has started, the reader knows that "the old people always said that a bad thing might come into the house if the feet water was kept inside and not thrown out" (Keegan 2007, p. 123). Keegan's (2007) story, therefore, begins by appropriating part of an Irish fairy tale; a part which, indeed, is central to the understanding of the story. Most remarkably, however, her story emanates from this fairy tale structure she has purposefully selected as the source of her story.

On the other hand, the closing section is entitled "Some notes on folklore/stories" (Keegan 2007, p. 161). More practical in nature, this section provides readers with more convenient information, such as the fact that "placing the tongs across the pram is said to prevent fairies from stealing the child" or the fact that Wicklow people "are nicknamed goatsuckers" (Keegan 2007, p. 161). While information such as this is not strictly necessary to comprehend the story, it does help readers gain a better understanding of the different characters' behavior. Paradoxically, being the more logical, explanatory section also highlights the folktale nature of the story proper. From beginning to end, the reader is conditioned into accepting the narrative pace and structure of the Irish folktale adapted by Keegan (2007).

There are two clear markers which qualify Keegan's (2007) story as an adaptation of the Irish fairy tale: mode of narration and deployment of time and space. One of the main characteristics of the folk tale is that narration "passes gradually from *personal* to *impersonal* mode" (Carrassi 2012, p. 30). This means that the narration moves from a first-person anecdote to a third-person narrative on to a local legend to finally become a folktale. In turn, this affects the figure of the narrator, which goes from subject/witness to informant/retailer on to anecdotalist to finally become a storyteller (Foster 1987, p. 216f). This is certainly the case in 'The Night of the Quicken Trees' (2007), where the narrative voice keeps its distance from the narration while, paradoxically, retaining enough proximity to the facts narrated, which allows its voice to remain unquestioned. Indeed, this narrative ambivalence, which is maintained all through the narration, opens the story, "shortly after the priest died, a woman moved into his house on the Hill of Dunagore" (Keegan 2007, p. 125). While the beginning is certainly reminiscent of that of fairy tales, the deictic nature of the expression "the priest" should not pass unnoticed. This deictic usage implies that the narrator (and to some extent the reader) is – or should be – familiar with this figure. As it is the opening line of the story, there is no possible internal reference, which must, then, be placed elsewhere, outside the confines of the story proper. In fact, this figure remains elusive, being always referred to as "the priest", common ground for both the protagonist, the local community and the narrator, but alien to the reader, who is left in the dark as to his real name. Keegan's (2007) narrative, therefore, maintains that move between the first-person anecdote and the local legend.

In fact, this fluidity of her adapted/adopted folktale narrative voice becomes itself a representation of the tangled relationships of the characters. As will be explored later, Margaret's relation with the community is one of belonging-alienation. In her adaptation of the folktale narrator, Keegan (2007) produces a narrative voice which exemplifies this complex relationship as it is difficult to ascertain whether the reader is witness to the omniscient narrator, to Margaret's inner monologue or to Stack's thoughts. Thus, on Christmas Day, when Stack decides to invite Margaret over to dinner, the narration develops in the following way:

> He looked at the black eel writhing on the pan. It looked alive and, for a moment, he wasn't sure. He bucked himself up and walked up the path to the priest's house.
> Margaret wasn't dressed. She was scratching herself and thinking. She liked to roam around in her nightdress having a think, drinking tea in the mornings. She went to the toilet and made sure she was still bleeding. It was strange to be producing eggs again (Keegan 2007, p. 138).

Although the narration is always carried out in the third person, the focus moves from Stack to Margaret's perception. At the beginning of the scene, the reader is told Stack's inner thoughts ("he wasn't sure") and feelings ("He bucked himself up"). The narrative voice also describes Stack's movements ("[he]walked up the path") so the reader knows that Stack is outside Margaret's house, perhaps observing her as he had done before, "He liked being at her door knowing the woman [Margaret] was inside, asleep and safe" (Keegan 2007, p. 136). The beginning of the next paragraph, focused solely on Margaret, is confusing from a narrative perspective, however. The first two sentences constitute a description of her state at that moment ("wasn't dressed", "was scratching and thinking"). They could, therefore, be Stack's perception from the outside. In fact, coming directly after the narrator's description of his movements, it is the more logical assumption. However, the following sentence, being a description of Margaret's likes, comes across as a narratorial description more than Stack's perception. This is reinforced by the subsequent sentence as not only does it describe an intimate scene, but it also refers to information which Stack does not possess ("she was still bleeding"). The paragraph finishes by focusing on Margaret's inner thoughts, "it was strange to be producing eggs again" (Keegan 2007, p. 38).

This narrative structure complicates the reading experience insofar as it is, at times, difficult to ascertain from whose point of view the reader perceives the story. However, it exemplifies the complex relationships between the different characters. Not only does this structure characterize Keegan's (2007) writing within the "mosaic or composite quality" (Boehmer 2005, p. 219) attributed to postcolonial women's writing, but it also epitomizes the emphasis on "the multiplicity of Irish history and [...] the contradictory nature of Ireland in [...] conscript[ing] the country into the linear narratives of developmental historical progress" (Flannery 2001, p. 22). The Irish folktale structure as employed by Keegan (2007) epitomizes the plurality of voices which historically conform the Irish narrative.

Time and space references are similarly deployed, moving between the concrete and the general, from being "originally specified [to] slowly generalized" (Carrassi 2012, p. 30). In this sense, there are two time considerations which need to be considered: the timeframe of the story and how the passing of time is marked as the story unfolds. Keegan's (2007) narrative appropriates both folktale structural elements, creating a narrative which can be interpreted in atemporal terms, a "contingent instrument, the historical interpreter of a timeless phenomenon" (Carrassi 2012, p. 73), and not only in the given context of a specific time period.

In 'The Night of the Quicken Trees' (2007), the timeframe remains diffuse, with no concrete indications as to when the story takes place. This, mixed with "her blending of tradition and superstition with modernity" (Morales-Ladrón 2021, p. 276), causes "the reader [to be] left confused with the characters' temporal dimension" (Morales-Ladrón 2021, p. 276). Rather than produce historically concrete time refences which could elucidate when the story is set, Keegan (2007) offers sparse hints that place the narration close to contemporary times, somewhere between the advent of the Irish Free State and the year 2007, when the story came out. The first such instance takes place when the character of Stack is introduced and the reader learns that he "did not like to think he would ever become like the new generation" (Keegan 2007, p. 128) only to specify later on which these maladies are, "they drank beer straight from the bottle, came back from America and Prague looking for pizzas, and couldn't tell a golden wonder from a Victoria plum" (Keegan 2007, p. 128). The narrator's introduction of Stack, apart from depicting him as a character anchored in the past, gives little to no hint as to the narrative timeframe. The rather obscure references to widespread travel opportunities or modern leisure activities, such as eating pizza, only ambiguously place the narration somewhere in the twentieth or twenty-first centuries. These references rather reinforce the abstractedness of the temporal frame than reduce its scope.

A slightly more concrete time reference takes place as the story advances. On Christmas Day, Stack invites Margaret over to dinner, an invitation she accepts despite her not wanting "to sit in that awful place eating fried snake" (Keegan 2007, p. 141). Although this meeting is, at first, rather awkward, as time passes by and she starts to enjoy the food, the conversation between them grows in confidence, "Stack bantered on. He criticized young people and turf, the Taoiseach, talked about New Year's resolutions and sunburn" (Keegan 2007, p. 142). The overt reference to the Taoiseach, a denomination in use Ireland since the enactment of the 1937 Irish Constitution, further narrows the temporal space of the story. There are, however, no further indications as to the narration's timeframe. Other references to modern appliances, such as the television, the radio or cars – like the previous mention of Prague or pizza – are vague enough to allow the reader's imagination to select a timeframe of their choice, one they can comfortably identify with.

This lack of concretion in the story, vaguely placing the action during post-independence Ireland, results in "a timelessness that is belied by the new twists Keegan brings to [it]" (Ingman 2018, p. 291), and allows a wider audience (in generational terms) to loosely identify with the timeframe, facilitating the acceptance of the narration itself. This is, precisely, one of the most remarkable characteristics of the folktale, which "bases its general validity on the capacity to maintain constantly alive the relationship of the individual with a series of elements that constitute his most deeply rooted identity" (Carrassi 2012, p. 184). Keegan (2007) appropriates this folktale structural device, constructing a narrative which allows for the depiction of minorities (and for the subsequent narrative interpretations) to be extensible to all the Irish postcolonial period and not only to a concrete historical time.

However, the most remarkable adoption and adaptation of the Irish folktale is how narrative time is conveyed to the reader. Carrassi (2012) argues that, in Irish folktales, time has a markedly diffuse character, as "the fairy tale is a phenomenon that disturbs an equilibrium imposed in a contingent space-time dimension" (p. 107). In other words, the narrative of a fairy tale does not follow the time logic operating in the real world. Although it would be an exaggeration to assert that this is what happens in Keegan's (2007) story, most certainly, in 'The Night of the Quicken Trees' (2007), time is difficult to measure. Yet in another adaptation of the Irish folktale, the passing of time is, almost without deviance, linked to a natural image. Thus, at the very beginning of the story, once Margaret has been introduced, the reader learns that "[i]t was autumn when she came. The swallows were long gone and any blackberry still clinging to its briar had begun to rot" (Keegan 2007, p. 125). As the story unfolds, similar other assertions are conducted. And so, "December came in wet. Margaret had never known such a rain. It didn't come down out of the sky but all skewed, on the wind" (Keegan 2007, p. 132), and "February turned into a March of many weathers" (Keegan 2007, p. 146). Time is present in the story almost as an extension of landscape, actualizing nature deployments in Irish folktales, where "the contours of the natural realm are often amorphous and the boundaries between the animal and human worlds are often blurred" (Smith 2019, p. 203), in the contemporary Irish short story. Time, therefore, condenses Margaret's reactions to her environment, but remains a diffuse way to control the chronological development of the narrative. This is supported by the stark and relatively short emphasis laid on the temporal mark, with the name of the month anthropomorphed in a short, simple sentence. Simultaneously, the natural imagery that follows the temporal marker is profuse in detail, with longer, compound sentences that help paint a clearer picture of the passing of time. In this way, Keegan's (2007) story manages to be concurrently detached from a too-specific marking of time while still appealing to a deeply rooted rural Irish identity. Keegan's (2007) story would, then, conform to the narrative structure of an Irish fairy tale, emanating from "Pre-Christian Irish culture [and] governed by the traditional type of memory" (Bondarenko 2014, p. 175), thus presenting the narrative as "a logically and chronologically ordered sequence [planned] in such a way as not to distract the listener from the main theme but also to preserve the storyteller's memory" (Carrassi 2012, p. 183).

Keegan's (2007) appropriation of the Irish folktale in 'The Night of the Quicken Trees' recuperates a more authentic Irish voice, one that deviates from mainstream nationalist discourse, but which helps create a more congruent national tale. By exercising "the recuperation of the mythic power of that folkloric superstition" (Smith 2019, p. 195) and using it to narrate the stories of ostracized communities, Keegan's (2007) narration acts as a catalyst for undermined voices. As the next section elucidates, Keegan's (2007) narration exposes the marginalization of dissenting discourses exerted under the domineering influence of the Catholic Church in post-independence Ireland.

Embodying the Irish nation: superstitious beliefs, the Catholic Church and national discourse

Keegan's (2007) appropriation of the fairy tale narrative facilitates the story's criticism of post-independence Ireland's univocal nationalist agenda. Carrasi (2012) argues that one of the defining features of fairy tale narratives is its forming "an ideal middle ground, in which Myth, Legend, and History can flow together and interact" (p. 43). 'The Night of the Quicken Trees' (2007) fulfils that requirement as it opposes the concept of an established religion against superstition and traditional beliefs, where the former is presented as a metaphor for the univocal, official Irish Republic while the latter represents marginal Irish discourses. Keegan's (2007) narrative achievement is to present them on a par, as the folktale validates superstition as a legitimate – and ultimately more authentic – form of perceiving the world. Therefore, Keegan's (2007) narrative reclaims the legitimacy of dissenting voices, portraying them as equally acceptable as the official national discourse, since they deploy "the idiom and voice of the local language, rooted in the local environment, to summon up a world and a vision" (Innes 2007, p. 32).

In 'The Night of the Quicken Trees' (2007), the Roman Catholic Church is established as the figure of authority at the onset of the story. The narrative voice describes the house thus, "[t]he priest's house stood on the highest point of the hill" (Keegan 2007, p. 125), attaching to the building – and its inhabitant – a domineering position over the whole community. This leading pre-eminence in community affairs is, in fact, embodied in the priest, who acts as a metonymic figure for the Catholic Church and for the Irish Republic. This institutionalization is conducted via naming or, indeed, not naming him as all throughout the story he is only ever referred to as "the priest". Innes' (2007) contention that the "naming of people and places or allusions to them […] become an assertion and (re)creation of this intimate inside community" (p. 201) acquires greater relevance in this narrative. While this institutional marker configures the priest as an entity within the immediate local community, it distances him both from the reader and from Margaret despite their intimate attachment. Although his presence is a perennial feature in the story, the priest is ultimately perceived as an alienating figure casting a shadow over the narration despite not partaking in it. Thus, the figure of the priest is used to both portray the power and influence of the Church over the whole community and to criticize said influence.

It is Margaret's meandering inner thoughts (deftly conveyed by a present-time narrative always undercut by past interferences) that first provide readers with a glimpse of the Catholic Church as a figure of authority. Thus, Margaret recalls how the priest "was her first cousin [and] he used to come to their house every summer to make the hay" (Keegan 2007, p. 129). What follows this introduction is a bucolic image of youth and love, "[h]e would come with the fine weather, sit on top of the hayrick, at her side, dig new potatoes, sharpen his appetite, pull scallions and eat them raw" (Keegan 2007, p. 129). The recurrence implied in the modality ("would come") followed by the asyndeton of farm-related verbs reinforces the positive connotations of the adjectives "fine" (attached to the weather) and "new" (attached to produce) and of the lusciousness implied in words related to physical satisfaction ("appetite" and "eat"). This overall connotation of innocence is further strengthened by references to physical purity, like the fact that Margaret "was a teenager" (Keegan 2007, p. 129) or natural purity, "[s]kies were blue back then" (Keegan 2007, p. 129). Added to this is the fact that the narration distinctly clarifies the nature of the priest and Margaret's relationship:

> He said they would marry, that they would get the bishop's permission, rear Shorthorns and have two children, a pigeon's clutch. Margaret could see him coming in from the fields with a handful of clover, saying the meadow was without comparison (Keegan 2007, p. 129–30).

The priest's promise, implied in the modality used for prospective future actions, is coupled with Margaret's vision of their potential future life together. The two syntactic elements put together result in a reiteration of the overall bucolic connotation of the remembrance. Again, there is lusciousness in word choice, this time stemming from an overt blooming nature ("rearing" and "having children") as well as from the pleasant, lush connotations derived from his holding a handful of clover (both in terms of sexuality and material prosperity).

This bucolic image is terminated at the end of the paragraph, "[a]nd then he went off to the seminary, became a priest, became the pride of a family who no longer called him by his name" (Keegan 2007, p. 130). The abruptness of the coordinating conjunction "and" in combination with two simple short sentences helps in breaking the previous bucolic, promising cadence of the remembrance. Likewise, the emphasis on the verb "become" in such a context implies a certain disbelief of the subsequent expression "pride of a family". This is further enhanced by the fact that they stopped calling him by his name. Thus, the act of becoming a priest, "the priest", in Keegan's (2007) fiction, terminates his previous character, obliterating any prior instances of familial and, indeed, romantic intimacy.

This transformation, however, implies accessing power structures capable of transforming the very nature of family relationships, as the narrative unveils. For although the previous sentence terminates the paragraph (and Margaret's bucolic remembrance), this is not closed by a full stop but by a colon. What follows it is, indeed, the priest's realization of his newly acquired status:

> 'Another drop of gravy, Father?'
> 'Do you think there's such a place as limbo, Father?'
> 'Did my father say where he was going, Father?'
> Even though he came back every summer to make the hay, he never again sat on the ditches combing knots out of her hair, talking about the children they would have. Summers passed and the whole family, instead of putting on the record player and opening the stout when the hay was safe on the loft, would kneel and answer his rosary (Keegan 2007, p. 130).

This recently acquired status as a representative of the Catholic Church implies not only (apparently) infinite wisdom, as gathered form the combination of profane and religious questions posed to him, but also the submission of the community, and its essence. It further epitomizes the Catholic Church's efforts to exercise "a monopoly on definitions in order to control a diverse, unstable reality" (Boehmer 2005, p. 159), paradoxically resembling previous acts of colonial interventions. Most tellingly, Keegan (2007) opposes the common noun "father" to the priest's title "Father", implying that the priest's figure garners more reverence, more command than the semantically related term representing the head of the family. This is further reinforced by an image which juxtaposes past happiness (epitomized by music and "opening the stout") and the now recurring act of obeisance implied by the affirmation that "the whole family [...] would kneel and answer his rosary" (Keegan 2007, p. 130). It is, therefore, the community, epitomized in the figure of the family, that must answer him. The priest's access to the hierarchies of the established religion, therefore, denaturalizes family relationships, thus marginalizing dissenting discourses. However, his figure also ushers in criticism of the established church, which is opposed to superstition and traditional folkloric beliefs.

This opposition and validation of folkloric beliefs is conveyed in a dual way, through the narrative deployment of the figure of the priest and via Margaret's inner perception of the two belief systems. On the one hand, the priest's figure, already established as a figure of authority, is partially debased as he is proven to be a flawed priest, "[n]either she nor the priest could help themselves. She felt him on top of her, panting, rolling over onto his stomach, zipping himself up, ashamed" (Keegan 2007, p. 140). An act that should be the epitome of love, of an intrinsic union, expressive of "the thrill after a decade of sitting on ricks of hay, eating scallions, him leaving the first primrose on the saddle of her bike" (Keegan 2007, p. 140), becomes instead a stark expression of a sexual encounter. This reading is, indeed, encouraged by both the syntax and the diction of these contrasting sentences. While the second one uses the continuous tense to concatenate elements of a similar length, with a diction reminiscent of ebullient nature, the first one displays a shorter, descending concatenation of elements finished in a past participle ("ashamed") that undercuts any possibility of a positive reading. Yet, Margaret's interpretation of the same act, always aligned with nature and folk beliefs, renders the possibility of a different reading, "[b]y breaking his vows of celibacy it felt possible that he might, somehow, make others" (Keegan 2007, p. 140). In doing so, Margaret embodies the alternative, suppressed other of the nation, "revealing some of the alternative possibilities that are closed down in the call for a homogeneous version of the country" (Gunning 2013, p. 83).

Further still, the priest's influence – and by extension that of the Catholic Church – is embedded in negative, uncanny connotations. His shadow is, in fact, everlasting, conditioning both the narrative (by the constant interruptions of present-time narration with reminiscences of the past) and Margaret's behavior, as she acknowledges, "[t]he greatest lesson the priest had taught her was the lesson of where one step can lead" (Keegan 2007, p. 134). His influence is so pernicious that Margaret feels the need to expurgate him by magic actions. Thus, all through the narrative, she continually burns his belongings, a process that gradually increases in proportion to the priest's narrative influence. In fact, the story begins with Margaret's reaction to the fact that "[t]he house smelled of the priest. [She] dragged anything she didn't want [...] and set fire to it" (Keegan 2007, p. 125). This expurgatory act, however, does not suffice, for the priest's presence closes in around Margaret as the narrative develops.

Just after she has been to Stack's house and before they have an intercourse, Margaret finds "a litter of black mongrel pups [...] running across the floor" (Keegan 2007, p. 143). This image instantly produces the interruption of present-time narrative with a priest-related past reminiscence, "[t]here were dogs in the graveyard the night she walked all over the priest's grave" (Keegan 2007, p. 143). From this, Margaret concludes that "[t]he priest was jealous, but the priest was dead" (Keegan 2007, p. 143). The simultaneity of the assertion, using the past simple for both "dead" and "jealous" places both adjectives on a par, incurring in a temporal paradox that can only be explicated via the uncanniness of the priest. This is further heightened by the fact that Margaret "felt an awful chill and pulled the cardigan over her nightdress" (Keegan 2007, p. 143). As a final act of expurgation, and once she finds out that she is pregnant with Stack's child, Margaret "pulled the priest's bed out of the room, took it down to the field, and doused it with paraffin. It was slow to burn at first, then blazed and turned into a bed of ash" (Keegan 2007, p. 154). The allegory of this last act of expurgation yields a potent interpretation. Margaret's first and only intercourse with the priest took place "under the quicken trees" (Keegan 2007, p. 140). As the explanatory section clarifies, "[t]he quicken tree is another name for the mountain ash or the rowan tree" (Keegan 2007, p. 161). The contextual polysemy of the noun "ash" – eased by Keegan's (2007) usage of the singular and not the plural – allows for a metaphoric interpretation of Margaret's setting fire to the priest's bed. As this blazes up and the priest's bed is transformed into a "bed of ash", the one space that symbolizes Margaret and the priest's unholy union disintegrates. This effectively ends the priest's influence over both Margaret and the narration as the priest is mentioned no more.

This conflict between the established religion and traditional beliefs is further epitomized by Margaret's incongruous perceptions of the two. The fact that it remains an inner discourse reflects the extent to which dissenting voices were marginalized by standardized nationalist discourses as "the postcolonial 'national', 'liberal', and 'developmental' state establish[es] and sustain[s] asymmetric power relations to marginalise minorities in these states" (Shahabuddin 2021, p. 82).

This is reflected in Margaret's inner conflict between the established religion – identified with the dominant figure of the priest – and what she perceives to be her true faith: folk beliefs. Although there are several instances of this all throughout the narrative, two are noteworthy. The first one takes place towards the beginning of the story, when Margaret is still an outcast. Being Christmas Eve, Margaret starts pondering about her past, which, inevitably, leads her to the priest:

> She wondered if the priest had gone to Hell. The priest believed in the afterlife, in God and Heaven and Purgatory, in all that. [...] Margaret wondered if she would join him there but it seemed more likely that she'd be turned into a pucán or a dock leaf (Keegan 2007, p. 133).

Her dismissal of the established religion, implied in the concatenation of the different elements conforming the priest's beliefs and dismissively finished by the vague expression "in all that", is paired with her belief in a differing possibility for an afterlife. Keegan's (2007) appropriation of the Irish folktale here further strengthens this perception. Margaret employs the phrasal verb "turn into" and the Irish word for a male goat ("pucán") to provide an alternative to Catholic beliefs. There is a narrative parallelism with Irish legends, in which, often, characters are turned into animals as punishment. The folktale narrative structure, with its blurred boundaries between the animal and human worlds (Smith 2019, p. 203), further supports Keegan's (2007) vindication of alternative voices.

The second instance worth mentioning takes place when "February turned into a March of many weathers [and] Margaret's superstition deepened" (Keegan 2007, p. 146). After spending some months at the priest's house, her superstition intensifies as does her feeling of alienation from the community. Feeling the burden of both the past and the present, Margaret "drove to a chapel [...], lit a candle at the feet of Saint Anthony, knelt in the front pew and stared at the ambo" (Keegan 2007, p. 146). However, instead of praying, she "imagined the priest standing there, giving out sermons while her belly got bigger with his child" (Keegan 2007, p. 146). Both this and the previous instance reflect Margaret's dismissal of the official religion and her belief in traditional folklore. However, they also portray the silencing of such beliefs for Margaret still conforms to the rituals of Catholic faith, even if this is only done outwardly. Indeed, for the greater part of the narrative, Margaret's dismissal of the established religion and acceptance of her dissenting voice only happens in her inner monologue, as if "suspect[ing] that in the new, liberated Ireland [...], there may no place for those

[...] whose culture and origins are awkwardly alternative" (Baraniuk / Hagan 2007, p. 73).

It is only when Margaret burns the priest's bed and pulls down the wall that her liberation, both metaphysically and in terms of discourse, takes place. Margaret's pulling down the wall is, in fact, compared to a Christian ritual:

> She was there half the day. When she saw light at the other side it reminded her of the time her mother woke her as a child, on Easter morning so she could see the sun dancing, to witness the resurrection of Christ (Keegan 2007, p. 155).

Allegorically, then, pulling down the wall implies her resurrection, and, indeed, from that moment onwards the narrative changes. However, it is also relevant to remark that the narrative equals both Christian religion and traditional beliefs. This is epitomized in the pagan ritual of burning undesired elements to get rid of evil spirits (Sneddon 2022, p. 108) and its comparison with the resurrection of Christ.

As mentioned, after this act, the narration acquires a different tinct, with Margaret freely voicing and enacting her beliefs as manifested in her independent way of bringing up her child, "as a mother she was ferocious [and] she gave [the child] his own way at every turn" (Keegan 2007, p. 158). It is precisely in this action where her liberated discourse can be better appreciated, as it performs "a restorative connection with that which [head been] denied--the internal life" (Boehmer 2005, p. 187) of suppressed minorities. Thus, Margaret "wouldn't let [the child] go to school, said there was nothing the people of that parish could teach him that she couldn't teach better" (Keegan 2007, p. 159). Although Margaret's stance fully anticipates the final rejection by the community, it also bespeaks of her freedom to rear the kid her own way, thus enacting her dissenting perceptions of the world. Indeed, Michael is almost described in heroic terms for he

> never crawled. He got out of his chair one day and made it all the way to the front gate [...]. When the boy got hardy he went around the bogs with Stack, jumping ditches with a pole, wading in bog-water and was never sick a day in his life [...]. He could write his name backwards and upside-down (Keegan 2007, p. 158).

Thus, Michael becomes the ultimate validation of Margaret's discourse, as her belief in traditional folklore leads her to rear a child whose description is reminiscent of the heroes in the old Irish legends. As the next section unveils, Margaret's alternative discourse is, indeed, proven a more authentic Irish voice than the priest-driven discourse the community upholds, and which leads the latter to finally reject her.

Questioning a community-driven discourse

Keegan's (2007) denunciation of the suppression of dissenting voices under univocal discourses comes in full light when considering the relationship between Margaret and the local community. In doing so, Keegan's (2007) appropriation of the folktale plays a major role as it is through the usage of natural imagery commonly associated to this genre that Margaret's rejection is portrayed.

This alienation is marked from the very beginning of the story as in the second line she is described thus, "[s]he was a bold spear of a woman who clearly wasn't used to living on the coast" (Keegan 2007, p. 125). From then on, landscape and nature are continuously deployed to emphasize her not belonging to the community. However, this is not done by depicting an alienating nature but rather by contrasting natural landscapes and aligning them with characters. In this way, when her new abode is first described, the reader learns that "roads were narrow and steep" and that "every creature seemed capable or on the verge of flight" (Keegan 2007, p. 126). This sense of oppression, of the need to escape, is combined with a stark physical description of the hill itself,

> Dunagore was a strange place without so much as a tree, not a withered leaf to be seen in autumn, just the shivering bogland and the gulls wheeling around, screeching under restless clouds. The landscape looked metal, all sturdy and everlasting but Margaret, coming from a place of oak and ash, it was without substance (Keegan 2007, p. 127).

Nature in Dunagore is, then, anthropomorphic and it actively rejects Margaret, with gulls screeching and restless clouds. Adjectives which, at first, could transmit positive connotations, such as "sturdy" and "everlasting", are, instead, converted into negative appraisal of the landscape. Nature is epitomized as an alienating element, a place that invites Margaret to leave. Such a portrayal, repeated all throughout the narrative, underscores Margaret's inability to adapt to her new surroundings, but also the landscape's unwillingness to accept her. Paradoxically, even in these initial stages, Margaret is allegorically characterized as "oak", a tree "bestowed with magical properties" (Sneddon 2022, p. 107) in Irish folklore and which had been used as a synonym for God in the early Irish glossary *Dúil Laithne* (Bondarenko 2014, p. 73). These connections place her closer to a more authentic Irish voice. This assumption is further heightened by a natural description of her place of origin:

> There would be no shade in the summer, no fields of barley turning yellow in the month of August. The skies in the east would now be obscured by falling leaves, their heifers would be in the barn, dairy cows chained to the stalls (Keegan 2007, p. 127).

Keegan's (2007) narrative technique opposes the two landscapes, slowly transitioning the reader from a stark location to a luscious one. By first asserting the starkness in Dunagore via a parallel structure, the narrator facilitates the reader's acceptance of the mellowness of the subsequent prose, which becomes more elaborate and ornate. Natural imagery is also more profuse in description, conveying intimacy and homely comfort. This is effectively achieved both syntactically and semantically. As can be observed, the last sentence concatenates three phrases which are progressively reduced in length. Thus, it starts with a passive sentence, moves on to a shorter conditional mode to end with a phrase in which this is omitted. Parallel to this is an approximation from outer to inner space, starting with the outer "skies", moving on to the barns to end fixing the narrative on the stalls. In like manner, word choice contributes to this inward, homeward movement, by first focusing on the yellow barley fields, and the darkening skies, to move on to heifers, the barn and dairy cows. The natural imagery deployed here is farm-related, far from the threatening wild nature Margaret encounters in Dunagore, and reminiscent of "aboriginal closeness to nature and communal responsibility" (Innes 2007, p. 67).

Keegan's (2007) landscape is metonymic of origin and belonging, and, therefore, of acceptance and rejection, as a conversation between Margaret and Stack elucidates:

'What part of the country did you come from?' he said.
'Wicklow.'
'The goat-suckers,' he said. 'That explains it.'
'Did you ask me in to insult me?' (Keegan 2007, p. 141)

Embodied by Stack, people from Dunagore are depicted as dismissive of Margaret's place of origin, labelling it in derogative terms. Later in the same scene, landscape is overtly referred to:

'Do you not miss your own part of the country?'
'I miss the trees,' she said. 'I miss the ash.'
The quicken tree, the mountain ash, were all the one.
'Well, you can't be blamed for that,' he said. 'There's no fire like an ash fire.' (Keegan 2007, p. 142)

There are two noticeable elements in this conversation. First, the implicit recognition that Margaret's discourse is, somehow, more authentic than that of the community, as represented by Stack. The metonymic nature of landscape implies that Stack's acknowledgement that "[t]here's no fire like an ash fire" (Keegan 2007, p. 142) is also the recognition that Margaret's discourse bears more authenticity. The second thing is the paradoxical expression Stack interrogates Margaret with, "your own part of the country" (Keegan 2007, p. 142). While Stack asserts that they both belong to the same country, implicitly, he is also voicing

Margaret's marginalization in Dunagore. By referring to "your own part", Stack is – perhaps inadvertently – signaling that Dunagore is *not* her own, thus underscoring the fact that Margaret does not belong. By extension, Stack and Margaret's conversation summarizes a reality in opposition to the homogenizing mainstream nationalist discourse, where "persecuted minorities [have been] misleadingly documented by a hostile majority" (Hartnett 2011, p. 14). Despite there being one country, this has no univocal representation, as manifested in the differences enacted by landscape. Keegan's (2007) narration, therefore, vindicates these marginal discourses by "inventing narratives to put in the mouths of those silenced or forgotten by the dominant histories of the present" (Walder 2010, p. 119).

This has greater implications yet as both for nationalist and postcolonial discourses, landscape plays a crucial role. Indeed, the identification of landscape with the ethnographic community has been long attested (Innes 2007, p. 72). 'The Night of the Quicken Trees' (2007) confronts such unifying discourses by showing that this identification is far from homogeneous in a country like Ireland, where the strong "Catholic ethos of the nationalist movement and the new Republic after independence" (Röder 2017, p. 329) promoted a univocal image of the Irish. This monopolization of discourse has implied the marginalization of minority groups in the Republic, like Protestants and Presbyterians, who "had to contend with a state and a society hostile to their Britishness and either chose or were forced to undergo a process of denationalisation and de-ethnicisation" (Ruane and Butler 2007, p. 626), or – worse still – xenophobic behaviors towards other groups, such as the Traveler community, "with decades, if not centuries, of stereotypes, negative media representation and poor government treatment" (Hartnett 2011, p. 2).

'The Night of the Quicken Trees' (2007) portrays such rejections through the ambivalent reception Margaret receives in Lisdoonvarna. While it is true that Margaret does little to mingle with and integrate in the local community, doing "her best to keep people at arm's length, for people were nothing but a nuisance" (Keegan 2007, p. 127), it is also certain that the local community views her with suspicion, thus reproducing established hostility patterns associated with the Traveler community (Sovacool / Furszyfer Del Rio 2022, p. 2). This hostility pattern is first triggered as mere gossip, exemplified in the community's speculation about her origin, "some said her people were all dead and the priest was her uncle [...]. Others swore she was a wealthy woman whose husband had run off [...]" (Keegan 2007, p. 130). However, curiosity soon translates into dismissal. Thus, when a middle-aged man approaches her house to ask her to sign a petition, his interrogation runs thus:

Questioning Identities in the Postmodern Nation 97

> While she signed her name his eyes crawled over her frame.
> 'Would you be any relation to the priest?' he asked.
> 'Why, do I look like him?'
> He looked up at her nostrils, the gypsy eyes and the waiting mouth.
> 'You don't look like anybody,' he said (Keegan 2007, p. 129).

This verbal exchange illustrates the movement from curiosity to dismissal. But, perhaps, the most interesting part is the narratorial intervention, which allows readers to access the man's thoughts when appraising her by focalizing the narration through him. It is after his impression of her "gypsy eyes" that he utters the dismissive "you don't look like anybody" (Keegan 2007, p. 129). While there is nothing in the narrative that makes one think that she belongs to that particular ethnic community – or to the Traveler community –, it is the first overt (and only) reference to an ethnic minority in the narration. Most tellingly, this almost imperceptible reference generates the first overt act of rejection and is reminiscent of the dismissive treatment minorities (especially certain minorities) received in the first years of the Republic. While "the state-builders of the 1920s were committed to the idea of an efficient and inclusivist parliamentary democracy" (Jackson 2010, p. 273), social reality differed. Even though the newly drafted Irish constitution was designed as non-discriminatory, there was the widespread perception that it "may not make adequate provisions in order to rectify what we may regard as violations against minority rights" (Kirby / McBride 1981, p. 61). In this sense, Keegan's (2007) story unveils the social oppression minorities have been subject to in Ireland. This repression is deeply entrenched in the social and institutional hierarchies of the country (Kavanagh / Dupont 2021) and, while not legally supported, it manifests itself in daily (and, at times, violent) acts of discrimination.

Paradoxically enough, Margaret's only moment of acceptance is prompted via her identification with a minority, that of the Travelers. After having spent some time in Lisdoonvarna and still haunted by her past, Margaret decides to ramble through town. While walking, she notices that "a caravan was parked beside the vegetable stand. *Meet Madame Nowlan, Teller of the Future,* the sign read" (Keegan 2007, p. 147). After sitting alone in a pub and having mused over her circumstances, both past and present, she decides to visit Madame Nowlan, who "was eating a rock bun, pulling raisins out of the dough with her fingernails. She had blonde hair and a fake tan. A pot of tea was left out on the table" (Keegan 2007, p. 147). Madame Nowlan proceeds to read her leaves and give her counsel.

While there is no overt mention of the Traveler community, references to the caravan, to her way of earning a living by reading tea leaves and to the marginality of her existence (living in a caravan and parked on the outskirts of town) all point to said ethnic community, still depicted nowadays as living "on the periphery of society, in tents or wagons, where they supported themselves by trading, repairing, providing entertainment, or offering seasonal agricultural work" (Sovacool / Furszyfer Del Rio 2022, p. 2). Paradoxically, it is through Madame Nowlan's agency that Margaret is temporarily accepted by the community as she sends the first community member, "a dark-haired man with a troubled look" (Keegan 2007, p. 151), to be cured by her. Thus, Margaret becomes the unofficial healer of the community, as "the Nowlan woman in the caravan told me [...] you're a seventh child, that you have the cure" (Keegan 2007, p. 151). From then on, "the whole parish started to come" (Keegan 2007, p. 151), which effectually translates into "new spuds and rhubarb and pots of jam and bags of apples and sticks outside her back door" (Keegan 2007, p. 152). This last sentence summarizes Margaret's situation deftly. While the nouns mentioned point towards an unquestionably rural community, the polysyndeton points to an excessive, overbearing abundance. However, what is most remarkable is the way this overwhelming gratitude is syntactically ended by the adverbial expression "outside her back door" (Keegan 2007, p. 152). The fact that all these gifts are left not only outside her house, but, most significantly, outside her back door, implies that – despite such signs of gratitude – she remains marginal to the community, embodying how minorities are "still in search of identity and acceptance in their own countries" (Hartnett 2011, p. 17).

Oddly enough, her partial acceptance in mainstream discourse comes via her identification with a marginal minority. However, such acceptance is proven to be only a tolerated coexistence for as long as she is useful. Once Margaret frees herself from the overbearing presence of the priest, thus liberating her discourse as well, she stops performing her healing activities, "Margaret gave up on the parishioners' ailments and apparitions. She'd had enough of them" (Keegan 2007, p. 159). This, in turn, provokes the anger of the community, who "started doing her harm" (Keegan 2007, 159). This final section of the narrative reveals that behind the apparent aloof isolation imposed on herself and her child – Margaret "wouldn't let him go to school, said there was nothing people of that parish could teach them that she couldn't teach better" (Keegan 2007, p. 150) – lies the fear of the violent rejection of the community as "minorities are seen as a threat to the political and territorial integrity of the states they live in" (Shahabuddin 2021, p. 64). The narrative clarifies this point as the narrator unveils how once Margaret has decided to stop healing the community, she knows that "if she sent her child to school, he would suffer" (Keegan 2007, p. 150). This is reiterated just a few lines on, after the enumeration of the incipient acts of vandalism against her, "she herself could withstand anything but her fears for overed round the child" (Keegan 2007, p. 159).

The community's violent rejection prompts her to fulfil her promise that she would leave the house if harmed, keeping "her course, get in a boat and cross over to the Aran Islands, go as far west as she could without leaving Ireland" (Keegan

Questioning Identities in the Postmodern Nation 99

2007, p. 127). This assertion, stated at the very beginning of the narrative – and thus conditioning it – is, in fact, revealing of the inner paradox at the core of the story. Margaret is, indeed, representative of a more authentic Irish voice than the community at Lisdoonvarna. As seen, Keegan's (2007) protagonist is closer to the Irish folk tradition; her place of origin better aligns with traditional depictions of the Irish landscape, and – most remarkably – she is the only Irish speaker in the story as revealed by the fact that her mother sang to her in Irish (Keegan 2007, p. 132), that she recurrently listens to Raidió na Gaeltachta (Keegan 2007, p. 130) or that the fortune-teller advises her to "rear your next child in the Irish tongue" (Keegan 2007, p. 148). Symbolically as well, her journey west – to the Aran Islands – reinforces her perception as a more authentic Irish voice, as she settles in "the last 'wilds' of Ireland [...], the West as a repository of indigenous Irish culture" (James 2008, p. 16).

Her journey west to the Aran Islands is the ultimate validation of her dissenting, non-mainstream discourse. On the day she decides to abandon the community, "the day was calm [...]. The morning was fine, the sea glassy" (Keegan 2007, p. 159). Natural imagery, therefore, reinforces the positive perception of Margaret's discourse as does Stack's inner realization that "all he had to do to make his future happy was to climb into that boat" (Keegan 2007, p. 160). However, despite Keegan's (2007) narrative validation, the story's ending paints a stark portrait for dissenting voices as Stack decides not to jump on the boat and go back to the community, "Winter was coming. The turf would keep him busy and fit. There'd be long winter nights and storms to blot out and remind him of the past" (Keegan 2007, p. 160). As the narrative ends, Keegan (2007) recovers the stark natural imagery that characterizes the community to narrate Stack's return. The phrasal verb employed is also significant, as it implies that Margaret's presence and, by extension, her discourse, is to be obliterated. Taken as a whole, the story finishes with a validation of dissenting, minority voices. However, by the time the story reaches its end, this validation seems futile as the univocal, mainstream discourse is, once again, the only prevalent voice while a minority but more "authentic Gaelic ideal becomes increasingly alien in contemporary Irish culture" (Smith 2019, p. 205).

Conclusion

Keegan's 'The Night of the Quicken Trees' (2007) adapts the traditional Irish folktale to perform a vindication of suppressed minority discourses in post-independence Ireland. Keegan's (2007) deliberate usage of Irish folktale narrative structures to frame her own fiction supports the criticism of the univocality of the mainstream nationalist and Catholic-dominated discourse imperative since independence as epitomized in the figure of the priest and in the depiction of the local community. Through her representation of Margaret and the usage of natural images, Keegan (2007) upholds the legitimacy of dissenting voices, symbolized in the narrative validation of folk beliefs. These depictions are set in opposition to the portrayal of a flawed Catholic priest and the control exerted over the local community by the established Irish Catholic Church as an epitome of official national discourses. Mostly kept to the protagonist's inner monologue, these differing perceptions of reality are ultimately proven a more authentic Irish voice than the community-driven discourse sustained and conditioned by the official religion of the State.

Margaret's dual narrative identification facilitates this vindication and caters for criticism of the univocal, Catholic-sustained nationalist discourse. Thus, the character of Margaret can be read as an embodiment of the ostracism minorities have endured under such conditions, which is exemplified in in her marginal role in the community as a healer. This, combined with her identification with a more authentic voice than that of the Church-controlled community in Lisdoonvarna, and ultimately illustrated in her journey west to the Aran Islands, effectively performs a narrative vindication of non-mainstream Irish voices. Overall, Margaret's characterization can be interpreted as vindication of minority discourses and of the necessity to include such alternative voices into mainstream collective depictions of the national self. Thus, 'The Night of the Quicken Trees' (2007) exposes the marginalization of subaltern minorities in a postcolonial, Catholic independent Irish State. In brief, Keegan's (2007) fiction questions the univocal nationalist discourse present in post-independence Ireland and its strong embodiment by the local, rural, and Catholic Church-dominated community to the detriment of more authentic – albeit diverging – Irish voices.

Bibliography

Aosdána: Claire Keegan: 2022, available at: http://aosdana.artscouncil.ie/members/keegan [23.12.2022].

Baraniuk, Carol / Hagan, Linda: 'Ireland's Hidden Diaspora? Finding A Place for the Ulster-Scots in Ireland's National Tale', in: Éigeartaigh, Aoileann N. / Howard, Kevin / Getty, David (eds.): *Rethinking Diasporas: Hidden Narratives and Imagined Borders*. Newcastle 2007, p. 70–77.

Boehmer, Elleke: *Colonial and Postcolonial Literature*. Oxford 2005.

Bondarenko, Grigory: *Studies in Irish Mythology*. Berlin 2014.

Carrassi, Vito: *The Irish Fairy Tale: A Narrative Tradition from The Middle Ages to Yeats and Stephens*. Maryland 2012.

Connolly, Linda: 'The Limits of "Irish Studies": Historicism, Culturalism, Paternalism', in: Flannery, Eóin / Angus Mitchell (eds.): *Enemies of Empire: New Perspectives on Literature, Historiography and Imperialism.* Dublin 2007, p. 189–210.

Flannery, Eóin: *Ireland and Postcolonial Studies: Theory, Discourse, Utopia.* Hampshire 2001.

Foster, John W.: *Fictions of the Irish Literary Revival.* Dublin 1987.

Graham, Colin: 'Subalternity and Gender: Problems of Post-Colonial Irishness', in: *The* THE JOURNAL OF GENDER STUDIES: SPECIAL ISSUE: GENDER AND POST-COLONIALISM 1996/5.3, p. 363–73.

Gunning, Dave: *Postcolonial Literature.* Edinburgh 2013.

Hartnett, J.: *Historical Representation and The Postcolonial Imaginary: Constructing Travellers and Aborigines.* Newcastle upon Tyne 2011.

Ingman, Heather: 'The Short Story', in: Heather Ingman / Ó Gallchoir, Clíona (eds.): *A History of Modern Irish Women's Literature.* Cambridge 2018, p. 277–293. DOI: 10.1017/9781316442999.016.

Innes, C. L.: The *Cambridge Introduction to Postcolonial Literatures in English.* Cambridge 2007.

Jackson, Alvin: *Ireland 1798–1998 War, Peace and Beyond.* Oxford 2010.

James, Kevin J.: '"Wilds of Ireland": Tourism and Western Terrain in the Late-Nineteenth and Early-Twentieth Centuries', in: Allen, Richard C. / Regan, Stephen (eds.): *Irelands of the Mind: Memory and Identity in Modern Irish Culture.* Newcastle 2008, p. 12–31.

Kavanagh, Anne Marie / Dupont, Maeve: 'Making the Invisible Visible. Managing Tensions around Including Traveller Culture and History in the Curriculum at Primary and Post-Primary Levels', in: IRISH EDUCATIONAL STUDIES 2021/40 (3), p. 553–569.

Keegan, Claire: 'The Night of the Quicken Trees', in: Keegan, Claire: *Walk the Blue Fields.* London 2007.

Kirby, Peadar / McBride, Sean: 'Minorities in Ireland: An Interview with Sean McBride', in: THE GRANE BAG 1981/5 (1) Minorities in Ireland, p. 61–66.

Morales-Ladrón, Marisol: 'Gender Relations and Female Agency in Claire Keegan's Antarctica', in: STUDIA ANGLICA POSNANIENSIA 2021/56, p. 275–292. DOI: 10.2478/stap-2021-0015.

Röder, Antje: 'Old and New Religious Minorities: Examining the Changing Religious Profile of the Republic of Ireland', in: IRISH JOURNAL OF SOCIOLOGY 2017/25 (3), p. 324–333.

Ruane, Joseph / Butler, David: 'Southern Irish Protestants: An Example of De-Ethnicisation?', in: *Nations and Nationalism* 2007/13 (4), p. 619–635.

Shahabuddin, Mohammad: *Minorities and the Making of Postcolonial States in International Law.* Cambridge 2021.

Smith, Eoghan: 'Autonomy, Naturalism, and Folklore in Claire Keegan's *Walk the Blue Fields*', in: THE CANADIAN JOURNAL OF IRISH STUDIES 2019/42, p. 192–208.

Sneddon, Andrew: 'Gender, Folklore and Magical Healing in Ireland, 1852–1922', in: Atwal, Jyoti / Breathnach, Ciara / Buckley, Sarah-Anne (eds.): *Gender and History: Ireland, 1852–192.* London 2022, p. 104–116.

Sovacool, Benjamin K. / Furszyfer Del Rio, Dylan D.: '"We're not Dead Yet!": Extreme Energy and Transport Poverty, Perpetual Peripheralization, and Spatial Justice among

Gypsies and Travellers in Northern Ireland', in: RENEWABLE AND SUSTAINABLE ENERGY REVIEWS 2022/160, p. 1–18.

Walder, Dennis: *Postcolonial Nostalgias: Writing, Representation, and Memory*. London 2010.

Frank Ferguson

Writing Around the State: Memory Cultures in Contemporary Northern Irish Writing

It is early spring in Bellaghy, a small village in what to some is Northern Ireland and what to others is the North of Ireland. The hawthorn hedge boundaries of the fields that border the village are bursting through with vivid lime-green twists of new leaves. In the Seamus Heaney HomePlace café in the thin but expectant sunlight, I meet with my team of creative writing workshop facilitators. Here in the once heavily fortified Royal Ulster Constabulary barracks we sit in a transformed space now dedicated to the work and life of Seamus Heaney and serving, it must be said, very good coffee. It is a bright and inviting building that welcomes the public as a museum, exhibition space and performance centre; a building now altered utterly from its former role. As we prepare for the day ahead of talks and workshops for secondary school pupils who are studying Seamus Heaney and Robert Frost as part of their A Levels, I am struck by the energy and talent of my team. All of whom are under thirty years of age and represent those who have grown up under the Belfast/Good Friday Agreement. Their lives to date have not been dictated by the restrictions and limitations of the Troubles as mine had been at their age. It is fair to describe it as a difficult peace that they have grown up in, but it has been one that has offered multiple possibilities that seemed beyond the reach of my generation. This place, despite everything else that is currently going on in Northern Ireland, suggests that there is hope and that literature and education can play important affirmative roles in creating lasting peaceful change and reconciliation.

I am also struck by the diversity of the group drawn from east and west Belfast and in one case by way of Lithuania. The talk is open, fluid and engaged that demonstrates the connections that have been made in Belfast and elsewhere in Northern Ireland in the last twenty-five years – a far cry from the halting 1970s discourse between the communities depicted in Heaney's 'The Other Side' in which only discussions of the weather or grass seed might be broached (Heaney 1972, p. 36).

To live in Northern Ireland is to follow the sense of life in Narnia at the beginning of Clive S. Lewis's *The Lion, the Witch and the Wardrobe* (2023, p. 8).

A world exists in wintry stasis in which Christmas never appears. The devolved assembly is in hibernation. Long term discussions rumble on about the settlement of Brexit and on the agreement which is required for Northern Ireland's separate status. A new framework has recently been proposed between Rishi Sunak, the British Prime Minister and the European Union, but we await the Democratic Unionist Party's response to this. Post Covid malaise lingers within the state and the global financial predicament precipitated by the crisis in Ukraine hits hard in a province already made vulnerable by Covid and long-term economic instability. The potential imagined by the Good Friday/Belfast Agreement of a quarter of a century ago appears fragile (Tannam 2020). And yet for all the darkness and indeterminacy in the social and political spheres. Positive voices continue to make themselves heard in literature and the arts. In particular, in the field of memory cultures there exists a profound range of writing on this subject that acts as powerful advocates for negotiating, comprehending and celebrating identities (Dawson 2007). The borders that seem so difficult to maintain or move beyond become more positive within writing. No longer loci of confinement they operate as places of access for individuals and communities whose energetic mobility point not to entrenched histories, but opportunities, hybridity and hope.

In this chapter I will explore how a range of writers have sought to move beyond the political, cultural, and linguistic confines of the state of Northern Ireland in their work either through adopting a literature of mobility, distance or evasion. At the time of writing there is much interest in the situation of religious/cultural orientation of the citizens of Northern Ireland. For the first time in the history of the state of Northern Ireland, Protestants are in the minority, based on the most recent UK Census figures (Northern Ireland Statistics and Research Agency 2022). This has occasioned much discussion and heightened calls for a plebiscite to determine if unification of Ireland is now the majority view (McClements 2022). Such calls may be premature given the voting patterns for Unionists, Nationalist/Republicans and non-aligned appear to remain narrowly ahead (Lowry 2022). How then is one to try and fathom the situation and gain an insight into how writers deal with this world that seems to be torn between demographic and cultural change and permanent statis? Much examination has been carried out on the literary imagination of Irish Protestants and more recently this has been further developed by the discussion on Ulster-Scot language, literature, culture and identity (Dawe / Longley 1985; Sloan 2000; Hutchinson 2018; McKay 2005; Mitchell 2022). How then are some of these writers examining the current situation?

I will take as my starting point the work of the poet, critic and memoirist Gerald Dawe. I will examine how he has embraced his northern Protestant heritage while simultaneously finding accommodation with his southern and western Irish cultural inheritances. His family history and individual Irish peregrination acts as a means for him to engage with memory cultures in ways which both explore the inheritance of trauma and conflict but embrace memoir and events that are not determined by overarching metanarratives. The ability of some writers to operate across and beyond the old binaries signifies the growth of the recent adoption of 'Northern Irish' as a marker of identity in the province, which seeks to eschew, blur and counteract the binary of British or Irish identities (Garry / McNicholl 2015).

In addition, the period since the Good Friday Agreement has witnessed the development of a small, but vocal group of Ulster-Scottish writers who see their work inflected by the linguistic, social, literary and cultural imprint of Scotland. While some have claimed these writers may embody a new Unionist form of nationalism my survey of their work suggests a more complicated and more variegated range of voices emerging which confound and subverts many of the assumptions made about their political and cultural allegiances. Dawe has traced the impact of Scotland on his life and how this has played out in the cultural memory that shaped Van Morrison (Dawe 2008, p. 36). However, his reflection on the significance of Scotland has not ventured into linguistic experiment with Ulster-Scots in his poetry.

In a distinguished literary career that began in the 1970s, Dawe shows no indication of slowing down. Currently engaged in a touring exhibition of his poetry and developing a documentary on his life and writing with DoubleBand Films and the BBC his energies are unflagging. Indeed, it is energy and movement that might define his writing. His adult life has been spent in a series of moves anticlockwise across Ireland from his home in North Belfast, he moved to the New University of Ulster at Coleraine for his undergraduate degree, from there his postgraduate studies took him to Galway from which he began his university teaching career, before moving to Trinity College Dublin.

Visiting professorships in the United States and England added to his sense of continually expanding horizons. An author of sinewy, taut poetry built around carefully delineated imagery, his language has both candour and control. This sense of control has enabled him to explore his personal background and that of his community.

As much as his writing has focused on his present surroundings, it is his ability reexamine his personal and regional identity that provides the focus for this chapter. While now he may be at a point in his career where he is aware of the range of work that he has developed throughout his adult life, it is important to register this process of reappraisal and reimagination was also prevalent in his working practice:

> I wrote *The Lundys Letter* from the west; there are quite a few poems about the west In *Sunday School* and *Heart of Hearts*. Between *Sheltering Places* in 1978 and *The Lundys Letter* in 1985 I started to reimagine the Belfast Protestant background I had grown up in and wonder about my own family's diverse provincial and 'refugee' roots. As I was trying to understand my life in Galway, I was – ironically and simultaneously – discovering my own background in Belfast and what these terms mean – 'background', 'Belfast', 'my own' (Ferguson 2023, p. 54).

Indeed, it is important to recognise that the process of his comprehension of northerness came from and was precipitated by movement away from the places he was writing about. This awareness pushed on by a different, or a range of different situations insists that Dawe's memory culture is a process that can provide ways of understanding and interpretation of Northern Ireland and in particular the exploration of northern Irish Protestant identity and history. 'Memory cultures' is an operative term in a number of ways. It demonstrates memory's potential to generate multiple impacts that can be affirmative and positive. It also points to memory as being active and having powerful agency to both reaffirm and initiate culture in the present. Memory speaks culture into being which is a very important strength in states and or regions in a post conflict situation which are seeking to find mutual respect and recognition between various groups and factions. To culture, is to inculcate and perform the unlocking of a sense of aesthetic and/or personal, group, community or national selfhood. In the wider sense there is a belief, however unfounded that the world of Northern Protestantism has not been articulated to the same extent that other varieties have been. As Connal Parr has suggested:

> […] it is important to emphasize that writing has come from within the Ulster Protestant community itself. By failing to address this, academics and commentators continue to inadvertently maintain the fallacy that the Protestant working class in Northern Ireland has no culture but the Orange Order and Rangers F. C. a deficiency which has filtered through to historical writing and contemporary journalism, leading to an inaccurate, skewed vision of its history and potential (Parr 2018, p. 1).

Given the longstanding attempts to chart this writing and community by many commentators from the 19th century onwards, epitomised by the work of John Hewitt as poet, critic and book collector, it is disappointing to see that such statements need to be made by contemporary authors (McCormack 2015). It is hoped that current trends in addressing the role of memory and forgetting in Irish culture can assist in not merely the recovery of these narratives but the acceptance that such narratives have existed for a considerable time. Guy Beiner's championing of the concept of mythhistory is significant in this process of reconsideration:

> It is enlightening to rethink our relationship with the past in terms of mythistory and to question a steadfast conviction, which has been upheld dogmatically by many historians, that History (seen as a truthful representation of facts) must be irreconcilably divorced from Myth (considered a fictional fabrication). The iconoclast urge for demythologizing is an expression of a modern 'hermeneutics of suspicion', which harks back to the classical differentiation between symbolic mythos and critical logos, through which generations of scholars have devalued traditions, regardless of the vital role they continue to play in society and culture (Beiner 2018, p. 5).

The turn towards appreciating the *mythhistory* of the Protestant community may yet open further possibilities of widening comprehension of and facilitate reconciliation within Northern Ireland and beyond. However, to comprehend and appreciate is not necessarily to embrace or adhere to. Memory and remembering may permit recollection and a return to points in the past, but they may not necessarily have to guide the actions of person recalling.

Dawe's work investigates and tests the focal points of his Protestant past, though often with confounding results. He has spoken of fascination for the 'chaste' forms of language of his Protestant background and this is evidenced in an oeuvre that cherishes precision and economy of expression. The concept that his writing is chaste, draws upon imperatives of purity and avoidance of additional vanities or elaboration:

> I went briefly as a boy to the Fortwilliam Presbyterian Church on the Antrim Road. Early on then I was struck by the purity of language in the hymns, the iconography of the Empire in the flags; Old Testament stories and New Testament parables. There was also a sense of individual, even civic, responsibilities or morality that you could not just dump outside and leave at the church door [...] I'm not particularly interested, though, in either hitting on the church or exploring its ministry or environment; I've not been scarred by this formation within cultural Protestantism to either want to do that or to fake a Catholic 'Irish' sense of what I'm doing as a writer (Ferguson 2023, location 712).

Dawe's Protestantism has affected him at the point of language, iconography and narrative. It is interesting to note the impact of personal and group morality and ethics, but the areas which cause concern and others are lacking. It is informative to note that the sense of harm occasioned by the "Church" is something that is placed within Catholic Ireland. While too major an area to explore within this essay one wonders about the impact of organised Protestant religion upon the individual and community, is there one wonders a Protestant equivalent of Catholic Guilt and this underexplored phenomenon in Irish life north, south and in its diaspora. Dawe's examination of Protestantism takes him to examine the impact that it had upon Irish writing:

> There is the fascinating encounter between the renegade Joyce and Beckett in Paris; one tries to pull the entire world into the book and the other to flush it all away. Yet you still hear the whispered echo of the Church of Ireland hymnal or vespers – 'Now the day is

over, night is drawing nigh' – in Beckett's *Krapp's Last Tape*. In Beckett that takes on a shocking poetic charge; sung in church, it can sound just like another cliché. I think that chasteness, that austerity of language, is one inheritance of Protestantism for which I am thankful (Ferguson 2023, location 702).

Dawe's interpretation of 'Protestantism' has intriguing implications for revising the canon of Irish as well as British literature, and recalls the impact of the denomination upon Beckett as much as Belfast. Austerity and chastity provide a direct, refined language that has implications for his personal as well as national literary cultures.

The concept of directness has enabled him to reach back into the mindset of his northern Unionist inheritance to articulate aspects of its history that have often failed to register elsewhere in Irish poetry. In work that was inspired by the historian Anthony Terence Stuart the poem 'A Question of Covenants' articulates the background of the Home Rule Crisis in Ireland from the point of view of Unionists (Stewart 1969). However, demonstrating awareness of this does not suggest that he is an apologist for sectional interests or sectarianism. Poems such as 'The Clock on a Wall of Farringdon Gardens, August 1971' have provided strong condemnatory retorts to violence (Dawe 2018). Terence Brown noted at the time Dawe's "engaging sense of astonishment that the poet has managed somehow partially to escape all that an in unpatronizing pity for those whose life is bounded by such limited and limiting horizons" (Brown 1986, p. 78ff). However the poem, viewed from a greater distance seeks to find its way into the psyche of the unionist populace and comprehend their sense of sense of imperilment and encirclement as much as their patriotic ardour. They are reimagined by Stuart and Dawe as a people at the precipice of insurgency, hope and doubt. They are delineated not with any grand commemorative tubthumping purpose but in a tense tableau that envisages the weathered trope of a boat leaving Belfast Lough.

> The Patriotic turns to face
> an invisible sea. From Castle Place
> thousands swarm through side streets
> and along the unprotected quays
> just to glimpse Carson, gaunt as usual,
> who watches the surge of people
> call, *Don't leave us. You mustn't leave us*,
> and in the searchlight's beam,
> his figure arched across the upper deck,
> he shouts he will come back and, if necessary, fight this time. (Dawe 2018)

The observation of the quotidian has been an important part of Dawe's ability to turn everyday matter into poetry. In 'The Clock on a Wall of Farringdon Gardens, August 1971' he captures the aftermath of riot and community displacement by a focus on the remnants of a clock left behind:

> I am the clock on a wall
> of Farringdon Gardens.
> I stopped dead at 7.30. They
>
> tried to take me away
> from the burning. I remember
> the whooshing smoke.
>
> But in the rush
> I was left here
> as if nothing had happened.
>
> Part of my task is
> not to get panicked.
> I'm regular and reliable
>
> and wake each morning
> for work—
> a bulwark of my society […]. (Dawe 2018, location 31)

This takes the mantel clock, once such a familiar timepiece in an Ulster home and stops it dead—an indicator of the calamity facing many in Northern Ireland at that time who had been displaced, threatened or burned out of their communities.

However, Belfast in the succeeding decades, while never idealised or avoided as a topic of literary interest, ultimately is not depicted as a site of limitation and one Dawe seeks a Joycean escape from or pact with. He shares with other writers of the 1970s and 1980s a reticence to launch bluntly into rhetoric about conflict and identity (Brearton 2003, p. 100). The Belfast that engendered so much sense of bleakness and threat to writers such as Derek Mahon and Brian Moore, seemed to have thawed a little and left less of a distaste in Dawe's writing. His recent memoirs speak of a sense of optimism and potential radiating out through his secondary school years in stark contrast to the difficult period of the conflict:

> The brief spell of optimism – barely thirty years after the founding of the two states in Ireland and a mere decade or so after the end of World War II – lasted about ten years, from the late 1950s to 1968/69. It was the key formative period in my own upbringing, a generation in which young men and women witnessed the world recovery from global war in local terms (Dawe 2020, p. 80).

While there was a growing awareness of the situation in Northern Ireland worsening and conflict deepening, his teenage years focused on a Sixties world of music and dancing and a deepening appreciation of writers and writing. Life in Belfast, a port city with a burgeoning Rhythm and Blues Scene was a place of excitement and possibility:

So the Northern Irish experience can illustrate what happens when the roots of historical conflict, its social and political outcrop, is not resolved in and by democratic government. What the imagination does in part is to try to embody the complexity of what has happened and provide some imaginative form of inclusive redress (Dawe 2020, p. 81).

Belfast like Heaney's Bogland acts as a multi-layered and multivalent theme in Dawe's writing. However, if Heaney's Bogland is imbued with the sense of needing to dig downwards to excavate painful memory, Dawe's Belfast is both a mirror and lens to look outwards and beyond.

> Johnny in Carroll's Bar shouts
> 'Two pies, one direct' as snow
> falls like dust over Smithfield.
> Up in the corner on the TV screen
> moon man, lunatic, space cadet
> beams all the way in black
> and white to our moon-viewing. (Dawe 2018)

In his poem 'The Moon viewing room' we get a strong insight into how Dawe's memory cultures Belfast and provides connection to different places. In a poem that echoes Derek Mahon's 'The Snow Party' we get a very different type of party, set in a Belfast bar at the time of the Moon Landings (Mahon 1999, p. 63). Its nod to Belfast vernacularity pokes fun at the zen-like sensibility of a Basho inspired gathering. In the pub with its pies and bar talk a recognisable 1960s Belfast takes shape amidst the falling snow. The reminiscence of small television set connects to another very different memory of the moon viewing room in Shisen-dō in Kyoto. If Mahon's poem draws start contrast to the differences between early modern European sensibilities and the cultured gathering of Japan, Dawe's poem is another snow viewing party that seeks to connect an alternative timeline between Northern Ireland on the cusp of civil breakdown and a place dedicated to the zen like calm of a house dedicated to writers and to the observation of the moon.

> Now I have it at my window
> at whatever time it may be
> all at once I see the snow
> that will not last, the voice of a man
> in his prime, and the jabber of us all,
> in the crowded moon-viewing room. (Dawe 2018, location 1067)

If Mahon's Snow party, like Joyce's 'The Dead' snowy ending is one forever trapped within a past. Dawe's is one where rescue is possible and the peace of a Kyoto scene though intruded upon by hints of Belfast gawping, carping and "jabber" can be maintained through memorialisation, as can the equally distant scene from Carroll's bar.

Such hints at the Ulster vernacular in Dawe's work point to another development of memory culture in the North of Ireland. Dawe's animus is driven by the memory of place and the places and faces that appear from the past in new places. His writing offers testimony to the vernacular of place and moment with occasional deployment of words that affirm his personal background. In a wider sense the decades after the Good Friday Agreement have also seen the broader remembering of the Ulster-Scots tradition, not as some have seen as an ideological weapon or resurgence of an old form of Unionist political identity, but as an important literary language that has often existed beneath the surface of many writers from the North (Ferguson 2008). At present there is a slow steady expansion of writers who work solely or partly within the Ulster-Scots language or tradition with workshops, competitions and very significantly presses, journals and institutions willing to publish work.

This has been noted by Walker and Greer:

> The Ulster-Scots component of the culture, heritage and language of the north of Ireland has long been misunderstood or frankly treated with hostile ridicule, often in class-ridden terms from within unionist communities, but it reflects many of the ties that culturally bind the two places together. Significantly there is something of an Ulster-Scots literary revival under way, with writers such as Steve Dornan, Angeline King, Angela Graham, Robert Campbell, Al Millar and Anne McMaster writing fiction and poetry utilising, or playing with, variations of Ulster-Scots (Walker / Greer 2023, p. 211).

While not disputing the appearance of a new group of writers, the concept of an Ulster-Scots revival has been, it might be said, an ongoing process before the Good Friday/Belfast Agreement and in some cases the concept of a revival itself may be disputed, with the work of some writers such as Thomas Given and Larne writer continuing well into the 20th century (Montgomery 2003). The language of eternal revival has tended to obscure the work of other writers who has continued to work in this area for decades. It also draws attention to the question of how much a writer may be aware of the linguistic or literary tradition they are operating within. Who or indeed what are we reviving? Intriguing questions are raised. The passing of one of the movement's great founding creative writers and lexicographers, James Fenton, does not seem to have disrupted the new range of writers coming through, or have been commemorated to any great extent ('James Fenton Obituary' Madden 2021). As new writers emerge alongside new platforms to present their work what kind of Ulster-Scots literature is being created. And furthermore, what memory cultures do they invoke, utilise and expand upon. How do these writers fit into the world of established writers like Dawe?

If we focus upon the work of the group mentioned by Walker and Greer we notice a broad range of new writers with distinct authorial voices who deploy Ulster-Scots into their work in a variety of ways. They approach the field of the Ulster-Scots tongue in a manner that complicates the once held notion that Northern writers created better work when they engaged in light renderings of Scots dialect (McIllvanney 2005, p. 216ff). This vision of "light" dialect "good" and "heavy" dialect bad has made for very reductive approaches to creative writing. It has also been articulated about Ulster-Scots writers and not from within Ulster-Scots writing. In a way that mirrors how the concept of Protestantism has been projected onto writers from a Protestant background, the actual experience may be markedly different. For Dornan and Millar, their Ulster Scots operates in much more nuanced and complex literary/linguistic spectrum both revel in uncompromisingly affirmative usage in their creative work. They are closest perhaps to James Fenton's approach in their determination to reach back into the linguistic and literary traditions that Ulster-Scots provides (Fenton 2000). Both have been winners/runners up at the Linen Hall Library's Creative Writing Competition (Savage 2022). This recent development in creative writing, held at Belfast's oldest subscription library and one with strong connections to Belfast's Enlightenment and radical past, is a powerful expression of how Ulster-Scots has been raised to public awareness and prestige.

> Oan an Egyptian Mummy in a Bilfawst Museum
> Here's a quare unco lang hame,
> for a heich-boarn dame o Thebes:
> hauf-unhapped, in a tomb o gless,
> for Bilfawst folk tae gove at.
> Yet here ye bide: baith blaw-in
> an residenter; a boady amang us,
> an a bein ayont oor unnerstaunin. (Dornan 2022, p. 18)

Dornan's knowledge and awareness of Ulster-Scots is profound as is his choice of subject that had been written on by previous Belfast poets such as Francis Davis, and John Hewitt (Smyth 2020, p. 40). Dornan could be said to be an inheritor both of Fenton and the Rhyming Weaver tradition in his opening section, playing as he does on faux country simplicity beholding the goings on of townspeople. The emphasis on "quare unco lang hame" stresses the double strangeness (queer, uncommon/ unusual) nature of the coffin (lang hame). It also requires the reader to examine the glass case in which this sarcophagus is placed and to view as both coffin and exhibit. We are faced with another type of *boady* (person/body) preserved in a manner similar to the Tollund Man (Heaney 1972, p. 48).

> Ye cudnae hae credited an efterlife
> in Bilfawst:yer ceevilisation hadnae mapped

oor coulrife, dour, ootby airt.
Yet here ye bide, ye aye-bidin boady,
as generations o folk like us scud by
like wraiths through yer quait dwams.[1]

In an inversion of Heaney's 'The Tollund Man' the mummy figure, Takabuti appears in place as an ever-abiding fixture of Belfast life (a cold, dour, inaccessible place) noted by a fixed non sentient inhabitant from a civilisation that hadn't bothered to map Hibernia (or Ultonia-Scotia). This turns the tables on the vision of the bog person as a victim that calls attention to Irish victims and the disappeared. It is the victim that survives as generations of locals flit by like ghosts in her quiet dreams/*dwams*. Dornan's choice of *dwams* is interesting, holding as it does a sense of stupor and reverie, as well as slumbers. A recasting of the Sleeping Beauty myth, and more significantly the traditional Irish *Aishling* form in which Ireland is represented by a woman, Dornan Aishling figure is herself a silent alien figure locked literally beneath the glass.

Dornan makes great use of Ulster-Scots to question literary and linguistic traditions and boundaries. And yet for all his experimentation and iconoclasm, his laconic, sharply observed urban-based Belfast poem contains many similarities to Dawe's oeuvre. For all his forays into jousting with Irish literary archetypes, the Ulster side of his work indicates many connections with northern Irish poetic preoccupations. At home in postmodern play as much as working within the tradition of the tongue, he is also at home in Belfast memory cultures.

This is also evident in the work of Alan Millar. Like Dornan, Millar has been working as an Ulster-Scots writer and researcher for a number of years. This excavation of the tradition is demonstrated in his short story 'Sam an Jeck speel Parnassus tae see Rabbie Burns' (Millar, 2021, p. 17). The narrative is an adaptation of the journey the county Antrim poet, Samuel Thomson made to Robert Burns in 1793. The work plunges the reader into the language and locales of north east Ireland and south west Scotland in the eighteenth century. There is no compromise for the uninitiated Scots reader. The prose is uncompromising and deft. "[…] aule fly sun keeks oot ahint blak cloud" single syllabled, terse and tart it both captures the zesty kick of a windswept Scottish port, and the thoughtworld of Thomson running between place and linguistic registers as he gets his thoughts in order on his pilgrimage to see Burns. His mind is also caught up on the politics of the revolutionary 1790s, and revolutionary in the sense that he is, if not a proponent of United Irish politics then a sympathetic fellow traveller. He is also a man on an errand for Burns, along with his own collection of poems echoing burns 'Poems on Different Subjects.' If Dornan is taking a ludic sally

---

1 Dictionaries of the Scots Language/Dictionars o the Scots Leid 2023, 'Dwam', available at: https://dsl.ac.uk/entry/snd/dwam.

around Irish traditional forms and poetic lineages, Millar is hitting head-on one of the major accusations that Ulster-Scots poets have faced since the appearance of Burns in the literary marketplace – that they are mere impersonators of Burns. Millar's Thomson speaks back in a number of ways to deconstruct such claims. The retracing of steps, which hints at one of Sam Hanna Bell's depiction of the journey taken by Scots adventurers towards Ireland in his novel *Across the Narrow Sea*, portrays someone at home and simultaneously far removed from Scotland (Bell 1987):

> PORTPATRICK, jist aff tha boat, aule fly sun keeks oot ahint blak cloud. Sam runs finngers owre blue burd covers o his 'Poems on Different Subjects' just published; girn grunts partly in tha Scottish dialect; ainst content there's nae watter damage, rehaps in sark tartle an pits bak wi his victuals. Stannin, keeks shifty at tha rid coats ootbye; slings poke owre shauldler; Mr Muir wheeched frae this quay naw six months afore. Luke throu here tae, up an flit last year, then last week tha letter:
> "*I long indeed very much for your presence, but it would be very unpleasant travel to come and see me without another errand.*"
> Feelins scud ramstam thou kist; visitin Mr Burns on tha lang finnger nae mair. Partial fortune delivered twa guid errands, then a third added. Love, posey an politics mixt. Knuckle doon fand impatience, there's a lang dreich cauldrife Camino twixt Carngranny an them that bears tha gree; dirty politics on whur taels forbye.

Thomson is both poet and nobody, travelling through a Scotland that is sending soldiers over to Ireland to police the radicalised Presbyterians, Thomson's denomination. The language of the prose emphasises his strangeness and the heavy use of spiky, fricative consonants symbolises the difficult times in which he exists in. It is a world in which Dawe's 'jabber' has run riot. More inversions of what is expected occur in the use of 'standard' English, indeed almost neoclassical Augustan English in the dialogue, and Ulster-Scots in the main body of the writing. This reversal of the standard approach for the Scots kailyard novel in which the speech of the characters was marked out by its Scotch idiom and description and narrative was carried out in English (Nash 2007, p. 108). This enables a different type of focus to settle on Thomson's speech and thought patterns as his walking through Scotland and a land described in Scots becomes a means for him to deliver his collection of poems to Burns and also to conjure poetry as he goes. He comes across not as some Burnsian flunkey, aping a master's language, but as a layered, complicated and very human subject in his own right.

If Dornan and Millar demonstrate the continuation of work in a vein similar to James Fenton, Philip Robinson and others from the Ulster-Scots Language Society (Fenton 1995; 2000; 2009; Robinson 1997; 2009). Writing by Angela Graham signifies new directions in the tradition. A relative latecomer to work in Ulster-Scots, her 'A Heerd Tha Sodjer On Tha Radio' takes the deployment of Ulster-

Scots from the confines of the province of Northern Ireland to explore the recent removal of American troops from Afghanistan:

> His wurds [...] an A wus thair!
> Kabul, at a 'gate' in tha airdrome waa
> — a gap nae braider nor ma shoodèrs –
> fornenst a thrang o despert fowk,
> me atween thaim an 'oot'.
>
> A wumman, wi hir babbie
> ticht tae hir breesht,
> püt hir left han tae ma face,
> in that oul, oul leid that ses, aa tha worl roon,
> *Sodjer, be kine; tak peety on me* [...]. (Graham 2021, p. 15)

She has been vocal in gaining further recognition for Ulster-Scots within the literary languages of the British Isles. Never one to shy away from asking questions that have often not been asked in public about Ulster-Scots:

> Certainly, no one gains from setting one form of expression against another; or from over-zealous gate-keeping about standards (though these must exist or expression gets catastrophically unmoored from its roots); or – most insidious of all – who is to be allowed to write in Ulster Scots.
> That last was the pressure that threatened most powerfully to hold me back. But I have finished the first draft [of a novel] and it has been a wonderful experience to live with the characters, and particularly the Ulster Scots speakers, seeing the world through those eyes, speaking with that tongue.
> But perhaps the time has arrived when a new set of questions can be asked: Why not in Ulster Scots? Why not me? Why not now? (Graham 2021)

Her ambition to employ Ulster-Scots as a literary language transcends many of the popular suppositions held about those who work in this medium – she is neither from a Protestant, or a rural background. She forms part of a diverse writing community which offers new ways for the memory of minority language and culture to find fresh expression within Northern Ireland and beyond. For this nascent group of writers identity is a complex and broad spectrum that is transnational, pluri-confessional and post-confessional also. As their memory cultures step outside the backyard of what was once narrowly conceived as Ulster-Scots culture, they are moving towards confident and innovative ways to express themselves. However, whether the conditions exist for them to connect with the literary marketplace in the same manner as Dawe remains to be seen.

What is apparent it that there is an appetite to delve into the collective memory of language in Northern Ireland and fully explore the possibility of what this memory can facilitate. Graham's recent collection of short stories *A City Burning* in which stories about Northern Ireland, Wales and Italy provide a variegated, incisive examination of traumatic encounters and comic moments is close to Dawe's memorialisation of Belfast in his recent trilogy of autobiographies (Graham 2020). These writers testify that the recent and distant past can be both remembered and rebuilt in ways that step outside old disabling entrenchments. Memory's role in culture can both affirm but also redraw and reinvigorate the culture. Stephen Dedalus' description of history as a nightmare may need revision: history and a literary and literate mythhistory may yet prove a dwam that we could wake up from productively and peacefully.

Bibliography

Beiner, Guy: *Forgetful Remembrance*. Oxford 2015. Kindle Edition.
Brearton, Frank: 'Poetry of the 1960s: The Northern Ireland Renaissance', in: Campbell, Matthew (ed.): *The Cambridge Companion to Contemporary Irish Poetry*. Cambridge 2003, p. 94–112.
Brown, Terence: 'Review', in: THE POETRY IRELAND REVIEW 1985–86/15, p. 78–81.
Dawe, Gerald / Longley, Edna (eds.): *Across a Roaring Hill: The Protestant Imagination in Modern Ireland: Essays in Honour of John Hewitt*. Belfast 1985.
Dawe, Gerald: *My Mother City*. Belfast 2008.
Dawe, Gerald: *Selected Poems*. Oldcastle 2018. Kindle Edition.
Dawe, Gerald: *Looking Through You: Northern Chronicles* Dublin 2013. Kindle Edition.
Dawson, Graham. *Making peace with the past?: memory, trauma and the Irish troubles*. Manchester 2007.
Dictionaries of the Scots Language/Dictionars o the Scots Leid: 'Dwam'. 2023, available at: https://dsl.ac.uk/entry/snd/dwam [April 1, 2023].
Dornan, Steven: *Ulster Scots Writing Competition*. Belfast 2022, p. 18.
Fenton, James: *The Hamely Tongue: A personal record of Ulster-Scots in County Antrim*. Newtownards 1995.
Fenton, James: *Thonner an Thon: An Ulster-Scots Collection*. Newtownards 2000.
Fenton, James: *On Slaimish*. Newtownards 2009.
Ferguson, Frank: *Ulster-Scots Writing An Anthology*. Dublin 2008.
Ferguson, Frank (ed.): *Balancing Acts: Conversations with Gerald Dawe on a Life in Poetry*. Dublin 2023. Kindle Edition.
Garry, John / McNicholl, Garry: *Understanding the 'Northern Irish' Identity*. 2015, available at: http://www.niassembly.gov.uk/globalassets/documents/raise/knowledge_exchange/briefing_papers/series4/northern_ireland_identity_garry_mcnicholl_policy_document.pdf [April 1, 2023].
Graham, Angela: *A City Burning*. Bridgend 2020.
Graham, Angela: 'New Impetus in Ulster Scots Writing'. 2021, available at: https://angelagraham.org/2021/03/new-impetus-in-ulster-scots-writing/ [April 1, 2023].
Hanna Bell, Sam: *Across the Narrow Sea*. Belfast 1987.
Heaney, Seamus: 'The Other Side', in: Heaney, Seamus: *Wintering Out*. London 1972, p. 36.

Heaney, Seamus: 'The Tollund Man', in: Heaney, Seamus: *Wintering Out.* London 1972, p. 48.

Hutchinson, Wesley: *Tracing the Ulster-Scots Imagination.* Belfast 2018.

Lewis, Clive S.: *The Lion, the Witch and the Wardrobe* (The Chronicles of Narnia, Book 2) London 2023. Kindle Edition.

Lowry, Ben: 'Election 2022: The Unionist Overall Vote Stays Ahead of the Nationalist Total, Albeit Narrowly', in: NEWS LETTER 2022, available at: https://www.newsletter.co.uk/news/politics/election-2022-the-unionist-overall-vote-stays-ahead-of-the-nationalist-total-albeit-narrowly-3684559 [April 1, 2023].

McClements, Freya: 'Fresh Calls for Border Poll in Wake of NI Census Results', in: THE IRISH TIMES 2022, available at: https://www.irishtimes.com/ireland/2022/09/23/fresh-calls-for-border-poll-in-wake-of-ni-census-results/ [April 1, 2023].

McIlvanney, Liam 'Across the Narrow Sea: The Language, Literature and Politics of Ulster Scots', in: McIlvanney, Liam / Ryan, Ray (eds.): *Ireland and Scotland: culture and society, 1700–2000.* Dublin 2005, p. 216–20.

McCormack, William J.: *Northman: John Hewitt (1907–87) An Irish Writer, His World, and His Times.* Oxford 2015.

McKay, Susan: *Northern Protestants: An Unsettled People.* Belfast 2005.

Madden, Andrew: 'James Fenton, champion of the Ulster-Scots language, dies at 89', in: BELFAST TELEGRAPH 2021, available at: https://www.belfasttelegraph.co.uk/news/northern-ireland/james-fenton-champion-of-the-ulster-scots-language-dies-at-89/40053279.html [April 1, 2023].

Mahon, Derek: *Collected Poems.* London 1999.

Millar, Alan: *Winners of the Ulster-Scots Writing Competition.* Belfast 2021, p. 17.

Mitchell, Claire: *The Ghost Limb: Alternative Protestants and the Spirit of 1798.* Belfast 2022.

Montgomery, Michael: 'An Academy established and the task begun: A report on work in progress', available at: Ulster Scots Academy, http://www.ulsterscotsacademy.com/research/ulster-scots-academy-established.php [June 29, 2023].

Nash, Andrew: *Kailyard and Scottish Literature.* Amsterdam and New York, NY 2007.

Parr, Connal: *Inventing the Myth:* Oxford 2019. Kindle Edition.

Robinson, Philip: *Ulster-scots: A Grammar of the Traditional Written and Spoken Language.* Newtownards 1997.

Robinson, Philip: *Oul Licht and other Ulster-Scots poems.* Newtownards 2014.

Savage, Joanne: 'Linen Hall Library announces Ulster Scots writing competition.' 2022, available at: https://www.newsletter.co.uk/whats-on/arts-and-entertainment/linen-hall-library-announces-ulster-scots-writing-competition-3843720.

Northern Ireland Statistics and Research Agency: 'Census 2021 Main Statistics Religion Tables'. 2022, available at: https://www.nisra.gov.uk/publications/census-2021-main-statistics-religion-tables, [April 1, 2023].

Smyth, Damian: *Irish Street.* Matlock 2021.

Sloan, Barry: *Writers and Protestantism in the North of Ireland: Heirs to Adamnation?.* Dublin 2000.

Stewart, Anthony Terence Q.: *The Ulster Crisis: Resistance to Home Rule 1912–14.* London 1969.

Tannam, Etain (ed.): *Beyond the Good Friday Agreement: In the Midst of Brexit.* London 2020.
Walker, Graham / Greer, James: *Ties That Bind?: Scotland, Northern Ireland and the Union* Dublin 2023. Kindle Edition.

Michaela Marková

The Battles we refuse to fight today become the hardships our children must endure tomorrow: The ethno-political conflict and its legacy in selected contemporary Northern Irish novels for children and YA

Twenty-five years after the 1998 Peace Agreement, Northern Ireland remains "in numerous ways a place marked by instability, not only in the seemingly unending accumulation of political crises which have been greatly exacerbated by Brexit, but also in economic, social, and psychological terms" (McCann 2022). The anniversary of the hard-won peace deal has been marred by an impasse that has raised questions whether the conflict can ever be resolved, what are the reasons that prevent its resolution, and whether the need to move on is one people agree on. The bleak outlook had already been alluded to in the recent Ulster University collated report 'Transforming education in Northern Ireland'. This report states that education in Northern Ireland is "divided and splintered" (Milliken / Roulston / Cook 2021, p. 82f). Outcomes of the UU comprehensive assessment the report presents have been understood as an appeal for "enduring vested interests of the churches and the traditional political blocs" to be addressed (Meredith 2021). Indeed, the researchers have been reported to have argued that "[a]ppeasing and balancing the demands of […] opposing denominational, cultural and national vested interests has [sic] contributed significantly to the creation of a system that is divided, splintered and consequently overly expensive." Overall, they maintain that an "ambitious and radical transformation" of the educational system in Northern Ireland is needed (Meredith 2021). This is an important plea, since "in transitional contexts, where processes of denial of the past can entrench the reasons for the conflict and result in reappearing in future generations, education has a crucial role to play in reconciliation and in ensuring that the legacy of the past is addressed" (McEvoy / McEvoy / McConnachie 2006, p. 96). In the context of contemporary Northern Irish writing, this is important to consider in relation to the assumed call for resolution of the conflict allegedly argued for in the writing by the so-called "new generation of authors." It becomes even more urgent when one considers the claim that while "the educational context is arguably the key site in Northern Ireland" as related to conflict resolution, it is also one that "has yet to provide substantial evidence of success"

(Pelaschiar 1998, p. 81 f).[1] Although it was not its primary objective, the UU report endorses the persistent sentiment that unless the contentious issues related to the legacy of Troubles, are openly addressed, future of the region might be thwarted. As such, it echoes socio-political commentaries on the unresolved quality of the conflict, but the outcomes also problematize what the youth of Northern Ireland has wished for, that is less division between unionists and nationalists.

This sentiment, shared publicly even by world leaders from outside Northern Ireland, such as the former US President Barak Obama, warns that despite the fact that in 1998 people "voted in overwhelming numbers to see beyond the scars of violence and mistrust," and "clenched fists gave way to outstretched hands," "[t]here's still much work to do" and as "[t]his work is as urgent now as it has ever been, because there's more to lose now than there has ever been" (2013). The debates about the Northern Ireland protocol and post-Brexit Irish Sea border further attest to how all-pervasive and widespread this sentiment actually is. In fact, Sinn Féin's vice president Michelle O'Neill had warned that Northern Ireland would be in a very dangerous place had the post-Brexit Northern Ireland protocol been scrapped (Leebody 2022). Although the danger O'Neill had in mind was mainly possible retaliation from the EU, the failure of power-sharing arrangements following the 2022 Northern Ireland Assembly election proves just how contentious the status quo and future of Northern Ireland remain. Actually, "[t]he UK government has taken this [failure] as evidence that the protocol is disrupting the GFA and its institutions" (Spisak 2022). It thus seems that some are really invested in carrying the plea title of this chapter calls for out.

Despite the fact that Northern Ireland is "in transition from being engaged in an extended period of violent conflict towards becoming a modern democratic state," the disputes about the protocol, indeed, seem to suggest that "difficult cultural and relational issues [...] continue to generate inter-communal conflict" (Chapman / Campbell 2016, p. 115). What are the underlying reasons for such that would enable greater understanding of the open-endedness of the conflict. In other words, what has prevented greater cohesion of Northern Irish society? Timothy White asserts that since "the [Belfast/Good Friday] Agreement attempted to be as inclusive as possible in order to bring all potential spoilers into the peace process," there "was no systematic effort to ascertain truth from those who historically were associated with the violence of the Troubles," and that such has perpetuated mistrust and threatened "the continued implementation of the peace process" (2013, p. 97f). A truth commission in Northern Ireland, however,

---

1 One of the reasons for such failure, it has been claimed, was the assumption that "intergenerational change would [inevitably] transform historically sectarian conceptions of identity into less reactionary or hostile identities" (White 2013, p. 95). However, the development of civil society in Northern Ireland requires a more engaged effort.

Cillian McGrattan has argued, would not be as successful an agent of fostering reconciliation but would rather result in competition for truth (see McGrattan 2012, p. 455ff). Yet, White warns, "lacking such a confrontation of history," the Agreement had created "a truce that contains the historical antagonism without transforming the communal divide," and thus "gives fuel to spoiler groups, who [might] seek to undermine the peace process and efforts at reconciliation" (White 2013, p. 98). Hence the plea that calls for a change which would enable establishment of permanent positive peace has gained even more urgency.[2] It is a plea, the chapter will argue below, which informs Garrett Carr's texts.

The slogan which has currently appeared on numerous banners and walls around Northern Ireland – 'The battles we refuse to fight today become the hardships our children must endure tomorrow' – might seem to suggest that those who have come up with it had considered the aforementioned plea to address the contested Troubles legacy and seek to act accordingly. The contrary, regrettably, is true. The slogan embodies Unionist and Loyalist adverse reactions to the possibility of an effective trade border in the Irish Sea and/or of the separate status from the rest of the UK. In fact, it might be read as implied justification for the serious inner-city violent riots attributed to resentment among the British Loyalist community at the Northern Ireland Protocol which plagued the streets of Belfast in April 2021.[3] In relation to these riots, the Northern Ireland affairs committee has been told by a member of the Loyalist Communities Council who was arrested during the disturbances, Joel Keys, that "violence could not be taken off table when basic rights were under threat." Despite the fact that he said he "supported and respected the political process", he explained, "[t]he minute that you rule violence out completely [...] you're admitting that you're not willing to back up anything that you believe in" (O'Carroll / Walker 2021). Such behavior, which confirms claims that "threats that destabilize the identity of a group can lead to protective mechanisms buffering against the negative effects of a change" (Flack / Ferguson 2021, p. 187), is a manifestation of what has been regarded as collective angst: "a fear or apprehension [felt by members of a group] that past principles and values associated with their group are not transferred into the future" (Flack / Ferguson 2021, p. 187). Some have argued that "a deeper cause [for the 2021 riots] is a growing sense of grievance among Protestants that the Brexit deal and the Good Friday

---

2 White concludes saying that such positive, "sustainable peace cannot rely solely on power sharing but needs to include a process of reconciliation" (White 2013, p. 102).
3 The Loyalist Communities Council "formally withdrew support from the Good Friday deal in protest against the [Northern Ireland] protocol." When the chair of the LCC, David Campbell, was asked whether such withdrawal 'represented a threat of resumed violence', he was reported saying that "'[w]e are not in the business of issuing threats but we are in the business of issuing warnings'" (Pogatchnik 2021).

Agreement itself are failing to represent their interests" (Landow / McBride 2021). In fact, the recent "alienation" among many unionists allegedly "suggests the lack of a redefined sense of identity that is attractive and viable for those who feel as if their historic sense of identity has lost its meaning" (White 2013, p. 101).[4]

While it is perturbing that the consequences of Brexit might disrupt the carefully negotiated and delicate balance of interests embodied by the Belfast/ Good Friday Agreement, what the former Northern Ireland Commissioner for children and young people, Koulla Yiasouma, said in relation to the to the 2021 riots seems even more worrying. Yiasouma suggested that the behavior of some adults in relation to the unrest in the region almost amounted to child abuse as children were being coerced into participating in the riots by adults.[5] Such was confirmed by the senior Belfast policeman, Assistant Chief Constable Jonathan Roberts, who said that rioters, some as young as 13, "were encouraged and supported by adults, who stood by and clapped and cheered and orchestrated those children in becoming involved in violent disorder" (Pogatchnik 2021). This is worrying since "socio-political identities and in-group and out-group attitudes, which are central to the maintenance of prejudice and underpin many political conflicts [...] appear to be consolidated during childhood" (Muldoon 2004, p. 454), and such coercive behavior disrupts the logic of the peacebuilding process, as it prevents those without the same experiences of violence associated with the Troubles from developing a more positive view of the o/Other. In other words, even those who have come of age since the 1998 Agreement might thus not be able to develop more positive views of the other community, and hence "will be less willing to compromise and work with the other in society" (White 2013, p. 97).

Contrary to its original meaning, this chapter reads the slogan in its title as an incentive for settlement that is more in line with the appeal for "enduring vested interests of the churches and the traditional political blocs" to be addressed (Meredith 2021). It believes that in order to achieve sustainable peace in Northern Ireland, as White has claimed, fostering of a civil society that "will require groups to address their past and construct a shared vision of the future, thereby reducing sectarian identities and providing room for the other in their own identity" (White 2013, p. 102) is vital.[6] Transition to a more peaceful Northern Ireland, White continues, is possible.[7] It is a protracted process that will occur over gene-

---

4 Graham Spencer argues that the political leaders of unionism in favour of the 1998 Agreement failed to articulate a new vision of unionism that would be attractive to unionists (2006, p. 45 ff).
5 Speaking to BBC Radio 4, Yiasouma, in fact, described the situation as "criminal exploitation and coercion by adults of vulnerable and at-risk children and young people" (Harte 2021).
6 For a discussion of how civil society can be built in Northern Ireland, see Knox 2001, p. 13 ff.
7 Chapman and Campbell argue that "community/based restorative justice is a resource which should be harnessed for its potential for resolving conflict and reducing violence" (2016, p. 115).

rations as the "intergenerational change is quite slow but accumulates over time", and "it may eventually yield effective generational transformations of identities" (2013, p. 103). In fact, some have publicly appealed directly to the youth of Northern Ireland to be the change, saying that local politicians

> need you young people to keep pushing them, to create a space for them, to change attitudes. Because ultimately, whether your communities deal with the past and face the future united together isn't something you have to wait for somebody else to do – that's a choice you have to make right now [...] whether you reach your own outstretched hand across dividing lines, across peace walls, to build trust in a spirit of respect – that's up to you (Obama 2013).

Few would contest that improving community relations in Northern Ireland is self-evidently a good thing. However, McEvoy et al. argue that the specific historical framing of reconciliation as community relations they outline in their article 'Reconciliation as a dirty word' has limited efficiency of the process.[8] In fact, they maintain that despite the fact that reconciliation "has been a consistent feature of Northern Irish educational system for almost three decades [...], this approach has largely failed to deliver on its promises" (McEvoy / McEvoy / McConnachie 2006, p. 81). Some reasons for the arguable failure of Integrated Education's "experiment in contact" they discuss were: "a lack of shared understanding of the terminology of tolerance and reconciliation; a resistance o tackling issues relating to identity and difference in the classroom; an assumption that the 'integrated' ethos of the school will somehow be absorbed by the children without any direct strategy being employed on behalf of the school" (2006, p. 96f). McEvoy et al. suggest that "an alternative framework to the community relations paradigm should inform contemporary attempts to better educate our young people about reconciliation and what it means to be a citizen in a transforming polity" (2006, p. 82). They "contend that the developments within citizenship education present an opportunity for presenting a more grounded understanding of the meaning of reconciliation to the next generation", which enables transformation of reconciliation "from [what some deem] a 'dirty word' into a new language of 'political generosity'" (2006, p. 99).[9]

In *The Moral Imagination: The Art and Soul of Building Peace*, John Paul Lederach maintains that "artistic interventions have potential to fill a gap in which everyday language is inadequate to relay" experience of the conflict and its

---

[8] McEvoy / McEvoy / McConnachie explain that even the government policy 'A Shared future' that sought to endorse "respect for diversity and a recognition of [...] interdependence," remains "premised upon the assertion that current problems in Northern Ireland are a result not of inequality [...] but a culture of intolerance" (2006, p. 95).

[9] Such generosity, McEvoy / McEvoy / McConnachie maintain, requires for "an acknowledgement of the need to respect the rights of the other" (2006, p. 95).

legacy (Jancsó / Butler 2020). The chapter proceeds with a discussion of politics and poetics of narrative of conflict resolution in selected contemporary texts which deal with the legacy of the Troubles in Northern Ireland, Garrett Carr's *Badness of Ballydog* (2010), and *Lost Dogs* (2010), together with Sue Divin's debut novel *Guard Your Heart* (2020).[10] The texts are assessed as what Maria Pia Lara has called 'reflective judgements', examples of just literature that questions morality after the end of a/the conflict, including responsibility to rebuild. Lara argues that reflective judgements constitute the framework in which morality itself emerges, one that can assess moral, as opposed to legal, wrongs. This framework, an embodiment of restorative justice principles, is useful in helping communities return from violence.[11]

The chapter would like to argue that even if the texts might not seem to have achieved an actual change of the status quo, their import is more than aesthetic. The texts put forward, however implicitly or indirectly at times, the claim that transformation requires transition "from a concern with the resolution of issues [...] toward a frame of reference that focuses on the restoration and rebuilding of relationships", which is what, Lederach argues, genuine conflict transformation requires (2004, p. 24). In fact, one might go as far as to claim that the texts embody and/or argue for the "shift from identities based on resistance and defense to those based on cooperation and reconciliation," and thus fulfil what Siobhán McEvoy-Levy calls the "positive task of peacebuilding" (2001, p. 3). In 2001, McEvoy-Levy argued that "how and what children/youth think about peace processes and the task of reconstructing their societies after war", remained "almost completely unstudied" (p. 32). However, identifying and mapping such is of great importance as "the child's and/or youth's interpretation of events, processes, participants and outcomes in a conflict is the relevant variable in terms of psychological resilience" (p. 32). In other words, if children and youth partake in the critical evaluative process, they are more likely to cope with the conflict and its consequences psychologically. Moreover, what they think of the peace process, affects the prospects for peaceful future.

The ultimate question the chapter seeks to ponder is: whether the works seek to challenge hegemonic, monologic discourses of othering or monsterisation, whether they champion what could be termed the ethics of the other instead, or whether they actually affirm the aforementioned claim that "an [altogether new] alternative framework to the community relations paradigm" needs to be em-

---

10 Divin's text will be contrasted with the collection of Lyra McKee's journalistic writing, *Lost, Found, Remembered* (2020). Lyra McKee was the young journalist who was killed in Derry/Londonderry by the New IRA during the riots in 2019.
11 Sara Cobb argues that is precisely because moral judgements are foundational to any public policy, and because of this they are a critically important component to its formation (see Cobb 2013).

ployed as a strategy "to address both the conflict and the divided nature" of Northern Irish society. There is yet another important aspect related to restorative justice the chapter will attempt to illustrate: the texts embody, that which concerns the roles of children and young people in armed conflict, and the effects of such conflict and its aftermath on their development. This is quite significant since regardless of the growing body of literature dealing with such, not too long ago "neither children nor youth [would] appear as important variables in the literature on peace process" (McEvoy-Levy 2001, p. 2). However, such neglect is "counterproductive in terms of peace building particularly in the crucial post/accord phase with its twin challenges of violence prevention/accord maintenance and societal reconciliation and reconstruction", as "youth embody essential elements of both challenges" (2001, p. 2f).

And how do the protagonists translate or de-code the Troubles and its legacy? Carr's trilogy follows the stories of three teenagers – May, Andrew, and Ewan – who are brought together in the first novel in the eponymous Ballydog, which is "the worst town in Ireland". In comparison to portrayal of Northern Irish society in the early Troubles works, Carr's portrayal of Ballydog (as well as of the rural setting of the last book in the trilogy) does not appear to resemble any real (Northern) Irish locale related specifically to the conflict. Ballydog consists of a town square, which "was mainly just used for car parking", "a church, a school, a small housing estate" and is, throughout most of the story, rather uneventful (Carr 2010a, p. 2ff). In fact, Ballydog could be based on any small, fishing coastal town anywhere in Western Europe. This indeterminateness seems intentional, and it also appears to be a narrative strategy quite suitable to represent the Northern Irish predicament. First, it prevents the discourse of violence from gaining prominence, without diminishing the fact that the conflict has influenced life in all different places on the island of Ireland. Furthermore, it allows Carr to address the issues concerning the legacy of t/Troubled past his works deal with from a much broader, considerate perspective. In fact, it appears that the author is interested in universality of the issues concerning (re)conciliation and that he uses the (Northern) Irish context to illustrate the points about them he wishes to publicize.

This assertion concerning Carr's universalizing approach is confirmed by the language the author applies, particularly in his discussion of the 'badness' of Ballydog. Whereas Carr could have followed the example set by the Troubles thrillers in his portrayal of Ballydog (as well as the other locales he depicts), the expressions he uses are less macabre. The text declares early on that the town has a bad reputation. It subsequently attests that the situation is indisputably grave, yet its focus lies elsewhere. Instead of elaborating on the said graveness using ethno-politically loaded terms, the novel puts its characters into situations that make the readers consider whether they would 'hide' or 'take a stand' had they been faced with similar problems May, Ewan, and Andrew must cope with. Thereby, the novel requires the readers to employ their own imagination and engage their critical abilities in the assessment of the discussed issues, such as whether one should do good and why.

That the text strives for an unbiased, yet complex and challenging depiction is further evidenced by the narrative strategy employed to elaborate on the said badness, which corroborates the assertion. The chapters that depict May, Ewan, and Andrew's adventures are interspersed with those which portray stories parallel to that of Ballydog and its badness. Despite differences in context, these stories have a common denominator – an apocalyptic, devouring sea monster. The sea monster, however, is not what Derrida terms a sovereign which devours to become untouchable. It is a "destroyer" of cities, yet only of those that are evil and full of "cruel and greedy people". Indeed, the monster functions as a protective mechanism. It works "as a kind of [a] surgeon, cutting away parts of the world that had gone bad" (Carr 2010a, p. 34f).[12] Some might suggest that the monstrous remedial measure attests to Carr's positivist perspective concerning conflict (re)conciliation. On the contrary, the alternative 'monster' chapters do not serve to offer assurance that prospects for future are inevitably bright or that they will materialize effortlessly. Rather, the text is quite critical about what has necessitated the monster's existence – the fact that people have repeatedly ignored badness which, unchallenged, has been allowed to spread.

The Badness of Ballydog, however, seeks to inspire people to challenge this inactivity, which kept the monster alive for centuries. The appeal to act against badness inherent in Carr's story is the more severe and trenchant as, outside of the literary text, the conflicts are real but there is no helpful monster that would cut "away parts of the world that had gone bad" (2010a, p. 110). Only people can resolve conflicts, establish and develop ethical relations to prevent them, and hence avert a potential de-evolution of humankind. This assertion can be deemed to represent the overall message Carr's trilogy puts forward in relation to interpersonal relationships. The afore cited Report of the Consultative Group on the Past argues that there are many issues involved in dealing with the past as well as a variety of different approaches. However, common among these is the understanding that dealing with the past cannot be a one-off event or a quick fix. Dealing with the past is a process, and allowing this process to evolve is critical. The Report also states that "a reconciling society takes collective responsibility for the past instead of attributing blame and avoiding responsibility" (p. 13).

---

12 This points to the fact that Carr is interested more in the impact of othering than in simply elaborating the nature of this process. Contrary to the texts that might offer information conducive to one's understanding of the dynamics of monsterisation, Carr's trilogy focuses on detailing the consequences of such process and how to approach these.

Carr's novels can be read as a careful consideration of the imperative these principles of reconciliation the Report puts forward exemplify. In fact, the texts echo the Report in that they advocate collectiveness and continuity of reconciliatory work.

The alliance May, Ewan, and Andrew form is not initially very successful; the teenagers fail to protect the town against the sea monster's remedial act in *The Badness of Ballydog*. The teenagers, however, persevere in the efforts at improving social conditions. It is when the collectiveness of the acts they engage in expands in *Lost Dogs*, crossing the ethno-political boundaries, that their efforts are eventually rewarded. Active implementation of the aforementioned principles gains even more importance when considered in connection with intergenerational trauma transfer. It is a known fact that "the legacies of violence not only haunt the actual victims but also are passed on through generations" (Schwab 2010, p. 1). Indeed, inter-generational trauma transfer can cause that even those without a direct experience of a traumatic situation become what Gabriele Schwab calls bodies "in pain, leading a somatic experience severed from consciously or affectively lived history" (2010, p. 1). It is the second novel in Carr's trilogy, *Lost Dogs*, which is the most informative about the issue of trauma transfer, particularly as related to the Troubles. Although neither of the main protagonists directly experienced the conflict, the teenagers are all forced to deal with its legacy. In Ewan's case, to use Schwab's terminology, this legacy is close to causing his "soul murder and social death". In other words, the legacy has a profound, negative impact on Ewan's psychosomatic wellbeing. *Lost Dogs* details the process of Ewan's traumatization to (re)emphasize the need for engagement with the Troubles legacy. This argument against inactivity recurrent in Carr's trilogy contests the proposal put forward as part of the reconciliation process: that people should draw a line under the conflict and leave the past be. Carr's test, on the contrary, strive for people to actively engage in (re)conciliatory work as unresolved, the legacy of traumatic events is likely to persist and (re)surface. However critical, *The Badness of Ballydog* and *Lost Dogs* also allude to possible means one can employ in the struggle against the use of violence. To sum up these numerous allusions, one could say that it all depends on how inter-personal differences are viewed. Indeed, the texts seem to posit that if potentials envisaged for the future are to emerge, good relationships are crucial.

Over eight hundred novels that deal with the modern-day Troubles have allegedly been written to date. It is obvious that the number of sub-genres and narrative approaches employed in those Troubles novels might be as vast as their quantity. Nevertheless, as Troubles fiction scholarship proves, concepts exist which allow us to discuss the conflict in its complexity as they manage to capture the causes of the conflict, as well as of its endurance and resolution at the same time. One such concept, as this chapter has shown above, is the myth of the wild man, which epitomizes the process of monsterization or othering. It offers a critical reflection of Western humanity, manifesting how Western civilizations developed their identities in relation to 'the other.' The Troubles are often explained as a conflict of perceived inter-communal differences, which solidified Northern Irish society into the infamous two communities binary, the us ones against them ones. Hence the myth of the wild man presents an opposite lens through which to examine Carr's trilogy of the novels for young adults which, even if implicitly at times, addresses contemporary Irish and Northern Irish society. Carr's trilogy echoes the key principle of the Report of the Consultative Group on the Past and contributes to implementation of the imperative. The novels inform their intended young audience in a balanced way about society in need of coming to terms with its troubled past, not dissimilar to post-conflict (Northern) Ireland.

The chapter will now the politics and poetics of narrative of conflict resolution in Sue Divin's debut novel *Guard Your Heart* (2020). The way the chapter approaches the text is as what Maria Pia Lara has called 'reflective judgements.'[13] Lara argues that reflective judgements constitute the framework in which morality itself emerges, one that can assess moral, as opposed to legal, wrongs. This framework is useful in helping communities return from violence and it can be argued that Divin strives for her work to embody such. How do the protagonists of her novel translate or de-code the Troubles and its legacy? Divin's text offers a perspective of two young adults, who were born on the day the 1998 Belfast/Good Friday Agreement was signed, which echoes Salman Rushdie's work *Midnight's Children*. One protagonist, Aidan, is a boy from the Catholic, republican background. The other, Iona, is a girl from the Protestant side. Both live with their families, in their respective communities, in parts of the city that correspond with the aforementioned division. They are brought together at the beginning of the story in a rather brutally violent act, yet as the story progresses, they somehow manage to forge what turns out to become a rather solid romantic relationship. In the context of the Troubles writing, such premise echoes the early Troubles texts that were examples of the love-across-the-barricades subgenre, which has been criticized for its simplified portrayal of the conflict.

The text opens with what the boy calls a miracle as he had thought it unlikely he would be able to finish school, yet manage he did. His seemingly positive prospects for future are soon followed by a metaphor of a bridge which might be taken as a sign of resolved inter-communal hostilities, or at least a promise of brighter future for the two communities: "I found myself standing at the Peace Bridge, its white overlapping triangles like a handshake across the river [...] A bridge to help heal the divides of the past; to span the gap between the Protestant

---

13 See *Narrating Evil: A Postmetaphysical Theory of Reflective Judgment* (2007).

Waterside and the Catholic Cityside. Peace in concrete" (Divin 2021, p. 9). Nevertheless, life proves to be more complex, and the text confirms that it takes more than a handshake to encourage reconciliation, for some issues which have prevented it are more difficult to deal with and process than the protagonists might have wished for, and the bridge metaphor is now used to convey the contrary meaning than previously, as it has become "a bridge from nowhere for no one to cross" (2021, p. 10). To go back to the love-across-the-divide paradigm, and use it to assess the overall situation the relationship echoes: the characters do not become immediately as intimate as might be desirable, for at least one of them, but have to allow for hesitation, denial, failure and else. What makes their approximation the more difficult? Well, it is almost clichéd, but as the readers learn from Iona, the deeply ingrained fear of the other being different, and a representative of the enemy, seems quite debilitating:

> It wasn't that I wanted to think old-school, them and us, it was just there. By nursery I knew my 'good' and 'bad' colours. At primary school, I learned my letters – 'aitch' not 'haitch', my numbers – 'three' not 'tree'. Everyone was tattooed under their skin. 'What school are you at?' people asked. Answer 'Saint' anything and it was dead cert you were Catholic. 'Where are you from?' The killer question (Divin 2021, p. 22).

Connolly and Healy argue that by the age of three children in Northern Ireland are able to identify and attribute positive or negative characteristics to a Catholic or Protestant person. However, they also argue that children are able to play with and adjust such sectarian stereotypes (2004). If we allow for the possibility of a generation-related attitudinal change, the question is how far has the young generation departed from the old divisions?

Aidan's political consciousness seems to mirror the correlation McEvoy-Levy's research into roles youth have played in post-accord settlement has identified. McEvoy-Levy, referring to Jean Whyte (1998), confirms the supposition that the teenagers and young adults who are engaged in politics are often those "who have a strong Irish, or British identifications, family traditions of interest/involvement, and sharpened perceptions of fairness/unfairness of the political system" (2000, p. 89). Given his family republican background, it is not surprising Aidan should be interested in politics: "I'd have needed to be tapping a white stick to not see their [IRA] shadow, especially in a family like mine" (2001, p. 4). Nevertheless, his keen interest is generated by politics per se rather than by efforts to redress injustice his community suffered in the conflict. In fact, however limited his perspective of the republican perpetrators and their motifs is, especially when compared with McKee's account of the same, it is safe to say that Aidan does not want to tread in his father's steps and become a volunteer. Indeed, he is terrified at the thought, and hence initially reluctant to acknowledge the fact, that his older brother had joined the clandestine organization. Although Aidan does not fully express his strong condemnation of his brother's involvement, one gets the feeling he strongly disapproves of the way Seán was behaving. Given the negative consequences of their father's IRA membership for the family, Aidan seems to be at a loss to rationalize Seán's.

It is telling to contrast Divin's text with Lyra McKee's account of the sectarian politics she presents in *Lost, Found, Remembered,* since the late journalist came from the same city as the protagonists of Divin's novel and was close to them in age as well. McKee's account is not only more critical but it also is more complex. Despite the fact that the journalist does not shy away from using the terms such as terrorists or murderers to refer to those who had been previously actively involved in the strife, she allows for the fact that the youths who had joined the IRA or the UVF and other factions "had generally done so for what had seemed like good reasons at the time" and were not, contrary to popular belief, "servants of Satan himself" (McKee 2020, p. 18ff). In fact, she admits she "didn't see the ex-prisoners [in particular] as being beyond redemption", probably since many of them were "men and women struggling to reconcile their present selves to what their past selves had done" (2020, p. 20). Despite the fact that McKee "didn't agree with what they had done" (2020, p. 19), she seems to feel compassion for those who had been actively involved, probably since "all of them, enemies who'd fought on opposing sides [...] were facing the same struggles in the peacetime. They all seemed to loathe sleep because sleep brought nightmares. They all woke up screaming in the middle of the night" (2020, p. 21). At the same time, however, McKee understands that similar might not be possible for "a woman who'd watched her husband be gunned down, in front of their children, perhaps in their own living room." Hence, she admits she would not be able to stand in front of such a woman and "tell her that the men who'd done it were more complex than evil and more human than her grief would allow her to believe" (2020, p. 20). Her conciliatory attitude probably stems from the fact that even though she admits she "saw the tail end of the conflict," she "didn't see enough to make" her "bitter towards 'the other side'" (2020, p. 64). So, it seems is thus able to move further away from the legacy of the Troubles than Aidan, at least until the moment when her life was prematurely ended by the IRA in 2019.

In relation to the former paramilitaries and their motivation to take up the arms, it is important to note that "regardless of the levels of actual support for sectarian conflict, the maintenance of a sectarian conflict is assured if people [simply] 'understand' that their ethno-political identities make them potential targets and that communal deterrence is a safety mechanism" (McEvoy-Levy 2001, p. 22), inside as well as outside of one's community of belonging. This is something McKee's journalistic oeuvre seems to enable its reader to acquire a deeper understanding of than Divin's novel. While this might have been perhaps mainly because of its wider scope and proximity to objective style of writing, it is quite puzzling when one considers claims concerning Northern Irish writing concerning the prospects for future raised by, for example, Laura Pelaschiar, that a fictional text should struggle with something McKee achieves so well.

This, however, does not mean that *Guard Your Heart* offers a simplistic perspective, not at least in relation to the different reasons for which people might have become involved in the paramilitary organizations, before the ceasefires or now. In fact, it seems to confirm the claim that young adults might "get involved in (dis)organized street-level political violence much earlier than when they are afforded the privilege of genuine involvement in politics" (McEvoy-Levy 2001, p. 24). Iona's brother Andy seeks to belong to another group than just the music band he plays in. Yet he struggles to receive his father's support for his extra-curricular activities which relate to communal politics, and it is possible to assert that his lack of fulfilment is the reason why he partakes in the brutal beating Aidan receives from Andy's mates. Regrettably, Divin does not explore this lack of fulfilment in greater detail, which is particularly unfortunate as Andy and his friends are Protestants, and not much has been written about post-conflict political engagement of youth from this community (at least not as much in comparison with the discussions concerning the Catholic counterpart).

What are the readers supposed to take away from Divin's novel and how does such compare with some of McKee's observations? Well apart from the rather positive last two chapters that not only bring the young couple together after a brief hiatus, and send them on an adventure abroad, which might be read as the bright prospect for future, the title of the novel alludes to what the overall message is. Despite the fact that Aidan is told to – "Live like the world is your oyster, Aidan, like hope and dreams are possible" (2021 p. 16) – another piece of advice repeatedly appears throughout the narrative, and that is his mother's favorite biblical proverb: Guard your heart above all else, for it determines the course of your life (Proverbs 4:23). The proverb is obviously not talking about the physical heart that beats. It is referring to the mind, the will, or even the inner man. The mind and the will are where important life decisions are made. The proverb suggests that everything one does flows out of one's mind and as such it makes sense to put a hedge or guard around it so one can protect the things s/he does. However, some might also claim that forgetting what is behind and straining toward what is ahead, we might press on toward the goal to win the prize (Philippians 3:12–14). This understanding of the quote might seem rather limited/reductionist, as it would mean to draw a line under the past, which, according to principles of transitive justice those who strive for positive peace should not do, as trauma (if nothing else) has the tendency to resurface. This is something McKee's text seem to confirm: "When the conflict ended in Northern Ireland, the fight turned from guns to history books. 'Ended' was a euphemism, I thought, because it never truly seemed to end, so much as it changed shape"

(2020, p. 15). Hence the title of Divin's novel might seem positive but it is also a warning. The question remains who is the real target audience? Despite the difficulties he has been through, Aidan seems to be more than capable to decide what his life goals are, and what he should do to achieve them. In fact, through Divin's elucidation of the said difficulties or obstacles Aidan encounters while trying to make his dreams come true, the warning is indirectly aimed at the older generations. Those who lived through the Troubles, yet those who are unable to make peace with the past. McKee's text, yet again, unpacks such criticism, outlining several reasons for the failures of the peace process:

> We didn't sign up to a war and get sold out by a surrender. Instead, politicians, hoping to sell the peace deal to our parents, made three promises. The first promise, they barely delivered on: peace [...] It wasn't the peace promised, just an absence of all-out civil war.
> [...]
> The second promise was prosperity. Peace, we were assured, would bring a thriving new economy. It never appeared. It didn't matter what qualifications you had, the most plentiful work was to be found in call centres, answering or making calls for a minimum wage. They were egalitarian shitholes; middle-class kids with PhDs mixed with kids with no GCSEs, and they all earned the same for doing the same grunt work.
> [...]
> The third promise the politicians made and broke was the one that hurt the most. It was felt mostly in the areas that had already been ravage, the ones where the gunmen continued to roam. Your children, they'd told your parents, will be safe now. With the peace deal, the days of young people disappearing and dying would be gone. Yet this turned out to be a lie, too (2020, p. 33f).

This allows for an answer to the question whether it is possible to read the text as an example of just literature, as that which questions morality after the end of a/ the conflict, including responsibility to rebuild. Even if none of the discussed texts might not seem to have achieved an actual change of the status quo, their import is more than aesthetic. All put forward, however implicitly or indirectly at times, the claim that transformation requires transition "from a concern with the resolution of issues [...] toward a frame of reference that focuses on the restoration and rebuilding of relationships," which is what, Lederach argues, genuine conflict transformation requires (2004, p. 24). In fact, it is possible to go as far as to claim that the texts embody and/or argue for the "shift from identities based on resistance and defense to those based on cooperation and reconciliation," and thus fulfil what McEvoy-Levy calls the "positive task of peacebuilding" (2001, p. 3). There is yet another important aspect related to restorative justice the texts embody, that which concerns the roles of children and young people in armed conflict, and the effects of such conflict and its aftermath on their development. The texts, read as reflective judgements, do provide the framework in which morality emerges, one that can assess moral, as opposed to legal, wrongs.

Applied in the Northern Irish context, these reflective judgements can lead to learning, which, in turn, might improve policy even in a place to which the belonging is contested.

Bibliography

Carr, Garrett: *Badness of Ballydog*. New York 2010a.
Carr, Garrett: *Lost Dogs*. New York 2010b.
Chapmann, Tim / Campbell, Hugh: 'Working Across Frontiers in Northern Ireland: The Contribution of Community-based Restorative Justice to Security and Justice in Local Communities', in: Clamp, Kerry (ed.): *Restorative Justice in Transitional Settings*. London 2016, p. 115–132.
Cobb, Sarah: *Speaking of violence*. Oxford 2013.
Connolly, Paul / Healy, Julie: *Children and the Conflict in Northern Ireland: The Experiences and Perspectives of 3–11 Year Olds*. Office of the First Minister and Deputy First Minister 2004.
Divin, Sue: *Guard your heart*. London 2021.
Flack, Patrick / Ferguson, Neil: 'Conflict Transformation: Relinquishing or maintaining social identity among former Loyalist combatants in Northern Ireland', POLITICAL PSYCHOLOGY 2020/42:2, p. 183–200.
Jancsó, Daniella / Butler, Austin: *The Poetics of Reconciliation*. Torkel Opsahl Academic EPublisher 2020/98.
Knox, Colin: 'Peace Building in Northern Ireland: A Role for Civil Society', SOCIAL POLICY AND SOCIETY 2001/10:1, p. 13–28.
Lara, Maria. Pia: *Narrating Evil: A Postmetaphysical Theory of Reflective Judgment*. New York 2007.
Lederach, John Paul: *The Moral Imagination: The Art and Soul of Building Peace*. Oxford 2004.
McEvoy-Levy, Siobhan: 'Communities and Peace: Catholic Youth in Northern Ireland', JOURNAL OF PEACE RESEARCH 2000/37:1, p. 85–103.
McEvoy-Levy, Siobhan: 'Youth as Social and Political Agents: Issues in Post-Settlement Peace Building', in: KROC INSTITUTE OCCASIONAL PAPER 2001/21.
McEvoy, Lesley / McEvoy, Kieran / McConnachie, Kirsten: 'Reconciliation as a dirty word: Conflict, community relations and education in Northern Ireland', JOURNAL OF INTERNATIONAL AFFAIRS 2006/60:1, p. 81–106.
McGrattan, Cillian: 'Spectres of history: Nationalist Party politics and Truth Recovery in Northern Ireland', POLITICAL STUDIES 2012/60:2, p. 455–73.
McKee, Lyra: *Lost, Found, Remembered*. Belfast 2020.
Muldoon, Orla T.: 'Children of the Troubles: The Impact of Political Violence in Northern Ireland', JOURNAL OF SOCIAL ISSUES 2004/60:3, p. 453–468.
Pelaschiar, Laura: *Writing the North: The Contemporary Novel in Northern Ireland*. Trieste 1998.
Schwab, Gabrielle: *Haunting Legacies: Violent Histories and Transgenerational Trauma*. New York 2010.

Spencer, Graham: 'The Decline of Ulster Unionism: The Problem of identity, image and change', CONTEMPORARY POLITICS 2006/12:1, p. 45–63.

White, Timothy: 'Generational change and redefining identities: Post-conflict peacebuilding in Northern Ireland', THE CANADIAN JOURNAL OF PEACE AND CONFLICT STUDIES 2013/45:2, p. 95–117.

Whyte, Jean: 'Young Citizens in Changing Times: Catholics and Protestants in Northern Ireland', JOURNAL OF SOCIAL ISSUES 1998/54:3, p. 603–620.

Internet sources

Harte, Lauren: 'NI riots: Children's commissioner says influence of adults in disorder 'amounts to child abuse"', in: BELFAST TELEGRAPH 2021/4:11, available at: https://www.belfasttelegraph.co.uk/news/northern-ireland/northern-ireland-riots-childrens-commissioner-says-influence-of-adults-in-disorder-amounts-to-child-abuse/40300331.html [10.12.2022].

Landow, Charles / McBride, James: 'Moving past the Troubles: The Future of Northern Ireland Peace', available at: https://www.cfr.org/backgrounder/moving-past-troubles-future-northern-ireland-peace [10.12.2022].

Leebody, Christopher: 'Northern Ireland would be in a 'very dangerous place' if protocol is scrapped claims Sinn Fein's Michelle O'Neill', BELFAST TELEGRAPH 2022/May 17, available at: https://www.belfasttelegraph.co.uk/news/politics/northern-ireland-would-be-in-a-very-dangerous-place-if-protocol-is-scrapped-claims-sinn-feins-michelle-oneill/41657076.html [10.12.2022].

McCann, Fiona: 'A Review of Northern Irish Writing After the Troubles: Intimacies, Affects, Pleasures (Caroline Magennis, 2021) ', 2022, available at: https://www.estudiosirlandeses.org/reviews/northern-irish-writing-after-the-troubles-intimacies-affects-pleasures-caroline-magennis-2021/ [10.12.2022].

Meredith, Robbie: 'Education in NI 'divided and splintered', says Ulster University report', BBC News, available at: https://www.bbc.com/news/uk-northern-ireland-56089069#comments [10.12.2022].

Milliken, Matthew / Roulston, Stephen / Cook, Sally: 'Transforming education in Northern Ireland. Coleraine: Ulster University', available at: https://pure.ulster.ac.uk/ws/files/105744826/Integrated_Education_Fund_Transforming_Education_in_Northern_Ireland_Briefing_Papers_Collection.pdf [10.12.2022].

Obama, Barack: 'Remarks by President Obama and Mrs. Obama in Town Hall with Youth of Northern Ireland', available at: https://obamawhitehouse.archives.gov/the-press-office/2013/06/17/remarks-president-obama-and-mrs-obama-town-hall-youth-northern-ireland [10.12.2022].

O'Carroll, Lisa / Walker, Peter: 'Senior loyalist says NI post-Brexit tensions 'most dangerous for years'.' THE GUARDIAN, available at: https://www.theguardian.com/uk-news/2021/may/19/senior-loyalist-says-ni-post-brexit-tensions-most-dangerous-for-years [10.12.2022].

Pogatchnik, Shawn: 'Northern Ireland leaders condemn violence, disagree on why people are fighting', available at: https://www.politico.eu/article/northern-ireland-riot-disagree/ [10.12.2022].

Pogatchnik, Shawn: 'Violence against Northern Ireland protocol isn't 'off the table'', available at: https://www.politico.eu/article/eu-warned-summer-violence-northern-ireland-protocol-uncahnged-brexit-uk-loyalist/ [10.12.2022].

Proverbs 4:23, accessed at Bible Study Tools, available at: https://www.biblestudytools.com/proverbs/4-23.html [10.12.2022].

Report of the Consultative Group on the Past, available at: https://cain.ulster.ac.uk/victims/docs/consultative_group/cgp_230109_report_sum.pdf [10.12.2022].

Spisak, Anton: 'Fixing the Northern Ireland Protocol: A Way Forward', available at: https://institute.global/policy/fixing-northern-ireland-protocol-way-forward [10.12.2022].

Thierry Robin

Borderline Troubles in *Resurrection Man* and *Breakfast on Pluto:* Remembering Northern Ireland before the GFA

> You need the crossing of bodies for the border to become real, otherwise you just have this discursive construction. There is nothing natural about the border; it's a highly constructed place that gets reproduced through the crossing of people, because without the crossing there is no border, right? It's just an imaginary line, a river or it's just a wall
> (Biemann 2002, p. 99f).

The notion of *trouble(s)* proves to be a protean concept, as the following list of definitions given in the *Merriam Webster English Dictionary* reminds its readers. It may mean:

1: the quality or state of being troubled especially mentally
2: public unrest or disturbance
3: an instance of trouble
4: a state or condition of distress, annoyance, or difficulty
 a: a condition of physical distress or ill health: ailment
 b: a condition of mechanical malfunction
 c: a condition of doing something badly or only with great difficulty
 d: *dated, informal:* the state of being pregnant while unmarried
5: an effort made
6a: a cause of distress, annoyance, or inconvenience
 b: a negative feature: drawback
 c: an unhappy or sad fact ('Trouble')

In enunciative terms, '*the* Troubles' with a capital 'T' and a final 'S' indicating the plural form, following the deictic determiner 'the', implies an understanding and a positioning of the concept of 'troubles' within a specific geopolitical space on the one hand and a specific series of events interconnected through the agency of causality in time, that is European History here, on the other hand. Through the definite article 'the', one immediately recognizes the anaphoric marker of conceptual preconstruction that is the digraph 'TH-' that establishes some shared knowledge between co-enunciators[1], or authors and readers alike in this case. Here, the deliberately vague, allusive and elusive but well-known euphemistic expression 'The Troubles' – reinforced by the plural phrasing – obviously refers

---

1 See Rotgé 2001, p. 9 for the following quote: "[…] the use of the determiner *the* for example is a sign of an anaphoric operation; it connects linguistic material together in order to produce meaning."

to the ethno-nationalist conflict which took place in the Northern part of Ireland from the late 1960s to 1998. 1998 is the year of the Good Friday Agreement (GFA), signed in Belfast, usually seen as the actual beginning of the peace process and henceforth of the end of the very same 'Troubles'.

The political quandary – no to say quagmire – characteristic of the so-called "Six Counties", inherited from the 1921 Partition – itself resulting from centuries of British settlement in the whole island, has recently come back to the forefront of the news and current political debates in Europe and the UK. It has underlined the problematic nature of a border which is supposed to be more tangible again and conversely re-harden the division of the island while EU integration had either erased it altogether or made it quite flexible, not to say figuratively *soft* and nearly invisible as Katy Hayward explains:

> The transformation of the Irish border as a physical and symbolic divide has been integrally connected to the role of the European Union (EU). At one level, the EU has indirectly helped to nullify the border's impact as a line of dispute between two states. At another, the EU has attempted to directly address the division caused by the border between two communities (Hayward 2011, p. 31).

This territorial moot point, once neutralized by the European ideal, has now morphed yet again into a seemingly never-ending source of contention. This questions the feasibility of an Irish backstop, potentially blocking the full-blown effects of a British neo-nationalist agenda epitomized by Brexit, before the COVID 19 pandemic in turn partly eclipsed the ongoing political imbroglio in turn eclipsed by the war in Ukraine and so forth. But the issue of defining identities through borders remains fundamental.

Borders, denial and Freudian death drive narrated in (Northern) Irish fiction

As explained, 'The Troubles' with an S constitutes a periphrastic understatement that replaces the blunt reality of a civil war where thousands of people – including many innocent civilians – were murdered ('Summary of Status') and nearly 50.000 maimed (see 'Chronological List')[2] because of the controverted existence of a border on a relatively small otherwise peaceful island, where the Freudian 'narcissism of minor differences'[3] factor looms large. This euphemism about the

---

2 Only in Northern Ireland, approximately 47,541 people were injured over 30 years.
3 This concept of *narcissism of small differences* ('der Narzissmus der kleinen Differenzen' in German) involves the thesis that communities, human groups, nations with adjoining territories and historically close relationships are unexpectedly more prone to engage in feuds, bouts of sarcastic ridiculing not to mention full-blown wars because of the hypersensitivity to

'Troubles' characterizes an official colonial-tinted narrative, marked by denial as analyzed by Stan Cohen in his famous 2002 essay entitled *States of Denial* – aptly subtitled 'Knowing about Atrocities and Suffering'.

> Denials draw on shared cultural vocabularies to be credible. They may also be shared in another powerful sense: the commitment between people –whether partners [...] or entire organizations– to back up and collude in each other's denials. Without conscious negotiation, family members know what *trouble* spots to avoid, which facts are better not noticed. [...] But the facts are too brutal to ignore. They have to be reinterpreted, using techniques like minimization, *euphemism* and joking: 'If the force of facts is too brutal to ignore, then their meaning can be altered. The vital lie continues unrevealed, sheltered by the family's silence, alibis, stark denial. The collusion is maintained by directing attention away from the fearsome fact or by repackaging its meaning *in an acceptable format*' (Cohen 2001, p.64 [my emphasis]).

The very word 'trouble', as shown in the definition given above, proves to be particularly apt to foster innuendo through its vagueness and multiple meanings, from mere physical discomfort and annoyance to strife, riots, terrorist attacks and slaughter. In linguistics, this corresponds to an ample *notional gradient*, which ignores any clear-cut boundaries, notably to offer Stanley Cohen's "acceptable format" to the outsider's eye. By Culioli's standards, as this essay intends to explain, the notional domain noted /troubles/[4] presents properties echoing the difficulty for any speaker to place a notional boundary accurately delineating the unpalatable essence of those so-called Irish "Troubles" from their multiple remote contradictions and palpable expressions. These boundaries proper may be defined by their evasiveness, their gradually jarring properties depending on *who* narrates the Troubles and *when* (see Boely 2002, p. 217). In other words, enunciative frontiers echo the arbitrariness and abstraction of national borders and the ideological viewpoints supporting them at different stages of the historical process. By blurring them through euphemism, one achieves the denial strategy spotted by Cohen:

> Vocabularies of political justification should not require the sad tales of sex offenders, alcoholics or 'compulsive' shop-lifters. Far from entailing a defective capacity to heed constraints, ideological crime denies the very legitimacy of these constraints. But even when people do appalling things for noble reasons, they may still search for a culturally recognizable language to evade conventional judgement. The result is a potent combination: in part ideological, in part defensive neutralization. This may escalate into a

---

minor or small details allowing for differentiation between otherwise close peoples, communities, nations. One may profitably cite the infamous instances of conflicts opposing India to Pakistan, Greece to Turkey, Ruanda to Burundi, Serbia to Croatia and since the grim winter in 2022 Russia to Ukraine. See Freud 2002 [1930], p. 131 and p. 305.

4 According to Culioli's Theory of Predicative and Enunciative Operations, notions are noted between slashes. See /dog/ in Ranger 2018, p. 28.

hermetic self-righteousness. *People facing total moral condemnation for carrying out atrocities manage to maintain a self-image of being good* (idealistic, sacrificing, noble, brave) or else just 'ordinary people' (Cohen 2001, p. 63).

Sadly, these lines about ordinary people committing atrocities could perfectly portray Victor Kelly, McNamee's sadistic self-righteous loyalist protagonist in *Resurrection Man*.

Last but not least, to finish with this protracted but necessarily nuanced introduction, the Troubles also illustrate what Sigmund Freud encapsulates in the concept of *death drive* or *Todestrieb* in his 1920 essay entitled *Beyond the Pleasure Principle* (Freud 1987, p. 316). In fact, 3,720 people were killed because of the conflict initially caused by the partition of Ireland (see McKittrick et al. 2007, p. 1552). Those *Troubles* show the wildly ample spectrum of pain caused by competing discourses based on opposite nationalist identity dynamics in a small European territory forcibly shared between Unionists and Republicans. This shows the ever-shifting gap between reality and the ideologies trying to harness and control it. This ontological gap between language and the *real* is a fruitful postmodernist field of research, long theorized by Brian McHale.[5] The Troubles from Belfast to Derry and their litany of endless attacks and gratuitous retaliatory barbarity translated into maimed bodies, maimed communities, maimed territories. But paradoxically, this tragic death toll initially fueled by and imbued with traumatizing inflammatory discourses have inspired a multiplicity of works of art, be they literary or filmic. Let us mention a few instances of that cornucopia of complex representations of the Troubles. They range from Bernard McLaverty's 1983 acclaimed novel *Cal* successfully adapted onto the screen by Pat O'Connor the following year, to Owen McCafferty's darkly funny 1998 play on childhood and sectarian violence entitled *Mojo Mickybo* turned into a film called *Mickybo and Me* by Terry Sloane in 2004, or Steve McQueen's 2008 multi-award winning *Hunger*.

In this chapter, the two Irish novels under scrutiny stand out as ideal pathways to investigate this dodgy twofold border – in narrative and territorial terms. They were written in the 1990s. Both feature, question, renew and transgress the usual notion of borders by resorting to the same vantage point offered by the queer outsider, the maverick protagonist who crosses boundaries, moral limits, set categories. Adopting a postmodernist aesthetic agenda based on the jarring discrepancy between language and reality, they transgress rules to wander through dangerous areas, ideologies and organizations, right in the heart of Europe, to draw our attention onto how collective identities may run amok. McNamee especially, shows how a conflict is deeply encoded in names and topography. Belfast "has withdrawn

---

5 See McHale 1987, p. xii for the following quote: "Postmodernist fiction differs from modernist fiction just as a poetics dominated by ontological issues differs from one dominated by epistemological issues."

into its placenames. Palestine Street. Balaklava Street. The names of captured ports, lost battles, forgotten outposts held against inner darkness" (McNamee 1994, p. 3).

Novels and films: McCabe's neo-delusional bog Gothic[6] vs McNamee's factional Gothic

First, *Breakfast on Pluto* – the novel by Patrick McCabe (1998) – was turned into a movie by Neil Jordan in 2005. Second, Eoin McNamee's sectarian piece of *faction*,[7] entitled *Resurrection Man* (1994), was adapted for the screen by Mark Evans in 1998.[8]

Neil Jordan[9] is a prominent Irish film-director. He has worked repeatedly on Irish History and politics with *The Crying Game*, which featured the lethal cat-and-mouse game played between IRA Provos and the British Army in the 1980s, and which got an Academy Award for Best Original Screenplay in 1992. In 1996, his *Michael Collins* – a period movie dealing with the Irish War of Independence [1919–1921] – was awarded a Golden Lion in Venice the same year it was released. Welsh director Mark Evans is by no means as famous or successful as Jordan is, but his work, which is notably placed within the confines of Wales, makes it relevant to study collective identities amongst British nations,[10] and the conceptual imaginary boundaries allegedly differentiating them. Analyzing identities requires we should pay attention to affects so this chapter will also show to what extent a psycho-analytical approach to the postmodernist blurring of ontological boundaries de-

---

6 McCabe has characterized his own prose as alternately neo-delusional or 'Bog Gothic', a mixture of fun horror and Irish small-town life – see O'Mahony 2003 and Pacini 2015.
7 Faction *per se* is a portmanteau word, blending fact and fiction. Truman Capote is generally credited with creating the true crime genre or 'the real-life novel' with *In Cold Blood* (1966). See, also, Lawson 2007.
8 Evans was born in 1963 in Cardiff, Wales. He studied for a history of art degree at the University of Cambridge, and then took a year out before taking a one-year course in film at the University of Bristol, along with a future famous British film-director, namely Michael Winterbottom. His career was initially marked by his Welshness. His film entitled *House of America* (1997) illustrated the cultural era known as *Cool Cymru*, which sought to promote Welsh figures, themes and identity.
9 Neil Patrick Jordan was born in Sligo in 1950. He is undoubtedly one of the most successful Irish film directors these days in addition to being a screenwriter, novelist and short-story writer. His first book, *Night in Tunisia*, won a Somerset Maugham Award and *The Guardian* Fiction Prize in 1979. He has also won three Irish Film and Television Awards, as well as the Silver Bear for Best Director at the Berlin International Film Festival for *The Butcher Boy* (1997).
10 See *House of America* (1997) set in a depressed Welsh mining town, *Hunky Dory* (2011), a musical set in Swansea or *Cymru Fach* (2008), a satire on various aspects of the Welsh community and culture (media, education and politics) he produced, directed by Gruffydd Davies.

fining identities reflects the way linguistic borders are construed in close communities. To do so, Culioli's enunciative theory comes in handy just as Ricœur's hermeneutics of the subject may help us reconcile this generic postmodernist quality of Northern Irish works of art. Narrative identities to Ricœur are based on split metaphors – mirroring split communities – as explained by Katarzyna Weichert:

> Ricœur's metaphor theory shows how the images are generated and how, in metaphorical process, discursive and sensual dimensions are intertwined. In this way, a metaphor occurs as a linguistic event which takes place between what is verbal and nonverbal. It is a linguistic creation and it works as a script for visualization. An image delivery takes place by organizing perceptions from previous experiences and synthesizing them in new constellations – content of experience (Weichert 2019, p. 65).

Both screen adaptations here are fairly faithful to their original literary *paper* models, as regards their narrative arc and general atmosphere. Let us note in passing that the author of *Breakfast on Pluto* – Patrick McCabe – was the co-screenwriter and has a cameo in the film as Kitten's creative writing teacher.[11] Eoin McNamee was actually the screenwriter of the movie adapted from his own novel. However, similarities are also limited.

While *Resurrection Man* is a somber fictionalized account of real sectarian murders which happened in Belfast, *Breakfast on Pluto* is an entirely fictional novel whose whimsical kitsch quality is probably most effectively rendered through the baroque casting of Cillian Murphy as Patrick Braden. Braden is an orphan boy, who very early takes to crossdressing while navigating the remote spheres of IRA activism and British counterterrorism services. McNamee's Kelly and McCabe's Braden are thus poles apart

Victor Kelly, the character created by McNamee – based on the real Protestant Loyalist activist and infamous psychopath called Lenny Murphy (1952–1982) – is the central character in both the novel and the movie entitled *Resurrection Man*. This title takes after an expression that ominously used to refer to body snatchers, in the 19th century, who stole and sold corpses for dissection or anatomy lectures in medical schools in Victorian England. Elaborating on the same macabre motif, academic Steve Baker argues that the film can be interpreted as a neo-Gothic vampire film, "situating it within a loyalist self-image of vampirism" (Baker 2004, p. 78).

Far from this supernatural gruesome vampiric reference, Patrick *Pussy* Braden is an eccentric Catholic cross-gender character in *Breakfast on Pluto*. He travels a vortex of violence in McCabe's homegrown so-called Bog Gothic[12] literature, a

---

11 See the full cast of the movie: https://www.imdb.com/title/tt0411195/fullcredits#cast [24.06.2023].
12 On McCabe's 'Bog Gothic', see Hughes, Punter and Smith 2013, p. 359.

mixture of stereotypical and kitsch Irish elements. Mirroring the novels, the two films explore the way one can relate to and make sense of tragic History through the opposite itineraries of two men, from childhood to adulthood, as both grapple with their sense of belonging to a community defined in more or less exclusive terms.

Linguistic borders and political identities

To the critical viewer, both films unwittingly interact as the two complementary sections of the same notional domain of /Irish masculinity/.[13] Both protagonists offer opposite interactions with enunciative boundaries. In McCabe's world, borders are crossed to seek fun and love. In McNamee's work, borders are synonymous with hatred, threat and death: you cross them to kill. Both stories rely on the *Bildungsroman* structure and narrative arc. This arc, rife with obstacles and boundaries, is where Culioli's notional domain comes in gloriously yet again. His linguistic theory is inspired from mathematical topology. It is based on *topoi* as defined by limits, frontiers, and the ensuing implicit co-constructed notions of otherness and converse identities, applied to semantics. In this theory, the frontier is not just crucial, it becomes an organizing center to make sense of words and events around oneself. Let us quote:

> The notional domain is constructed from the notion. It enables the enunciator [here that is the writer or the movie-maker] to structure the class of occurrences which is associated with a particular notion [e.g.: all the militants who may be regarded as nationalists make up the notion of /nationalist/. All those occurrences [i.e. actual people advocating nationalism] make up the corresponding domain. The notional domain is organized around an occurrence which serves as a reference, a prototypical occurrence, which is called the organizing centre [your ideal/perfect nationalist / psychopath / terrorist you name it, with all the adequate features of what such a creature should involve]. The notional domain is divided into three zones:
>
> - An interior, made up of occurrences entering into a relation of identification with the organizing center, therefore possessing all of the properties that constitute the notion.
> - An exterior, which is in a relation of disconnection with the organizing center, and therefore has none of the properties of that center.
> - Lastly a boundary (or frontier), a hybrid zone containing occurrences having properties both of the interior and the exterior and entering into a relation of differentiation with the organizing center.

---

[13] 'Notions,' as defined by French theorist Antoine Culioli, are conventionally noted between /slashes/.

In this model, which is based on mathematical topology, the exterior stands for strongly contrasting values (or 'strong otherness') and the boundary for weakly contrasting values ('weak otherness' – not really, scarcely, just enough) (adapted from Gilbert 1993, p. 69 ff; own translation and emphasis).

Braden and Kelly, while situated across from each other as regards their Irish male identity, incidentally shed light on the anomalous history of partition and sectarian division in Northern Ireland. In our corpus, these boundaries take on various forms, such as the divide between communities, denominations, social classes, political parties, sexual orientations, genders, accents, nationalities, personal aesthetics. Culioli's Theory of Enunciative Operations allows us to deconstruct the stereotypical binaries that underpin *Weltanschauungen* in general –and the Troubles in particular– by achieving the visualization of identity-dynamic reverse-engineering of representations. His famous gradient featuring the variable presence of a given property noted p inherent in a subject, or its opposite, as shown in the following diagram:

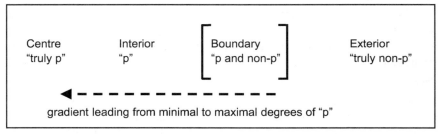

Source: Ranger 2018, p. 31

Recently, there has been a plethora of books treating of the *Irish border* and its legacy of schizoid intractable binaries opposing an allegedly hard border to a soft one. Let us mention in passing: Dermot Ferriter's *The Border: The Legacy of a Century of Anglo-Irish Politics* (2019), Cormac Moore's *Birth of the Border: The Impact of Partition in Ireland* (2019), Ivan Gibbons'*Drawing the Line: The Irish Border in British Politics* (2019), Richard Humphry's *Beyond the Border: The Good Friday Agreement and Irish Unity after Brexit* (2018), Donnacha Ó Beacháin's *From Partition to Brexit The Irish Government and Northern Ireland* (2018), Henry Patterson's *Ireland's Violent Frontier The Border and Anglo-Irish Relations During the Troubles* (2013), Patrick Mulroe's *Bombs, Bullets and the Border: Ireland's Frontier: Irish Security Policy, 1969–1978* (2017).

This should not lessen the importance of these older contributions to the same topic, elaborating on the same imaginary line dividing the Irish landscape: Colm Toibin's autofictional *Bad Blood: A Walk Along the Irish Border* (2001) or its more recent counterpart by Garrett Carr: *The Rule of the Land: Walking Ireland's*

Border (2017). More broadly, the border is a recurring central theme in contemporary Irish literature of all kinds and genres, from James Gordon Farrell's posthumously acclaimed *Troubles* (1970), which was retrospectively awarded the Lost Man Booker Prize in 2010 and narrates the genesis of the border to Brian McGilloway's compelling and dark thriller *Borderlands* (2008). The question lying at the heart of all these artistic works – be they poetic, visual, fictional, autobiographical – is how the existence of a border may be viewed either as unnatural (that is Patrick Braden's viewpoint) or vital (i. e. Victor Kelly's opinion).

"What's in a name?"

Victor Kelly in *Resurrection Man* is a violent, bloodthirsty, paramilitary Protestant activist living in Shankill, the political heart of Northern Irish unionism. He thinks of himself as a British fighter. He is represented as stereotypically heterosexual, brutal and hellbent on revenge. Whereas Patrick Pussy Braden is a sweet-mannered Catholic transvestite living in the imaginary border town of Tyreelin, situated in the Republic. Pat craves acceptance and an actual sense of belonging. He couldn't care less about politics though he cannot escape the Troubles and keeps being chased by all the protagonists of the conflict. He is overtly gay. These two protagonists doubtless embody – rather steeply at that –, the stereotypical symbolic dyad opposing female and male agents in trite representations of colonization. Usually in imperialist discourses, male figures (here Victor, the Protestant Northerner) are described as powerful conquerors whereas the natives or colonized are portrayed through feminine, female or effeminate bodies – Patrick Pussy Braden satirizes that conservative viewpoint on gender roles by being overtly, flamboyantly gay *and simultaneously* a stubborn rebel against all conventions.

Edward Said elaborated on this trope, typical of the 19th century, in his 1978 book entitled *Orientalism*. The very same trope of colonialism as rape "in which colonized territory is rendered dubiously coterminous with the stereotype of a precultural and female geography" was also perfectly explained by scholars like Sara Suleri (1992, p. 16). In our corpus, these two diametrically opposed protagonists take the representation of postcolonial Ireland to an allegorical level, which both solidifies and satirizes stereotypes through their extreme treatment of identity narratives.

Tropes and protagonists in our corpus on screen and paper navigate Culioli's gradient from their own archetypal 'organizing center' to unexpected borderline figures. The hypothesis that our two protagonists should be interpreted as archetypes verging on deliberate stereotypes is borne out by their names. 'Victor' here ironically refers to conquest and 'victory', whose most famous local manifestation dates back to William of Orange (see McNamee 1994, p. 65) and the 1690 battle of the Boyne for Unionists, while Patrick obviously refers to the homonymous 5th century AD Christian Saint who supposedly founded Ireland after being held captive by pirates and sold as a slave. Here language and literature both process and deconstruct these two figures to re-position them in the pivotal decade that the 1990s were. The die-hard loyalist turns into a conservative monstrous fantastic Dracula-like murderer while the queer would-be IRA activist becomes an ambiguous revolutionary fairy-tale creature and destabilizing cross-dresser. Play upon the characters' notional gender is mirrored through the transgression of usual literary genre boundaries. Displacing such classical boundaries – from crime fiction and Gothic tales or vampire stories to love stories, Bildungsroman/apprenticeship narratives, historical novels, thrillers, etc. allows writers and directors to dissect the fractured collective psyche informing the Troubles.

Neil Jordan analyses his movie emphasizing its joyous parabolic dimension:

> How does somebody survive a deeply aggressive world just by being himself? [...] In making the film, I wanted to turn it into a fairy tale, the fairy tale that the central character, Patrick, manages to create out of his own harsh life. As Pat McCabe and I worked on refining the script, in the back of my mind all the time was *Candide*. [Voltaire's fable of an eternal optimist who maintains that he lives in the 'best of all possible worlds' even as ruin and mayhem envelop him].
> Through this insane insistence on seeing the world as a beautiful place, Patrick never really loses even when he loses everything.
> [...]
> [To Jordan, despite all the tumult of Patrick's life, *Breakfast on Pluto* is darkly funny.] The events of the film are like tragedy, but the central character turns it into a comic reality. [...] It's a thing that comes out of the Irish storytelling tradition (https://www.sonyclassics.com/breakfastonpluto/breakfastonpluto.pdf).

As Jordan says, McCabe's work insists on the beauty of the world, even in the middle of the cruelest show of violence. *Breakfast on Pluto* ends up being a variation on the usual initiatory journey of an orphan who comes across villains. As Guillermo Iglesias-Díaz explains, this is done in a luminous though somewhat oddball manner:

> [F]antasy plays such a pivotal role in *Breakfast on Pluto* that the film could be considered a sort of fairy tale, especially as we listen to Kitten starting her narration, laying bare the traits of this popular genre: while she is walking a baby in a pushchair, the baby becomes her audience, as is usually the case with fairy tales, and two little robins will act as Kitten's help to co-narrate these first moments in the film. With the subtitles to translate their conversation, Jordan includes another generic twist, playing with the realistic convention inside this fantastic tale: subtitles are provided so that we can understand the little birds and have access to, as Kitten says, 'every secret behind every lace-curtain window.' As we follow their flight, we hear Kitten's voice starting her tale: 'I was born in a small town near the Irish border' (Guillermo Iglesias-Díaz 2022, p. 79).

Guillermo Iglesias-Díaz goes on to explain that Braden literally comes from the margins of his national community. Funnily enough, the viewers are then shown the church tower full of pigeon excrement, which is a first clue of Braden's problematic relationship with the foundations of his own national/notional 'Catholic' identity. The 'once upon a time' fairy tale codes are recycled here to warn the viewer/reader that any life-narrative put to paper or screen has to be taken with a pinch of salt. Identity narratives remain mere constructs to be criticized first by calling out unreliable narrators.

As opposed to this pastiche fairytale approach chosen by McCabe/Jordan, where Patrick Braden embodies Eros, one finds McNamee's grim, factional hybrid Gothic thriller. Billy Gray aptly reminds us McNamee's metafictional approach proves to be challenging to translate onto the screen:

> Both McNamee's fictional remediation of the Shankill Butchers' story and the subsequent cinematic adaptation of the novel – scripted by McNamee himself – initially received a somewhat mixed critical response. Admirers of the novel praised the manner in which it avoided the undesirable designation of "Troubles Trash", thereby *destabilizing the crass stereotyping* that has frequently bedeviled fictional representations of the Northern Irish conflict (Magennis 2010: 66). Others have commented positively on the text's use of metafictionality and admire the way it attempts to problematize the crisis of novelistic representation through the use of a self-conscious reflexivity, overt stylization and innovative *generic hybridity*. Dermot McCarthy, for example, has praised McNamee's attempt to examine the world of sectarian violence through post-structuralist tropes such as the *'decentered self'* and the crisis of signification (2000, p. 134).

The two movies also similarly deal with problematic origins. *Resurrection Man* relates the story of Victor Kelly, the leader of an Ulster Volunteer Force[14] unit in East Belfast – inspired from Lenny Murphy, a real paramilitary UVF Loyalist who led a group of men known as the Shankill Butchers. Murphy – in real life – became notorious for the kidnapping, torturing and murdering of randomly selected Catholic civilians between 1975 and 1977. Overall, 23 people[15] – including Protestants who disagreed with Murphy's methods or behavior – are known to

---

14 Parallel to the IRA on the mostly Catholic Republican side, the largely Protestant Ulster Volunteer Force (UVF) is an Ulster loyalist paramilitary group, which emerged in 1966 a couple of years before the period known as the Troubles even actually began. Its first leader was a former British soldier called Gusty Spence [1933–2011] who was one of the very first Loyalists convicted of murder. The UVF started a vicious armed campaign which lasted over three decades. Though it declared a ceasefire as early as 1994 and officially ended its so-called military campaign in 2007, a large number of its activists and members have continued to engage in and promote violence and criminal activities in the Six Counties. Today, as of 2020, this paramilitary organization is still classified as a terrorist group by the UK, the Republic of Ireland, and the USA.
15 For further details on each death, see https://cain.ulster.ac.uk/sutton/chron/index.html.

have been slain by the gang. These unfortunate victims were invariably subjected to paroxysmic sadistic violence, enacted principally through the extensive use of sharpened butcher's knives, hence their sinister name as a gang. A good instance of this Freudian death drive is to be found right from the start of Victor Kelly's gloomy career:

> Before he formed his own unit Victor sat in on several killings. In one they picked up a Catholic on the Springfield Road in a hijacked black taxi. He got *a bit of a digging* in the back and was moaning by the time they got him to a lock-up garage off the Shankill. They carried him inside. There was an acetylene torch in the corner of the garage. A battery leaked acid on to the floor. Victor wore a blue boiler suit and carried a shortblade knife that he'd got in the Army and Navy stores. There was a smell of butane in the air, a sense of limits reached.
>
> The body was found in a shop doorway on Berlin Street. *There were 124 careful knife wounds on the body.* Death was due to slow strangulation. The victim appeared to have been suspended from a beam while he was being stabbed (McNamee 1994, p. 17; own emphasis).[16]

Rather realistically in the movie or the book, Lenny Murphy is seen to have a psychopathic domineering personality (expressed through its fictional counterpart "Victor"), that leads him to indulge in extreme homicidal behavior. Martin Dillon documents this in detail in his journalistic investigation on the Shankill Butchers, which he presented under the form of a book, first published in 1989 (Dillon 1990). Kelly kills without the slightest suggestion of remorse. His pathological behavior is intimately linked to complexes concerning his own dubious heritage or insecure sense of identity. His father is commonly suspected of being 'a Fenian' or a *Taig* (a derogatory word in Hiberno-English for 'Catholic') because of his Catholic-sounding surname 'Kelly': "[There are] Rumours that your da's a Fenian, member of the Roman Catholic persuasion" (McNamee 1994, p. 105).

Victor's behavior is therefore marked by *Thanatos* or death drive. It echoes a deep fear of the return of the repressed (see Freud 1995, p. 28f), in the sense that his name might betray some interbreeding, some taboo intercourse between his ancestors that he refuses to consider. "Bearing the name of Kelly meant that he was always suspected of being a Catholic" (McNamee 1994, p. 4). A minor character, a tramp called Smiley, puts it simply: "I know you [...] for the bastard son of a bastard Catholic by the name of Kelly" (McNamee 1994, p. 201). Therefore Kelly keeps wanting to prove that he is immaculately Protestant, and has nothing to do with Catholics, whom he plainly hates like so many other loyalists whose speeches on 'popery' verge on full-blown paranoid prejudice:

---

16 Note the contradiction between the euphemism "a bit of a digging" and the final horror: "124 *careful* knife wounds".

"Catholics were plotters, heretics, casual betrayers" (McNamee 1994, p. 9). Yet the same Loyalists are reluctant to acknowledge their own fragmented identities, ranging from Free Presbyterians to Pentecostalists, as this excerpt shows:

> Afterwards he would go down to the Cornmarket to listen to the preachers and their recital of sectarian histories. They were thin men dressed in black with ravaged faces. They predicted famine and spoke in tongues. Their eyes seemed displaced in time. They would eat sparsely, sleep on boards, dream in monochrome. There was a network of small congregations and merciless theologies throughout the city. Congregations of the wrathful. Baptist. Free Presbyterian, Lutheran, Wesleyan, Church of Latter-day Saints, Seventh Day Adventists, Quakerism, Covenanters, Salvationists, Buchmanites. Pentecostalists. Tin gospel halls on the edges of the shipyard were booked by visiting preachers for months in advance. Bible texts were carefully painted on gable walls. Victor listened to their talk of Catholics. *The whore of Rome. There were barbarous rites, martyrs racked in pain. The Pope's cells were plastered with the gore of delicate Protestant women. Catholics were plotters, heretics, casual betrayers* (McNamee 1994, p. 9; own emphasis).

Kelly's name keeps nagging at him. It reminds him his own family story might not be that simple altogether. It urges him to do something to compensate for that tainted loathsome identity revealed by his odd-sounding name (by his own racist standards). Therefore, he finally does so by literally attempting to get rid of *real* Catholics in the *real* world, by simply killing them. This element of perverted onomastics suffices to make him a *notional* outsider within his own national community, having him cross the boundary between sectarian identities in the 'wrong' direction. As Dillon further explains:

> Lenny Murphy was a belligerent child and by the time he was ten years old he was threatening other children and removing their pocket money from them at knifepoint. [...] He is remembered by a classmate as follows: We all called him Mick because we believed he was a '*Taig*'. With a name like Hugh Murphy there was little doubt. He never called himself 'Hughie' as most kids would have done because *Hughie Murphy would have certainly made him a Catholic.* [...] He was a tough wee nut [...]. He wasn't particularly bright. Another thing that struck me was that he never talked about his father [...]. He was devious (Dillon 1990, p. 5; own emphasis).

Interestingly, this quote underscores the essentially linguistic dimension of identity construction, especially in Northern Ireland. Mere names can make you a Protestant or a Catholic to the public eye. It is enough to sell you out: "Hughie Murphy would have certainly made him a Catholic." This scarily short-sighted, arbitrary construction of sectarian violence –summarized by Shakespeare in his famous 'What's in a name?' cue[17] – makes the novel oddly gripping, not through actual events but rather through words and their disturbing distance from reality.

---

17 As Shakespeare shows in *Romeo and Juliet* (II, 2, l. 45f), what someone or something is called

Deconstructing images of hatred

Curiously, the whole movie scripted by McNamee and shot by Evans, though darkly lyrical it may be from time to time, always sticks to facts and a rather predictable visual style, which eludes that linguistic confusion, fierce metafictional irony and decentered-self approach praised by Billy Gray. One exception though – and one of the few noteworthy instances of the reflexive play originally meant by McNamee in the book – may be found in the soundtrack towards the end of the film, when Victor is eventually cold-bloodedly shot dead and eliminated by the British special services and the IRA. An extract from Act II, scene 2 entitled 'La Vergine Degli Angeli' from Giuseppe Verdi's opera *La Forza Del Destino* (*The Force of Destiny*, 1862) is played in the background to render the ironic reflexive narratorial effect produced by the parody – not pastiche this time – of the *mater dolorosa* motif in the final description in the book. That's the moment when Dorcas –Victor Kelly's mother – actually makes up the fake story showing herself kneeling down beside her dead son's body while in fact, she was never allowed to have direct access to her son's corpse. She actually learned about her son's death watching TV:

> *She had not been allowed past the incident tape.* In the distance she could see soldiers standing beside a Land- Rover. Victor's body lay on the pavement, his face turned away. His jacket was pulled up exposing his back so that she wanted to pull it down for him. *Later that night when she turned on the television news she felt as if she was watching something old-fashioned.* Archive footage of an eerie killing; a slum murder. [...] She told him how she had knelt beside her son's body in the street until the police arrived (McNamee 1994, p. 231).

This juxtaposition emphasizes yet again the chasm opposing lyrical discursive clichéd representations to sordid callous facts. The reference, in Verdi's opera, is obvious and underlines the action of fate when reality looks more like sheer neurosis as regards Kelly's final 'fate' and demise. Throughout the book and the film, Victor strives to escape his overwhelming sense of 'lack,'[18] or uncertain identity, by committing heinous acts of extreme violence against a religiously defined *Other*, supposedly to be found in the exterior of his own Loyalist Prot-

---

or labeled – e. g., 'Montague' or 'Capulet', 'Murphy' or 'Johnson' – is arbitrary compared to their, or its, intrinsic qualities. In Shakespeare's 1597 play, Juliet Capulet bemoans Romeo's last name of Montague, her family's sworn enemies: "What's in a name? That which we call a rose /By any other name would smell as sweet." McNamee captures that shallow bigoted dynamics of the Troubles based on nametags.

18 The leitmotiv of *lacking* is hammered throughout the novel and its diverse characters – see McNamee 1994, p. 17, 20, 48, 55, 72, 86, 89, 108, 111, 108, 120, 166, 194, 207, 214 etc. – making the whole novel and film insist on what is not there, some sense of frustration whilst *Breakfast on Pluto* is conversely about acceptance.

estant notional field. His wild uncontrollable predisposition for frantic violence (or his extremist reading of Unionism) eventually isolates him within his own paramilitary group. His own community gradually comes to view him as an undesirable element. So much so that he is eventually done away with by paramilitary rivals working in collusion with prominent members of the British Special Branch. The problem remains that while the novel's language is elaborately reflexive and shows the delusional erratic nature of Kelly's acts through sophisticated tropes, the film slowly turns into a voyeuristic ultra-violent B-movie. It is probably difficult to adapt a metafictional novel relying on cinematic tropes into a film. Something is lost in the translation into the very medium which was supposed to be ironically mimicked – namely the gangster movies mentioned in the book – to assert the distance between Kelly's wild immature ego and its trite representations and foul consequences. For instance, in the film, how do you render an original simile phrased like this in the novel: "Victor Kelly felt an expression cross his face like in a film" (McNamee 1994, p. 230)? The de-centered self-perspective associated with the problematic film-within-the-film formidable tropes probably proved too big a challenge for Mark Evans.

In *Breakfast on Pluto* (the film), Jordan's hero, Patrick *Pussy* Braden shares with Victor Kelly – in addition to an inadequate name (the obstreperous trivial 'Pussy' echoing the awkward – by loyalist standards – Catholic-sounding 'Kelly') a problematic father, since Patrick's father is indeed a Catholic priest played by Liam Neeson. His real mother has simply abandoned him. The whole movie describes Patrick's quest for her. This leads him to London, a place that is rife with terrorist attacks and bombings planned by the IRA in the 1970s and early 1980s. McCabe's narrator sums up the narrative arc as follows, in his prelude to the novel:

> 1922; *a geographical border drawn by a drunken man*, every bit as tremulous and deceptive as the one which *borders* life and death. Dysfunctional double-bind of *border*-fever, *mapping out* the universe into which Mr Patrick Braden, now some years later found himself tumbled. Distracted by the bombs and bullets, *eviscerations*, nightly slaughter. And ultimately deciding to devote his life to a cause and one alone. That of ending, once and for all, this ugly state of perennial limbo. To finding – finally, and for us all! – a *map* which might lead him to that *place* called home. Where *all borders* will ultimately vanish and *perfume* through Tyreelin Valley, not come sweetly drifting. [...] an end to abandonment rage and lust for vengeance, through a terrorized London [...]. Such are the dreams of Paddy Pussy, transvestite prostitute (MacCabe 1998, p. xf, own emphasis).

In the passage above, the twofold isotopy of place and borders unwittingly underscores how much each film represents each complementary or antagonistic view or series of *topoi* in the conflict: "evisceration" vs "perfume". In *Resurrection Man*, Belfast is patrolled by British paratroopers as if the city's form and structure were "untrustworthy, possessed of a dubious topography which required constant surveillance" (McNamee 1994, p. 84).

In that respect, the beginning of each movie sheds light on that symmetrical construction. After watching the two opening sequences[19] closely, two clear-cut opposite sets of "markers" and linguistic "operators", to quote from Culioli, may be spotted. The following table aims to summarize the whole set of binaries observable in each film:

Table 1

Breakfast on Pluto (2005)	*Resurrection Man* (1998)
1. Set in the Republic (South)	1. Set in the Six Counties (Northern Ireland)
2. Imaginary characters and plot	2. Characters and plot based on fact/real history
3. Presence of communal markers (the Catholic church, its steeple, the village, crowds, marches and demonstrations)	3. Fragmentation of the community. Only streets, rooms or individuals are shown.
4. Essentially a *1st person narrative:* Patrick is the one who tells the story of his life. In the movie, this translates into loads of monologues and the systematic use of voiceover.	4. Essentially a *3rd person narrative*. Victor's life is obliquely narrated, accounted for by others –his mother, journalists, accomplices, policemen, Special Branch agents etc.
5. A charismatic but absent illegitimate father (a Catholic priest played by Liam Neeson)	5. A dull but present legitimate father (a Protestant layman played by obscure actor George Shane)
6. A glib, talkative, flamboyant protagonist	6. A silent, taciturn protagonist
7. An absent but kind mother	7. An overbearing castrating dour mother
8. Cartoonesque special effects (e.g. the colourful robins inserted in the opening sequence reminiscent of Walt Disney's *Bambi*, 1942)	8. Noirish aesthetics, drab and dull colours, typical of 1950s gangster movies such as John Huston's 1950 *Asphalt Jungle*.
9. Bright hot colours (pink, purple etc.)	9. Prevailing cold dark colours (black, gray, blue…)
10. Blue sky	10. Overcast, grey sky
11. Prevailing wide shots and tracking shots: openness and movement.	11. Prevailing close-ups, if a tracking shot is used, more often than not its movement is made up for by slow-motion
12. Homely elements in the setting: the kitchen, the bottles of milk, the vision of the village and community as a whole in wide shots.	12. Impersonal setting: a dead-end street, a garage mechanic's, a basement, a prison cell…
13. Open air perspectives	13. Stifling closed spaces
14. Stereotypically gay and/or effeminate elements/props: dresses, a pram, high-heels, makeup, lipstick etc.	14. Stereotypically manly or "tough guy" props: leather jackets, tools, strong alcohol, blades and guns, cigarettes held in cupped hands or between middle knuckles instead of fingertips
15. Milk	15. Blood

---

19 See extracts from *Resurrection Man* (the film) 00:40 to 03:32 and then 04:00 to 05: 50 m and *Breakfast On Pluto* (the film) 00:30 to 3:30 m and 04:28 to 05:15 m.

Table 1 *(Continued)*

Breakfast on Pluto (2005)	***Resurrection Man*** (1998)
16. A deliberately vintage mawkish soundtrack: *Sugar babylove* by the Rubettes (1974)	16. A gloomy/sinister soundtrack made up by tolling bells and the martial-like telegraphic sounding credits reminiscent of a hail of bullets shot by a sub-machinegun.

All these elements point to opposite sections of the notional domain of /Irishness/, where tropes are so many divergent locating operators that contextualize two antithetical visions of the 'Troubles.'

Violence through razor sharp boundaries is the option encapsulated by *Resurrection Man*, while peace, inclusion and the blurring of the very same borders is the agenda promoted by Jordan, echoing MacCabe's aesthetic project "Where *all borders* will ultimately vanish and perfume through Tyreelin Valley". The notion of crossing, bridging, suppressing the border is omnipresent in the original book *Breakfast on Pluto* (MacCabe 1998, p. 7, 18, 53, 82, 158, 160). All politicians talk about getting into a lorry to drive across the border to take over the North. On page 82, the border is only mentioned for Irwin to cross it. Pussy Braden's old classmate Pat McGrane crosses the border to visit his girlfriend (MacCabe 1998, p. 53, 158, 160). In a word, McCabe deals with the border as something that must be transgressed or ignored so as to reunite individuals.

In *Resurrection Man*, it is the opposite idea of clear-cut impassable limits that is underscored. Catholic refugees camp at the border but do not dare enter loyalist territory to find shelter.

> It was around then that Victor started to see the first graffiti appearing in the derelict Catholic streets that had been burnt out before the army were sent in. The television had shown the occupants camped at the border fifty miles away, living in tents. The parents in food queues advancing shabbily. He was impressed by the graffiti. It was a rumour of approval in the narrow streets. Resurrection Men 1. Taigs 0. It confirmed that he was on the right track. It was the first sign of a legend taking shape, a dark freight in the soul of the city (McNamee 1994, p. 133).

The whole world of the Six Counties is construed by the narratorial voice as based on the very notion of separation, alienation, brutal fragmentation. Lines and boundaries are not to be tampered with. They indicate whole districts that are to be demolished or isolated, as in the following passage imbued with an aesthetics of division, havoc and constraint: "There were lines on the map too, indicating rivers, areas which had been demolished, suggested escape routes following a bomb, zones of conflict, boundaries, divisions within the heart" (McNamee 1994, p. 13).

Urban geography is marked by an isotopy of discord and obliteration: "Burnt-out streets, divided streets, memorial streets" (McNamee 1994, p. 220). Belfast

City is crisscrossed with "one hundred and sixty-four checkpoints" (McNamee 1994, p. 19). This geography – that stands as the equivalent for Culioli's exterior field to the notion as explained by Graham Ranger[20] – which has been linguistically built and internalized by the narrator here, is one of strict exclusion. Between two killings, Victor Kelly is shown driving his car along invisible but powerful borders again:

> He was driving carefully along the *edges* of Catholic West Belfast. She [Heather, his girlfriend] had never been this close before although she had seen these places on television. Ballymurphy, Andestown. The Falls. Names resonant with *exclusion*. Now they were circling the *boundaries*, close enough to set foot in them. Victor drove up into the foothills until they were looking down on the west of the city, its densely populated and mythic new estates, something you didn't quite believe in (McNamee 1994, p. 45, own emphasis).

Again, names are important identity markers of the same rejection and ostracism. Ballymurphy and Anderstown sound irretrievably Catholic or Republican to Kelly's ears.

Towards a postmodernist aesthetics of derealization

The boundaries between communities in Northern Ireland are so rigid in McNamee's work that they look like monumental geological rifts or even mythical entities from a world beyond reality: "mythic new estates, something you didn't quite believe in" (McNamee 1994, p. 45). These metaphors, based on disbelief, also echo back to the derealization Victor Kelly suffers due to his hatred and alienation. The experience of derealization separates a person from the outside world that they perceive as lacking vividness or emotional coloring. The following definition proves adequate to describe his behavior:

> Derealization […] is experienced as the sense that the external world is strange or unreal. The individual may perceive an uncanny alteration in the size or shape of objects (macropsia or micropsia), and people may seem unfamiliar or mechanical. Other common associated features include anxiety symptoms, depressive symptoms, obsessive rumination, somatic concerns, and a disturbance in one's sense of time, [i]n some cases, […] loss of feeling(American Psychiatric Association 2004, p. 488).

---

20 On the notion of geography seen as complex topology related to the notion of belief, see: "Central to linguistic activity is the operation of categorization, as speakers seek to match prelinguistic, cognitive representations (or, *what a subject means*) and linguistic representations (*how to say it*). This is presented within the Theory of Enunciative Operations as an operation whereby occurrences are situated relative to a complex topological space called a *notional domain*" (Ranger 2011, p. 8).

The narratorial trick to underscore this twofold phenomenon of derealization and fragmentation is to show characters from East Belfast who find it hard to believe in the existence of West Belfast, which verges on lunacy to the average reader. To Kelly, you do not "quite believe in" the existence of Catholic neighborhoods. Even if it takes only five minutes to drive from Shankill Road to the Falls, Heather has never set foot inside the Catholic districts and has only seen them on TV, where you might as well see pictures in the news from Canada or Papua New Guinea. Defamiliarization is also a technique used by McNamee to show how repression works. It is achieved through the postmodernist insertion of images (whether from TV or moving pictures) presented as fantasies whose ontological status remains ambiguous within the fiction. Ricœur's concept of split metaphors (See Ricœur 1978, p. 143ff)[21] again helps to account for the disjunctive potential of images both referring to reality and to radically new imaginary contents at the same time. Precisely due to that ambivalent, reversible power of pictures (of dread or desire), there are tropes and motifs, which are strictly identical in both movies, especially the very *mise-en-abyme* of screens and cinema in both films.

Revealingly, it is James Cagney, the Irish American actor (1899–1986) who played the tough guy in *Public Enemy* (1931), who features prominently in *Resurrection Man* whereas it is Mitzi Gaynor (born in 1931), the famous US actress and dancer in *South Pacific* (1954), who acts as a role-model in *Breakfast on Pluto*. Yet unexpectedly, the similar trope of the movie within the movie ultimately reinforces the contrast between the two films. While Patrick Braden fantasizes about an absent mother whom he imagines, looks like Hollywood star Mitzi Gaynor and aspires himself to look like her,[22] Victor Kelly is introduced as a James Cagney wannabe. This is achieved in a seminal scene where the projection room Victor visits as a child with his father, is described in terms reminiscent of the womb, a world in limbo where you are not affected by the outside world and gain access to your most secret desires. His father introduces him to that world of phantoms and shadows on the screen in an old cinema called the Apollo –whose ironic mythological subtext, conveyed by the name 'Apollo,' will not be lost on the reader:

> Once he took Victor up to the projection room during the matinee at the Apollo cinema on the Shankill Road. The projectionist was Chalky White who had been to school with

---

21 To Ricœur, metaphor theory posits "a problem arising on the boundary between a semantic theory of metaphor and a psychological theory of imagination and feeling. By a semantic theory, I mean an inquiry into the capacity of metaphor to provide untranslatable information and, accordingly, into metaphor's claim to yield some true insight about reality [meaning having informative value]" (1978, p. 143).

22 The whole 199-page-long novel is peppered with mentions of Mitzi Gaynor, p. 8, 23, 69 (twice in the same page), 74, 122, 177, 199.

James. Chalky was six feet tall, stooped, with carbon residue from the lamps in his hair and his moustache. There were two big Peerless projectors with asbestos chimneys leading into the ceiling. There were aluminum film canisters on the floor and long Bakelite fuseboxes on the wall. The air smelt of phosphorous, chemical fire.
Chalky showed Victor a long white scar on his arm where he had accidentally touched the hot casing.
'Laid it open to the bone', Chalky said. He showed Victor the slit in the wall where the projectionist could watch the picture. He talked about film stars he admired. Marion Nixon, Olive Brook. Victor liked Edward G. Robinson and James Cagney in Public Enemy. *When he looked through the slit he could see Laurence Tierney as John Dillinger laid out on a morgue slab like a specimen of extinction.* [...] After the Apollo Victor worked hard at getting the gangster walk right. It was a combination of lethal movements and unexpected half-looks. An awareness of G-men (McNamee 1994, p. 5, own emphasis).

This excerpt works like a Freudian primal scene (see Freud 1975, p. 62, 92)[23] which is both proleptic and prophetic. It allows Victor to see through a slit in the dark, from a hot room, a confusing though precise violent image of what he aspires to be and will eventually turn into, as an adult: a bloodthirsty criminal, a delusional 'public enemy' who strangely feeds upon frustration, narcissism and a thwarted craving for grandeur and belonging. The scene is allegorical. The message is conveyed through a cogent motif, as is often the case with McNamee. In *The Ultras*, another faction by McNamee, the eye motif is introduced right from the start of the book –through a scene of dissection performed by the protagonist's father, who happens to be an eye-surgeon. It hints at Robert Nairac's future fatal career as a British spy (McNamee 2004, p. 6f). In *Resurrection Man*, this delusional voyeuristic death drive will lead Victor to his loss, as the projectionist explains in the Apollo scene: getting too close to the whole apparatus allowing for the shadows to appear on screen "laid it open to the bone," meaning excruciating pain and fatal retribution. In a word, 'trouble' and frustration are all Victor will ever get by identifying with screen chimeras or elusive gangster figures. His final death is a ferocious anticlimactic scene he cannot watch or anticipate: "He did not see one of the men leave cover and walk over to him and put his foot in his neck and shoot him through the back of the head with a snub-nose revolver. There were no words, got him at last. No last rueful gangster smile, goodbye world" (McNamee 1994, p. 230).

This wry cinematic motif also lays bare the tenets of both books and movies as suggested previously through McHale's postmodernist ontological readings. Both adopt and share a relativistic postmodernist stance as regards truth and

---

[23] To Freud, the expression 'primal scene' refers to the sight of sexual relations between the parents, as observed, constructed, or fantasized by the child and interpreted by the child as a scene of violence.

History as Linda Hutcheon aptly analyzed in *A Poetics of Postmodernism: History, Theory, Fiction:*

> In the nineteenth century, at least before the rise of Ranke's 'scientific history,'[24] literature and history were considered branches of the same tree of learning [...]. Then came the separation that resulted in the distinct disciplines of literary and historical studies today [...]. However, it is this very separation of the literary and the historical that is now being challenged in postmodern theory and art, and recent critical readings of both history and fiction have focused more on what the two modes of writing share than on how they differ. They have both been seen to derive their force more from verisimilitude than from any objective truth; *they are both identified as linguistic constructs, highly conventionalized in their narrative forms, and not at all transparent either in terms of language or structure; and they appear to be equally intertextual, deploying the texts of the past within their own complex textuality* (Hutcheon 1989, p. 105f, own emphasis).

The idea that truth and History are "linguistic constructs" – similar in essence to Culioli's reversible enunciative notions – is crucial to understand both *Breakfast on Pluto* and *Resurrection Man*. According to Paul Ricœur, "Narrative identity takes part in the story's movement – or History's movement at that – in the dialectic between order and disorder" (Ricœur 1996, p. 6 [translation modified 'movement' instead of 'mobility']).

That construction can be made either to heal or divide. McCabe and McNamee offer two narratives for Northern Ireland. The latter heads towards aporia and historical nostalgia for the dead British Empire of the colonial era: "By day the city seemed ancient and ambiguous. Its power was dissipated by exposure to daylight. It looked derelict and colonial. There was a sense of curfew, produce rotting in the market-place" (McNamee 1994, p. 16). The other vision by McCabe points towards reconciliation, the merger or suppression of the very same barriers between clans, tribes, groups, denominations constitutive of the composite notion of Irishness.

Through their complex handling of a double temporality (that of personal childhood and the broader timeline of the Troubles through numerous flashbacks), these two stories show to what extent the strategy according to which that narration is plotted – to borrow the notion of emplotment[25] from Ricœur again – determines a logic of hatred/restriction or appeasement. The two narratives

---

24 Leopold von Ranke (1795–1886) was a German historian, considered one of the founders of modern source-based history. He set the standards for much of later historical writing, introducing such ideas as reliance on primary sources (Empiricism), an emphasis on narrative history and international politics (*Aussenpolitik*).

25 This is what Ricœur says about characters, events and the sense that can be derived from stories: "Th[e] function of emplotment relies on a framework of rules within which the intelligibility resides, and as a consequence we may speak of a schematism of the narrative function" (Ricœur 1990, p. 68).

problematize what Culioli calls a "gradient orientation."²⁶ In other words, each story embodies a notional pointing movement that either crosses the notional boundary towards otherness and peace (in McCabe's work) or bounces back onto obsessive neurotic sameness (in McNamee's).

A conclusion beyond notional and national binaries

To conclude, it makes sense that the main protagonist in *Breakfast on Pluto* should be a transgender person and that so many gates, doors, windows, thresholds should be passed or opened in the book and its screen adaptation. The whole idea of a border having to be crossed or even transgressed is brought forward in the prelude written by McCabe – to him "all borders will ultimately vanish" (1999, p. xi). Doors are constantly opened in the novel (over thirty times in less than 200 pages). Visually, this is rendered through the recurring motif of closed spaces – houses, confessionals, cars, backstage rooms, peepshow cubicles, prison cells, stifling suits, IRA caches – being abandoned and left behind. Far from being Manichean narratives *per se* though, these two novels actually emplot the ambivalent possibilities of the *Zeitgeist* towards the very end of the Troubles in the 1990s, at a moment which can be characterized retrospectively as a tipping point.

The Troubles were typified, right from the start in 1968, by an increasingly restrictive reference to a sectarian definition of belonging in both communities. That is what gives the dualistic nature inherent in all periods of conflict, imposing a simplistic often zealous binary of 'us against them.' This is potentially illustrated through a multifarious range of oppositions which are so many oversimplifications and generalizations: 'Catholics vs Protestants,' 'Nationalists vs Loyalists,' 'Republicans vs Unionists,' 'proletarians vs middle-class people,' 'colonies vs Empire,' 'North vs South,' 'Celtic vs Saxon,' 'Dublin vs London,' 'West Belfast vs East Belfast,' 'Eire vs Britain,' 'Gaelic vs English,' 'hurling vs Cricket', etc.

Another final difference consists in the immediate context of production or collective narration. To quote from Culioli's theory yet again, what matters is the situation proper and the moment in history when the enunciation of those identities takes place. This situation is defined by the year when each book was written or *emplotted*: 1993–1994 for McNamee's noirish metafiction versus 1998

---

26 For further information on this point, see Culioli 1995, p. 60, e. g., "[…] when we construct our gradient, one direction is headed towards a less and less strong (or a weaker and weaker) degree [of a given quality or typicality of a given entity] up to a posited last, imaginary, point" (1995, p. 60f).

for McCabe's eccentric fairy-tale pastiche. This year of creation is a crucial factor that determines the form and message of each ensuing movie.

In Culioli's theory, the situation of uttering is the absolute origin of locating operations. It comprises two co-ordinates. On the one hand there is the enunciator (that is the narrator chosen by the author or the viewpoint favoured by the director). On the other hand, you find the moment of uttering – the spatio-temporal parameter – in other words the timeframe chosen in Northern Irish history from which to narrate events. In this case, the time co-ordinate proves decisive as regards the way the Troubles are construed retrospectively.

Resurrection Man was conceived while still informed by a logic of military confrontation promoted by the UVF and the IRA Provos, even if Sinn Féin was increasingly promoting a political rather than a violent solution to the Troubles.[27] On the contrary, *Breakfast on Pluto* was clearly influenced by the political agenda displayed by the Good Friday Agreement signed in Belfast on 10 April 1998. That treaty sought to end the Troubles even if, to McCabe, as shown in the beginning of Jordan's movie, peace is always a work in progress or a permanent construction site, as the tragic Omagh terrorist attack in August 1998 sadly showed.

These two movies also expose the narrativist procedures that establish History and truth, through deconstruction and metafictional or metacinematic pastiche. To McNamee in 1994, History is impersonal: "offspring to the grisly night, [a] rank, allusive narrative, […] a strange tale" (McNamee 1994, p. 233). While to McCabe, in 1998, History is an inclusive promise, as can be seen at the end of the prelude (dating back to 1999): "The war over, now perhaps *we* too can take – however tentatively – those first steps which may end unease and see *us* there; home, belonging and at peace" (McCabe 1999, p. xi).

Despite the modal markers of uncertainty, including "perhaps", "can", "may", "tentatively", it is rather apt that Jordan's movie should begin and end with the image of a baby in a pram. Evans's, on the contrary, starts with tolling bells and concludes with a final shot at night, showing the dead body of Victor Kelly sprawling on the front garden of his parents' house. The Troubles lead to a mere cul-de-sac in the latter. They give way to a *Renaissance* in the former work once the logic of denial and repression has started being deconstructed both on the ground, in hearts and speeches. In a word, the way borders are constructed and narrated have implications, which may debunk or conversely harden not just *notional* but *national* boundaries, reminding us, if needs be, that aesthetics and politics do rhyme – more often than not – with linguistics.

---

27 On this issue, see Keefe 2018.

Bibliography

American Psychiatric Association: *Diagnostic and Statistical Manual of Mental Disorders DSM-IV-TR* [Text Revision]. Washington DC 2004.

Baker, Stephen: 'Vampire Troubles: Loyalism and Resurrection Man', in: Barton, Ruth / O'BRIEN, Harvey (eds.): *Keeping it real: themes and issues in Irish film and television.* Wallflower 2004.

Biemann, Ursula: 'Performing the Border. On Gender, Transnational Bodies, and Technology', in: Sadowski-Smith, Claudia (ed.): *Globalization on the Line.* New York 2002, p. 99–119.

Boely, Christian: 'La Traduction des verbes marquant un processus avec altérité qualitative', in: Guillemin-Flescher, Jacqueline (ed.): *Contrastive Linguistics and Translation*, T.6. Paris 2002.

Breakfast on Pluto, [blurb] [https://www.sonyclassics.com/breakfastonpluto/breakfastonpluto.pdf], [24.06.2023].

'*Breakfast on Pluto* (2005) Full Cast & Crew', [https://www.imdb.com/title/tt0411195/fullcredits#cast], [24.06.2023].

Carr, Garrett: *The Rule of the Land: Walking Ireland's Border.* London 2017.

'Chronological List of Deaths', in: Conflict Archive on the INternet – cain.ulster.ac.uk, [https://cain.ulster.ac.uk/sutton/chron/index.html], [24.06.2023].

Cohen, Stanley, *States of Denial–Knowing about Atrocities and Suffering.* Cambridge 2001.

Culioli, Antoine: *Cognition and Representation in Linguistic Theory.* Amsterdam, Philadelphia 1995.

Dillon, Martin: *The Shankill Butchers* [2nd ed.]. London 1990.

Evans, Mark, *Resurrection Man*, DVD, 101 m., UCA Universal Pictures, 2004 (UK 1998).

'Faction', *The Oxford Pocket Dictionary of Current English.* Available at https://www.encyclopedia.com [13.07.2023].

Farrell, James Gordon: *Troubles.* London 1970.

Ferriter, Dermot: *The Border: The Legacy of a Century of Anglo-Irish Politics.* London 2019.

Freud, Sigmund: *Das Unbehagen in der Kultur* [1930] / McLintock, David (trans. & ed.): *Civilization and Its Discontents.* London 2002.

Freud, Sigmund: *Drei Abhandlungen zur Sexualtheorie* [1905] / Strachey, James (trans) / Marcus, Steven (ed.): *Three Essays on the Theory of Sexuality.* New York 1975, p. 62ff.

Freud, Sigmund: 'Jenseits des Lustprinzips' [1920] / Strachey, James (trans. & ed.): 'Beyond the Pleasure Principle,' in: *On Metapsychology.* London 1987.

Freud, Sigmund: *Über Psychoanalyse* [1910] / Strachey, James (trans. & ed.): *Five Lectures on Psycho-Analysis.* London 1995.

Gibbons, Ivan: *Drawing the Line: The Irish Border in British Politics.* Dublin 2019.

Gilbert, Éric: 'La théorie des Opérations Énonciatives d'Antoine Culioli', in : Cotte, Pierre & al. : *Les théories de la grammaire anglaise en France.* Paris 1993, p. 69–74.

Gray, Billy: 'A thrilling beauty'?: Violence, Transcendence and the Shankill Butchers in Eoin McNamee's *Resurrection Man.*' ESTUDIOS IRLANDESES: JOURNAL OF IRISH STUDIES 2014/9, p. 54–66.

Guillermo Iglesias-Díaz, Eugenio, 'Trans-gendering the Irish Na(rra)tion: Neil Jordan's *Breakfast on Pluto*'. Estudios Irlandeses: Journal of Irish Studies 2022/17, p. 77–89.

Hayward, Katy: 'The EU and the transformation of the Irish border', in: Ramsbotham, Alexander / Zartman, William (eds.): Accord 2011/22, special issue: *Building peace across borders*, p. 31–34.
Hughes, William / Punter, David / Smith, Andrew: *The Encyclopedia of the Gothic*. Malden (MA) & Oxford 2013.
Humphry, Richard: *Beyond the Border: The Good Friday Agreement and Irish Unity after Brexit.* Dublin 2018.
Hutcheon, Linda: *A Poetics of Postmodernism History, Theory, Fiction.* London 1989.
Jordan, Neil: *Breakfast on Pluto*, DVD, 129 m., Sony Pictures Home Entertainment 2006 (Ireland UK 2005).
Keefe, Patrick Radden: *Say Nothing: A True Story of Murder and Memory in Northern Ireland.* Croydon 2018.
Lawson, Mark: 'The King of Faction', in: *The Guardian*, 12 Nov 2007, https://www.theguardian.com/commentisfree/2007/nov/12/comment.film [24.06.2023].
McCabe, Patrick: *Breakfast on Pluto* [1998]. London 1999.
McGilloway, Brian: *Borderlands*. London 2008.
McHale, Brian: *Postmodernist Fiction*. London 1987.
McKittrick, David / Kelters, Seamus / Feeney, Brian / Thornton, Chris / McVea, David: *Lost Lives*. Edinburgh 2007.
McNamee, Eoin: *Resurrection Man*. London 1994.
McNamee, Eoin: *The Ultras*. London 2004.
Mulroe, Patrick: *Bombs, Bullets and the Border: Ireland's Frontier: Irish Security Policy, 1969-1978.* Dublin 2017.
Moore, Cormac: *Birth of the Border: The Impact of Partition in Ireland.* Dublin 2019.
Ó Beacháin, Donnacha: *From Partition to Brexit The Irish Government and Northern Ireland.* Manchester 2018.
O'Mahony, John: 'King of Bog Gothic', in: *The Guardian*, 20 August 2003, https://www.theguardian.com/books/2003/aug/30/fiction.patrickmccabe [24.06.2023].
Pacini, Andrea: *ContamiNazione e Trauma: personalità liminali nei romanzi di Patrick McCabe.* Thesis defended at the University of Florence: 2015, 10.13140/RG.2.1.2493.2728. https://www.researchgate.net/publication/303245866_ContamiNazione_e_Trauma_personalita_liminali_nei_romanzi_di_Patrick_McCabe [24.06.2023].
Patterson, Henry: *Ireland's Violent Frontier The Border and Anglo-Irish Relations During the Troubles.* London 2013.
Ranger, Graham: *Discourse Markers: An Enunciative Approach.* Cham (Switzerland) 2018.
Ranger, Graham: 'Surely not! Between certainty and disbelief,' Discours, A journal of linguistics, psycholinguistics and computational linguistics 2011/8, https://journals.openedition.org/discours/8416 [13.07.2023].
Ricœur, Paul: 'The Metaphorical Process as Cognition, Imagination, and Feeling,' Critical Inquiry 1978/1:5, p. 143–159.
Ricœur, Paul / Kearney, Richard (ed.): 'Reflections on a New Ethos for Europe,' in: *The Hermeneutics of Action.* London 1996, p. 3–15.
Ricœur, Paul: *Time and Narrative* (vol. 1). Chicago 1990.
Rotgé, Wilfrid: 'Desperately looking for a core value,' in: Anglophonia 2001/9, p. 7–21.
Said, Edward: *Orientalism*. London 1978.
Shakespeare, William: *Romeo and Juliet* [1597]. Levenson, Jill L. (ed.). Oxford 2008.

Suleri, Sara: *The Rhetoric of English India*. Chicago 1992.
'Summary of Status of the person killed', in: Conflict Archive on the Internet – cain.ulster.ac.uk, [https://cain.ulster.ac.uk/sutton/tables/Status_Summary.html], [13.07.2023].
Tóibín, Colm: *Bad Blood: A Walk Along the Irish Border*. London 2001.
'Trouble', available at https://www.merriam-webster.com/dictionary/trouble [24.06.2023].
Weichert, Katarzyna: 'The Role of Image and Imagination in Paul Ricœur's Metaphor Theory', Eidos, a Journal of Philosophy and Culture 2019/7, p. 64–77.

Liliana Sikorska

Vanquishing mirages: nations and nationalisms in Barry Unsworth's *The Rage of the Vulture* and Orhan Pamuk's *Silent House*

In 1992, in his seminal work, *The End of History and the Last Man*, Francis Fukuyama predicted the end of narrow-gauge nationalisms and the eventual victory of liberal democracy (Fukuyama 1992), the system which was to ultimately rewrite history by substituting political-nationalistic trends with economic preoccupations, in Europe and elsewhere. The termination of the cold war and the dissolution of the Soviet Union in 1991 indeed created a vision of the new Europe, while the ensuing expansion of the European Union in the early 21st century, which included countries like Poland and Hungary, seemed to carry the assurance of international cooperation and, in the Schengen area, visa free traffic. The unrest in Ukraine in 2013 and 2014, the on-going war between Russia and Ukraine in the Donbas region, the European migration crisis resulting from the war in Syria in 2015, Brexit in 2020, as well as the migration crisis of 2021 and the full-scale Russian military aggression against Ukraine, clearly demonstrate that we are far from envisaging "that there are no countries", to paraphrase John Lennon's song 'Imagine.' Thus, instead of concentrating on re-building the world after the global pandemic of Covid-19 and opening up borders, the contemporary world-politics resonates with conflict-based creeds, redolent of earlier xenophobic tendencies that can be found in the two texts selected for further analysis. The present paper examines Barry Unsworth's *The Rage of the Vulture* (1982) and Orhan Pamuk's *Silent House* (1983), novels depicting Turkey and Europe in times of change. Unsworth shows the end of the Ottoman Empire mainly through the eyes of a British man who becomes entangled in the Armenian cause, but offers also the point of view of the Sultan Abdul Hamid II.[1] Pamuk narrates the transformation of Turkey after the takeover by Mustafa Kemal Atatürk through the memories of an old woman and the experiences of her grandchildren. For both Unsworth and Pamuk, the vicissitudes of the image-making are tied with the (re-)construction of the national identities of com-

---

1 Out of respect for the position of the Turkish ruler, I am using the capital letter. The quotations are faithful to the writer's original spelling.

munities. Both novels vanquish mirages. While simultaneously challenging and endorsing the processes of secularization, they depict the clashes of religious and nationalistic ideologies strikingly current today.

Etymologically, the word 'nation' comes from the Latin "noun *natio*, which, in turn, is derived from the Latin verb *nasci* meaning 'to be born from'" (Grosby 2005, p. 44). On the one hand, the idea of 'being born'[2] points to the relationships within a family, community and society, but on the other, it signifies territoriality (Grosby 2005, p. 33). These two cruxes lie at the core of the creation of empires, including the Ottoman empire. What is more, the former concept is bound with the primal distinction between 'us' and 'them', enemies and allies, as Vamik Volkan terms them (Volkan 1988),[3] originating in the works of Plato, who divided humanity between Hellenes, the Greeks, and *barbaroi*, the barbarian people from Asia minor. His was a linguistic, more than a cultural distinction, because barbarians were those who did not speak the Greek language.[4] They were "not only foreign to the Hellenes but also their enemies by 'nature.'"[5] Such theories instilled in the ancient Greeks the fear of strangers, xenophobia (Khair 2016, p. 2f). As it transpires, for Plato, kinship has been understood in terms of ethnicity and language, but also through locations inhabited by culturally distinctive groups. The latter idea, that of territoriality, implies the existence and continuity of a relatively uniform society throughout time (Grosby 2005, p. 20). Ethnic, and by analogy, national cultures, are cemented in the collective consciousness through shared history, language, literature as well as through symbols, namely, flags, anthems and monuments, in themselves enhancing that collectivity. The conviction that "a nation understands itself, and, by so doing, constitutes itself" (Grosby 2005, p. 60), forms the foundations of current theories of nationalism, which, in its most basic understanding "refers to a set of beliefs about the nation" (Grosby 2005, p. 5).

---

2 Grosby presents ethnic and civic nations: the ethnic criterion assumes the birth of the parents in a given territory, [while] the civic nation guarantees any person born in a given territory entitlement to citizenship "irrespective of the origin of language or religious beliefs of one's parents" (Grosby 2005, p. 33).

3 Volkan, a Turkish Cypriot, sees identification and hostility as the extreme cases of the juxtaposition between us and them suggesting that people need to identify with one group and strengthen this group's identity by their hostility toward the other group. Similarly, Jonathan Glover links ethnic and religious conflicts to sociobiological hypothesis, according to which "certain behavior patterns may result from genetically programmed dispositions that had survived value in an earlier environment" (Glover 1997, p. 15).

4 Tzvetan Todorov discusses the origins and persistence of such divisions in the past and today in *The Fear of Barbarians*. He defines who a barbarian is and outlines the development of the perception of 'barbarians as strangers' and 'barbarians as cruel people' relating his analysis to the notions of culture and civilization (Todorov 2010, p. 14–34).

5 In *The Republic*, Plato, uses the term *génos* to refer to the sense of cultural collectivity of the Greeks (Grosby 2005, p. 3). Plato stresses the need to differentiate between "a citizen and a resident alien, or even visitor from abroad" (Plato 1998, p. 303).

Aware of the idealization of the concept of a nation, Benedict Anderson in his seminal investigation of nationalism draws attention to the contemporary paradox of "[t]he formal universality of nationality as a socio-cultural concept," which he sees as the necessity to possess "a nationality, as he or she 'has' gender" (Anderson 2006, p. 5). Nonetheless, Anderson identifies a nation with an "imagined community", because despite social inequalities "the nation is always conceived as a deep, horizontal comradeship" (Anderson 2006, p. 7). While classical communities were linked by sacred languages and religions, the nationalistic trends, originating within the empires, brought to the fore the theoretical discussions on the philosophical, sociological and ethnic nature of present-day "nationhood" (Anderson 2006, p. 13). Despite the fact that empires, i.e. "[the] Roman and [the] Ottoman, have sought to unify their peoples as a political alternative to nations" (Grosby 2005, p. 4), at the turn of the nineteenth and twentieth centuries European empires witnessed the birth of a number of anarchistic and pro-self-rule movements, advocating the fight for freedom of the subjugated nations.[6] These movements, which found their violent release in various insurrections, were the culmination of the nineteenth century developments pertaining to collective identities and geared towards the liberation of hitherto suppressed ethnic groups.[7] Their members were ready to kill and die for what they thought was the higher good, for their "imagined communities" (Anderson 2006, p. 7).

For Anderson, however, those devotion has remained "the central problem posed by nationalism", namely "what makes the drunken imaginings of recent history (scarcely more than two centuries) generate such colossal sacrifices?" (Anderson 2006, p. 7). Patriotism, recognized as the noblest of sentiments, promotes the idealized perception of one's nation and constantly rekindles the duty of one's absolute loyalty subsumed in Horace's *"Dulce et decorum est pro partial mori"*, sweet and noble it is to die for one's country (Horace 1999, p. 96).[8] The early twentieth century revolutions effected by nations struggling to be free, besides ending imperial, and frequently alien, oppression, were commonly recognized as positive forces. Nonetheless, the aftermath of these efforts, instigated

---

6 For more, see Hoffman 2006. Hoffman locates the contemporary terrorist movements with the social and political awakening of ethnic groups in the nineteenth century. Drawing on the movements towards modern age citizenship and statehood, the author shows the fluctuation of the meaning of the word terrorism, and, for that matter, nationalism (Hoffman, 2006, pp. 3–20).

7 Andrew Vincent states that this idea "went into abeyance during the mid to later twentieth century, since the collapse of the Berlin Wall in 1989 and the changing political landscape of international politics, there has been, once again a surge of positive interest in nationalism (amongst other forms of group particularity). Many have seen this as a hopeful prospect for the twenty-first century" (Vincent 2002, p. 5).

8 This quotation is more commonly associated with Wilfred Owen's poem 'Dulce Et Decorum Est', the poet's anti-war manifesto (Owen 1972, p. 55).

the birth of radicalism, and, in effect, ensued the redefinition of the concept of a 'nation' and its ideological tour de force, 'nationalism.' The extreme nationalism in Germany, for example, resulted in the creation of national socialism and the totalitarian ideology in Soviet Russia, instituted to defend the communist system, divided the nation into the 'white Russians' and the 'Red Russians'; the latter group were the only true Russians during the Soviet rule.[9] Both examples are patent departures from the initial meaning of nationalism as patriotism, which hitherto unified ethnic and cultural communities through their belief in shared cultures.

In recent years the philosophy of nationalism surfaced in relation to the liberal theories of state, accompanied by the unsolved issues of loyalty and particularity (McKim / McMahan 1997, pp. 5f). Judith Lichtenberg cites five central arguments in defense of nationalism: The Flourishing Argument: human beings need to belong to a group; The Self-Determination Argument: the individuals possess a moral right to form self-governing associations; The Reparations Argument: nationhood is a means of rectifying historical grievances, of old rights and wrongs; The Pluralism Arguments: the world is a better place containing diverse cultures; and The Intrinsic Value Argument: the existence of a given culture is a good that ought to be promoted as it flourishes on a particular value (Lichtenberg 1997, p. 161). Lichtenberg's aforementioned points assume enlightened citizenship and the balance between the demands of the state and the needs of its residents. That is why Lichtenberg, while certainly endorsing the ideals of nationhood, is more skeptical about the practical implementation of those ideals. Paradoxically, both Abdul Hamid II and Mustafa Kemal Atatürk, the main characters of the novels chosen for further analysis, would have approved of the above-mentioned views: The Sultan on the basis of the Ottoman supra-nationality, and the President of the Republic of Turkey because of his glorification of ethnic Turkish identity. Peleg reasons that the new Republic was modeled on nation-states of Western Europe, particularly France. He emphasizes that the name: 'Republic of Turkey' rather than 'Turkish Republic' coincided with the founding elite's attempt to substitute Turkish identity for the previous Ottoman one (Peleg 2007, p. 169). "National identity, like personal identity," as Glover holds, "is constructed partly by means of a story about the past. The narrative used to shape national consciousness can contribute to conflict in a way not completely separate from the contribution of perceived characteristics" (Glover 1997, p. 23).

---

9 Contemporary 'Putinism' is based on the same premise, because totalitarian regimes cannot tolerate dissent, or even differences of opinion, and that is why President Vladimir Putin so readily represented Russia aggressive politics as a defense of his nation and its long-standing values, without, however, specifying what these values might be.

It comes as no surprise that communities and nations want to ensure the survival of language and ethnic over and above religious traditions.[10] In Glover's view: "The nation is often seen as at least the best defense of these things and sometimes as their embodiment" (Glover 1997, p. 19). 'Nationalism', thus, can be referred to a cluster of beliefs about the normative significance of nations and nationality. Undoubtedly, human identity is fashioned by one's family and within the public sphere, in which geography, history and culture intersect, but the idea of nationhood surmounts that of an individual. That is why, as McMahan asserts, "the members of the nation ought to control their collective affairs and that membership in the nation makes it not only permissible but in many instances morally required to manifest loyalty and partiality to fellow members" (McMahan 1997, p. 107).[11] Far from reaching a definitive conclusion, the existing discourses on nationalism, reverberate with the concurrent corroboration of the initial assumptions of nationalism – those of the struggles for liberty and self-governance of suppressed nations, and the disparagement of nationalism as "tribal conflict", whose results "can be seen from Belfast to Bosnia" (Glover 1997, p. 11).

The debatable position and ethos of the nationalist movements in the Ottoman Empire is depicted by Barry Unsworth in *The Rage of the Vulture*, the novel recreating, almost literally, the death throes of Abdul Hamid's realm. The title and the motto of the novel come from the first lines of Lord Byron's poem 'The Bride of Abydos': "Know ye the land where the cypress and myrtle / Are emblems of deeds that are done in their clime? / Where the rage of the vulture, the love of the turtle, / Now melt into sorrow, now madden to crime" (Byron 1970, p. 264). Using Byron's work, Unsworth clearly sides with the oppressed communities, yet, by allowing the reader to see the early twentieth century Turkey through the eyes of the last Ottoman Sultan, Abdul Hamid II (1842–1918),[12] the author challenges the dominating perspective of the British in the character of Henry Markham, an army officer stationed in Constantinople. Both individuals seem to be posing the

---

10 The immigrant diasporas were created in territories which offered legal protection to practice different religions. In Muslim countries, *dhimma* stood for "a social contract between Muslims and members of other religions – Judaism and Christianity– provided the latter accept the Islamic rule." *Dhimma* is mentioned in the Quran (IX, 29), which urges the non-believers to pay a tribute. The payment became a poll tax and gave the *dhimmis* a "definitive fiscal status" (Hiro 2003, p. 124f).
11 Identifying the reasons for partiality and impartiality, McMahan argues that members of the same nation are required to be partial to one another, as co-nationals they "must give some degree of priority to one another's interests over those of foreigners or nonmembers" (McMahan 1997, p. 109).
12 Different sources spell out the name of Abdul Hamid in different ways. I will use his name as spelled out by Unsworth in my analysis, but will stick to the original whenever quoting other authors.

same question – why does one continue in a country "maddened to crime", the query equally pertinent for the characters. The plot of the novel involves Markham over the past twelve years haunted by the memory of his dead Armenian fiancé, Miriam Kirkorian, and the Sultan, who senses the termination of his reign but cannot fathom the end of the empire, with which he was entrusted thirty-three years ago. Not knowing any other life, the Sultan wants to preserve his power and Markham keeps hoping for amends of the sin of betrayal (Unsworth 1991, p. 120). Through his contacts in the city, Markham becomes entangled with the Armenian cause. A speaker of Turkish, with a commendable knowledge of the East, he had always understood that western liberal principles would be difficult to implement in "a medieval theocracy like Turkey" and regarded diverse dissident societies as "Vultures of democracy." The vultures, however, are as much the new political groups as the European empires, stalling any radical activities in order to sustain the status quo. For Markham "[e]very diplomatic service in Europe was the same, playing the same game, following the same rules. Balance of greed, balance of fear. The last thing any of them wanted was the dynamism of internal change" (Unsworth 1991, p. 165).[13] Nonetheless, for either side the late spring and summer of 1908, as well as the following year, will be the time of irreversible transformation.

The opening of the novel offers an image of the rather dejected Abdul Hamid II, alone in one of the rooms of the Yildiz Palace observing his city and its inhabitants through a telescope. This pastime alleviates his solitude but is also related to his obsession of controlling and spying. Abdul Hamid is a curious character, sometimes caught between the need to become more progressive and his obligation to be orthodox, even in such a trivial matter as seeking solace in the harem. He would have liked to visit his latest favorite, but bound by tradition, he cannot barge into the women's quarters, as the etiquette demanded that he announced his arrival, and so in the end, he gives up on the idea (Unsworth 1991, p. 101). Looking towards the palace of Cheragan on the Bosphorus where "his mad brother Murad V had been immured for thirty years" (Unsworth 1991, p. 11), the sixty-six-year-old Sultan fears plots recalling his participation in the deposition of their uncle, Abdul Aziz.[14] Throughout his reign, Abdul Hamid II

---

13 Unsworth has a number of the characters, including Madame Wallish, who openly expressed her opinion that all European nations are 'vultures', discuss European politics regarding Turkey (Unsworth 1991, pp. 136–137).
14 Caroline Finkel spells his name as Abdülaziz when she outlines the accession of Abdülaziz's eldest son, Yusuf (Finkel 2006, p. 483). Abdul Aziz, who succeeded his brother, Abdulmejid, tried to put his own son on the throne, and this incited Murad and his supporters to overthrow his uncle. The coup d'etat that placed Prince Murad on the throne on May 30, 1876, was seamlessly planned so that Abdul Hamid would have never been implicated (Finkel 2006, p. 481).

dreaded political unrest, also because he was instrumental in the deposition and imprisonment of his brother Murad V, on August 31, 1876. Before the accession of Abdul Hamid II, there was no report concerning Murad's physical or mental frailty, but after the coup, he was pronounced unfit to rule.[15] As Murad V, the Sultan promised "constitutional rule and ministerial responsibility" (Finkel 2006, p. 482), the act which, alongside his pro-western lifestyle and his "lending ear" to one of the Young Ottomans returning from exile, Namik Kemal, were the reasons why he lost support, and Abdul Hamid II took his place. Macfie claims that most of the Muslim inhabitants wanted to live in a country where the Muslim supremacy is enshrined in the *Sheriat*, which asserted the position of the Sultan and the supremacy of the Muslim *millet* (Macfie, 1998, p. 15, Finkel 2006, p. 483).[16] At the time, the Ottoman empire did not desire westernization but moderate reforms concomitant with the upholding of Muslim traditions and Abdul Hamid II's politics seemed to have guaranteed those requirements.[17]

Cutting a fine and charismatic figure, young Abdul Hamid took the legendary Sword of Osman, the attribute of power of the Ottoman Empire and a symbol of his legitimacy as the Supreme Leader; his swift decision was initially saluted by his subjects as a promise of support towards judicious liberal improvements, best described through a version of the contemporary slogan: 'Let's make the realm great again.' As a monarch intent on strengthening the influence of the Ottoman Empire in Europe he readily received foreign royalties, for instance, Edward VII, heads of state, and businessmen. He developed rail and telegraph systems, giving the concession to build the Istanbul-Paris line, granting the country the famous Orient Express (Finkel 2006, p. 479).[18] Unfortunately, the Russo-Turkish War of 1877–1878, which exposed the weakness of the Ottoman Empire, forced him to

---

15 Edward S. Cresy in his *History of the Ottoman Turks* published in 1878, sides with the official history claiming that Murad "proved hopelessly imbecile" (Cresy 1961, p. 548).
16 In Unsworth's novel, Arturo Zimin, a Levantine spy, remarks that The Young Turks movement "has strong bases in Paris and Geneva. A person like that would make an excellent courier" (Unsworth, 1991, p. 130). Millet signifies the religious community (Macfie 1998, p. 15).
17 Sir Adolphus Slade, who in the Ottoman Army assumed the name of Mushaver Pasha, noticed that the reforms brought about by Sultan Mahmoud II (1785–1839, LS) incited a Moslem social revolution and "disturbed the foundations of the edifice reared by his ancestors, and altered the relations of Turkey with Christendom. Previously isolated…Turkey then entered the comity of nations, but on invidious terms, the terms of a stepchild in a numerous family" (Slade 2012, p. vii). Slade's is one of the few pro-Turkish narratives of the beginnings of the Ottoman Empire, which influenced their perception of the Kurds, for example. He also offers a detailed account of the war, which although victorious for the Ottomans and their Allies, contributed to the slow waning of the empire.
18 In the novel, Abdul Hamid is approached by two American businessmen offering him large sums for the privileges to drill for oil in Mesopotamia (Unsworth 1991, p. 101; Macfie 1998, p. 16f).

fall back on the only form of rule he thought would work in Turkey, the absolutist regime.[19] Macfie reckons that Abdul Hamid was "proclaimed Sultan in the midst of the Eastern Crisis, taking advantage of the mood of national humiliation and defeat that the war against Russia had evoked" (Macfie 1998, p. 15). The recurrent disturbances in the Balkans since 1875, and the loss of Egypt to the British in 1882, contributed to his preoccupation with security (Mansfield 2004, p. 114).[20] The incessant conflicts with the Kurds and the Armenians fostered his later dislike of liberalism.[21] In the novel, Unsworth recreates the atmosphere of hazard surrounding the Reval Agreement, which had been signed between Czar Alexander and Edward VII on June 10th. Even though the Germans were opposed, the signs of growing friendship between Russia and England unsettled the Sultan, who had a premonition that his former allies were "dismembering the Balkans between them" (Unsworth 1991, p. 178f). Abdul Hamid could sense, however, that, in the words of Somerville, a financier and member of the Ottoman Debt Commission, Europeans were: "[...] squabbling over pickings. We have made Turkey into an international danger-zone. The Government is debt ridden, the whole country is in decline" (Unsworth 1991, p. 142).[22] Mehmed Kâmil Pasha also spelled as Kiamil Pasha (1832–1913), who was four times the grand vizier after 1994, did display Anglophile tendencies, at the same time he was a fierce opponent of CUP and tried to crush it in 1912 (Züricher 2021, p. 426) The economic situation of the country, interlaced with reformatory movements and nationalist insurrections will be the causes of the ultimate dismantling of the Ottoman

---

19 In Egypt, by the end of 1870s, there were "new controls on the press, which developed into strict censorship during the reign of Sultan Abdul Hamid II (1876–1919)" (Rogan 2010, p. 171). Unsworth talks about the censorship of the press in Constantinople in relation to Hassan Fehmi's assassination.

20 Eugene Rogan offers an inciteful analysis of the Mamluk-Ottoman relationships in Egypt since 1600 (Rogan 2010, p. 44ff). In the nineteenth century the Ottomans introduced legal equality between Muslims and non-Muslim citizens so as to bar the European powers from interfering in Egypt (Rogan 2010, p. 119). Egypt was autonomous within the Ottoman rule; the difficult economic situation more than political developments, however, led to the establishment of the European rule in Egypt from 1878 (Rogan 2010, p. 132). Ismail Pasha, who ruled in Egypt between 1863 and 1879, through his diplomatic skills changed his title to khedive, a Persian title meaning viceroy, in 1867 (Rogan 2010, p. 123). When Richard Burton found himself in Cairo, in 1863, he saw the tensions between the Egyptians and their Ottoman rulers. No wonder, his representation of a stereotypical Turk is one: "[...] in frock coat and Fez, ill-dressed, ill-conditioned, and ill-bred, body and soul" (Burton 1964 I, p. 99; for more, see Sikorska 2021).

21 "Tribes are marked off from one another by some combination of ethnicity, religion, shared territory, language, and shared culture" (Glover 1997, p. 19).

22 For Arturo Zimin: "The British have no reliable sources of information in Constantinople" (Unsworth 1991, p. 127). Markham, based on his observations of Kiamil Pasha, the Grand Vizier, was, somewhat naively, convinced that the country was pro-British (Unsworth 1991, p. 298).

empire. What the Sultan could not have foreseen was that the price of the Republic of Turkey would be its Ottoman identity.

Although he was credited with the development of primary, secondary and professional schools, with one of them, Darulfunun, later becoming Istanbul University, he also tried to strictly control the curricula of schools to instill in the pupils Islamic morality and the Ottoman character (Macfie 1998, p. 15). In spite of his nationalistic tendencies, or perhaps because of them, Abdul Hamid's rule was marred by his drive for autocracy. The same man, who as a young crown prince worked with the group of liberals called the Young Ottomans, and who liked Arthur Conan Doyle's Sherlock Holmes stories and Jacques Offenbach's music, suspended the Parliament and reasserted the authority of the Sultan.[23] The historical Ahmet Izzet Furgaç (1864–1937) was Chief of General Staff after the 1908 revolution. He served in several cabinets in 1919–1920, but never joined the resistance in Anatolia (Züricher 2021, p. 426). His actions are rather ironically reviewed in *The Rage of the Vulture* by Mr Colin-Olivier from the French Embassy: "'Confident tyrannies can never last long [...] Fear is a great preserver, preservative, how do you say it?'" (Unsworth 1991, p. 136). Faced with unrest, Abdul Hamid II strayed from the path of reform and turned to the belief card appealing to the religious authorities for support and seeking confirmation of the accord between the *Sharia* law and the Constitution.[24] "An *iradé* (A Muslim ruler's official decree, LS) to this effect was published in the morning papers of Friday 24th July" (Unsworth 1991, p. 245). Unfortunately, his decree did not end the problems of his rule. The Sultan might have sensed "that more would be needed than an ultimatum from the Third Army Corps to turn an Islamic theocracy of five hundred years' standing into a modern democratic state on the French or English model" (Unsworth 1991, p. 249). Within the span of the next few months, Abdul Hamid, contrary to his oath, suppressed the Constitution, and supported the counter-revolution by enticing the mutineers with money and promises (Unsworth 1991, p. 416); these were later used as the main arguments for his deposition.

---

23 In his *Memoirs*, Izzet Pasha wrote about an audience with the Sultan when he heard Offenbach music playing. Izzet was trying to tell the Sultan what awaited him from the Young Turks. Abdul Hamid believed in the loyalty of the First Army Corps in Constantinople as well as the Anatolian peasantry. He thought that the palace guard, the Albanians, whom he describes as "trusty" and "the only troops in the Ottoman Empire, it was said not in arrears of pay", would not let him down (Unsworth 1991, p. 11). When asked for advice, The Grand Vizier expressed the opinion that the terms of the rebels should be accepted and the Constitution should be restored (Unsworth 1991, p. 242).

24 The Sultan formally addressed the religious authorities: "Could the Constitution be accepted without the Sheriat, the Sacred Law? The answer came in the accustomed single word of acceptance: *Olur*, [yes] it may be done" (Unsworth 1991, p. 244).

Cushioned by tight security, his 'trusty Albanians', the Sultan lived in constant expectation of burgeoning plots.[25] The Sultan's anxiety concerning security[26] resulted in his continual carrying of two pistols, and frequent changing of his sleeping arrangements. A ruler of the empire, he kept certain routes in the palace as only known to him; his fear imprisoning him in his own home (Unsworth 1991, p. 215). Furthermore, his paralyzing apprehension of political disorder strengthened the position of the secret police, and Umur-u Hafiye, whose network of informants, accredited instruments of the Palace, facilitated arrests and the exile of many contrary-minded politicians. The secret police became the most hated force of the empire. European agents in Constantinople were aware that the system worked through intimidation and blackmail, but they also witnessed its end with the assassination of the Sultan's agents in Monastir, Janinna, Aleppo and Smyrna (Unsworth 1991, p. 38). Unsurprisingly, in the novel, Abdul Hamid is an avid reader of the day's *djurnals,* the reports from the spies – the activity intermingled with monitoring newcomers, including those residing in Pera, the district of the European Embassies and business houses. "Files were kept on all foreign residents in Constantinople, civil and military. He knew the man's name and a certain number of facts about him. His name was Markhan and he spoke Turkish. Another unusual thing" (Unsworth 1991, p. 13). Markham likewise is mindful of the Sultan's "scrutiny of the world." The Englishman "[…] felt suddenly empty in that knowledge, drained of identity, as if the most vividly realized life was at the end of the Sultan's telescope" (Unsworth 1991, p. 30). The image of Abdul Hamid surveilling the city is, in a way, mirrored by Markham's wandering through Constantinople, observing the people, collecting information.

Working as much for the British government as to atone for his transgression, Markham is enthralled by the persona of the Sultan "with a sort of disguised fascination" (Unsworth 1991, p. 133). In the eyes of the Europeans, the final years of Abdul Hamid's rule were synonymous with "despotism and reaction" (Macfie 1998, p. 15), and such an almost undeservedly negative portrait is also offered in Unsworth's novel.[27] Predictably, Unsworth terms Abdul Hamid's reign as "long

---

25 In Richard Burton's *Personal Narrative of a Pilgrimage to Al-Madinah and Meccah*, Albanians are depicted as a "reckless brood", who "when they march are not allowed ammunition for otherwise there would be half of a dozen duels a day" (Burton 1964 I, p. 133). Burton's representation of them is akin to the stereotypical representations of the Saracen Sultans and their armies in the medieval Saracen romances. Such typecasts are then strengthened by the claims that "all Orientals hate drinking in any but a bright light." Notwithstanding, Burton gets drunk on 'Araki' with an Albanian Ali Agha, following the ritual of drinking and eating mint scented food (Burton 1964 I, p. 135).
26 The Europeans also knew that the Balkans are "riddled with secret societies of one sort or another […] it is a way of life with them" (Unsworth 1991, p. 164).
27 Interestingly, a similar depiction features in Orhan Pamuk's *Nights of the Plague* (2022), where the character of the Sultan, who imprisoned his brother and his brother's children in

and blood-stained", portraying the Sultan as universally dreaded and disliked, prone to outbursts of unnecessary violence, "maddened to crime" – to use Byron's expression again – just as the world envisioned him (Unsworth 1991, p. 11).[28] One of the examples of his predisposition for evil is his treatment of Midhat Pasha, called by Zeine "a most enlightened and courageous reformer" (Zeine 1961, p. xvf), the one who introduced the Constitution, and "whom Abdul Hamid had first exiled and then had strangled" (Unsworth 1991, p. 257). Although the attitude of the Foreign Office was to see "Turkey as a moribund imperial power, completely static, incapable of change" (Unsworth 1991, p. 163), such a representation was not entirely accurate. Change was coming and it was inevitable through the presence of a secret society, called the Committee of Union and Progress, in existence from 1905 onwards. By 1907, the members of the Committee were sending open communication to all European states "setting out their principles and aims" (Unsworth 1991, p. 164). Though their intention was not to dismantle but to modernize the empire, their actions, in the end, facilitated its dissolution.

Analyzing Abdul Hamid's reign, Caroline Finkel asserts that there are two competing views of Abdul Hamid II, one that interprets the last Sultan as "an obscurantist" and his reign as one of "a somewhat shameful past" from which Turkey was "delivered by [the] leadership and vision of Mustafa Kemal Atatürk" (Finkel 2006, p. 488). In such a framework, the Sultan's government is a prequel to the age of reform and secularization. The other approach, siding with the anti-Kemalist faction, sees Abdul Hamid II as a hero, "the sultan who reverted to a more conservative path after the experimentation of the *Tanzimat*, re-emphasizing the Islamic character of the Ottoman state and championing Muslims against the other peoples of the empire, the non-Muslims being seen in this reading as the root of the crisis which brought about the empire's collapse" (Finkel 2006, p. 488).[29]

Indeed, the slow waning of the Ottoman Empire after the Crimean war (1853–1856) and the unsuccessful war with Russia (1877–1878) was accelerated by the internal conflicts with Kurds and Armenians. The measures of security were raised because of an intelligence report that in 1899, at the end of Ramazan – during the feast of *Hirkai Sherif*, of the adoration of the Cloak of the Prophet –

---

the palace, is only slightly softened by the less hostile depiction of Murad's great-grand daughter. While in Pamuk's novel, one finds a critical portrait of the reigning monarch, Unsworth's work is imbued with unmitigated dislike of the Sultan.

28 Abdul Hamid knew that ministers were afraid of him, abiding by the particular protocol of leaving. "They went, taking care to move slowly, to keep their arms by their sides, remembering the fate of their colleague Hakki Bey who had been shot through the throat for forgetting to do this" (Unsworth 1991, p. 77).

29 *Tanzimat* is the period of reform 1839–1876 (for more, see Finkel 2006, p. 447f).

when Abdul Hamid was to show himself in public, he would be assassinated.[30] Armenians were thought to have pro-Russian sympathies, but the situation was much more complex, than a simple case of the Ottoman xenophobia. There were two Armenian nationalist organizations formed abroad, one in Geneva in 1887 and one in Tiflis in 1890, the latter flaunting more anti-Russian views. Both did not shy away from violence as a means to gain independence for Armenia. At the same time, as Finkel avows, "the Kurdish tribes were jealously independent" and were indeed part of the cavalry regiments, Abdul Hamid's *Hamiddiyye*, policing the region (Macfie 1998, p. 17). Positioning the Kurds against the Armenians is highlighted in Unsworth's novel. After the massacres of the 1890s, Markham had no doubt that Abdul Hamid "Vice-Regent of God on earth", ordered to kill the Armenians and "...with a word here and a word there and a few strokes of the pen brought death to fifty thousand obscure Armenians, in round figures, among them a girl named Miriam Kirkorian, whose fiancé had been not an Armenian but an Englishman [...]" (Unsworth 1991, p. 55).[31] Colonel Nesbit, British Military Attaché in Constantinople, offers a much more unsympathetic view of the situation, judging that abled bodied Armenians let themselves to be killed by "a few skinny Kurds." He voices an opinion that if one does not have the courage to fight one is "not fit to live" (Unsworth 1991, p. 55).[32] Such an avowal recaps the foundations of social Darwinism, widely accepted by the western bourgeoisie, and central to nineteenth-century racism (for more, see Khair 2016, p. 67f). Far from agreeing with Nesbit, Markham nonetheless recalled "a Circassian face, or possibly Kurdish" (Unsworth 1991, p. 123)[33] as one of the attackers. Even though Markham knew that the Armenians had enough cause "to want Abdul Hamid dead. He has done away with well over a hundred thousand of them in the course of his illustrious reign. Some say half a million." For the sake of the optics, the Sultan needed a scapegoat, a Christian minority group, otherwise, it might have

---

[30] The police raided all the suspected homes simultaneously, in order to search for chlorate potassium, even the smallest amount from which you could make a bomb. Unsworth, *The Rage*, p. 139. Abdul Hamid reveled in the reports from the spies, he also believed in depositions obtained through torture. "Abdul Hamid had ended up more frightened and confused than ever. Finally, he ordered all the water pipes in the Palace, well over a thousand of them, to be exhumed in his presence and replaced by others only a few inches below ground, so that any attempt to use them for purposes of assassination might be instantly detected [...]" (Unsworth 1991, p. 53).

[31] Miriam Krikorian was a student in London; Hartunian's sister married a man called Krikorian, they had three children, one of them was Miriam (Unsworth 1991, p. 301).

[32] Nesbit also suggested that Armenians were implicated in the assassination attempt of Abdul Hamid in 1905. (Unsworth 1991, pp. 304–305). His view is imparted by Madame Wallish who is of the opinion that "[...] Armenian societies make trouble for themselves" (Unsworth 1991, p. 140).

[33] Markham claimed that marriages between Turks and Greeks were not uncommon in the 1890s (Unsworth 1991, p. 279).

appeared that his subjects rebelled against the regime (Unsworth 1991, p. 141). What is interesting, however, is that the Sultan himself had an Armenian type of face, his biological mother Tirimüjgan Kadin had been, as Unsworth holds, "an Armenian slave girl" (Unsworth 1991, p. 107). Despite his dislike of the methods, Markham realized that Abdul Hamid wanted to preserve the old order, the respect for the national and cultural values of the Ottomans. It was clear that the Turks "like all races [are] renowned for their fidelity. They can be relied upon to commit atrocities too" (Unsworth 1991, p. 35). Suitably, the Ottoman Empire utilized the golden rule of the Romans: "divide and conquer."

The idea of multi-cultural countries respecting minority religions and customs was not in the Ottoman best interest. Armenians were Christians, their language derived from the western branch of Indo-European languages, and they harbored separatist dreams; while Kurds, who were largely Muslim (their language being of Indo-Iranian origin), similarly hoped for autonomy (Hiro 2003, p. 50, 281). Both were minorities in the Ottoman Empire: "Such groups almost inevitably resist integration and seek official recognition of their language and culture" (Kymlicka 1997, p. 59). Goodkin places the attachment to one's culture as the fundament of selfhood. "Communities, especially national communities, share 'understandings' not just in the trivial sense of sharing certain 'bodies of information' but also, more important, in the sense of sharing some idea of the significance to be attached to those things" (Goodkin 1997, p. 92). Both Armenians and Kurds were recognized as distinct ethnic groups within the empire, but were also associated with those rebuffing its sovereignty and therefore hampering the unification of disparate ethnic groups under the supremacy of the Turks. In the novel, Markham finds out that there were groups working towards the establishment of an autonomous Armenia "with a homeland in Eastern Turkey" (Unsworth 1991, p. 300), but neither the Ottoman Empire, nor the Republic of Turkey would have approved of the creation of an independent Armenia on Turkish soil. This view is articulated by Nejib, a Turkish officer, and member of the Committee of Union and Progress, who emphasized that there could never be a "union between Turkish and Russian Armenia." What is more, disillusioning Markham, Nejib was convinced that "many of those claiming to be Armenian patriots are socialist agitators from over the Caucasus, who would sell tomorrow. Capitalism is the enemy for them" (Unsworth 1991, p. 419). Unsworth essentially alludes to the nascent communist movement inside Turkey's sworn enemy.

Recognizing the potential clashes between ethnic groups, which are granted dissimilar degrees of autonomy, Judith Lichtenberg differentiates between the "nationalism of those who have succeeded in securing a state, or at least dominance within one, and the nationalism of those – within this state but having a different culture – who have not" (Lichtenberg 1997, p. 170). For her, the question remains "what [are the] legitimate claims each of these groups has and what to do when they clash" (Lichtenberg 1997, p. 170). In Nejib's assessment, the massacres fueled Europe's negative perception of the Ottoman empire by preventing the Armenians from being forgotten: "Once more the attention of Europe is fixed on the Armenian question" (Unsworth 1991, p. 419). The cynicism, echoing the centuries-old conviction legitimating the inferior position of non-Muslims in an Islamic state, is re-configured in Nejib's belief in a primal idea of "Turkey [...] for the Turks" (Unsworth 1991, p. 419), a country with a strong army and frontiers that can be defended.[34] Such a declaration, as Glover insists, is rooted in the "national self-image", which "is often (even if misleadingly) cast in terms of the tribal nation, [where] the favorable characteristics are easily thought of as ethnic ones" (Glover 1991, p. 23). According to contemporary individualist theorists the human individual is "truly universal, that is whenever one encounters human individuals, they are formally the same, regardless of race, gender, age, ethnicity or nationality." Thus, in Vincent's view, "[...] to assert a belief in the community or group as the true particular or individual shifts the whole onus of morality away from human individuals towards groups (of many and various types). This tends immediately to cast doubt on both moral and political individualism and traditional human rights theory" (Vincent 2002, p. 3). On the eve of the First World War and faced with the destruction of their homeland, many Turks acknowledged the value of cultural and religious ties promulgating the fight for national security and against the forces which sought to destabilize it.

This drive towards exclusive nationalism indicated certain tendencies in Turkish politics, which prompted Markham to infer that the massacres of the Armenians in 1890s were perfectly planned. "They began when the drums were beaten in the morning and stopped when they were beaten again at nightfall. You know, as if there were rules. Most of it was down in the Galata region – a very cosmopolitan district, yet not one Jew was killed, not one Greek. Only Armenians. Do you know why? They went round painting white crosses on all Armenian houses" (Unsworth 1991, p. 140). What Markham does not understand was the long-standing dislike of the successful Armenian merchants and financiers "with contacts outside the empire", who were feared, and so "forbidden to carry arms", their influences curtailed by the imposition of higher taxes "than other Ottoman citizens" (Wilson 2005, p. 133). Searching for the spark which inflamed the anti-Armenian sentiments, Markham does not mention the seizure of a bank in Constantinople in 1895 by Armenian revolutionaries, which brought on recurrent retaliations, continued throughout the first two decades of the

---

[34] Namely, as a way of contrasting different conceptions of group particularity (Vincent 2002, p. 4).

twentieth century (Wilson 2005, p. 133).³⁵ While blaming Abdul Hamid for the Armenian genocide, Markham's bitterness is also the result of his guilt. Seeing Miriam's violation and death, he only wanted to save his own life; for by announcing his English identity, he played "the traitor's part" (Unsworth 1991, p. 55), complicit in the Palace's actions:

> Into Markham's mind, unbidden, came leaping memories of what men not much different to look at had done, memories of what he had seen or had been told, images not separate but coalescing, blood cemented: clubbed Armenians, bleeding their lives away in the gutters of Galata; the human bonfires of Urfa; the lines of blinded Bulgarians. He shook his head very slightly to dispel these images, and the images went, but the collective agony pulsed still in his mind, slowly, like the slow beat of his own heart (Unsworth 1991, p. 35f).

However dedicated Markham might have been in discerning the real perpetrators of the extermination, however deserved was his penance (he was captured by the Sultan's soldiers and tortured in the palace), he was not important for the Armenians: "These people are interested in the collective idea. Set against the idea of an independent homeland for two and a half million Armenians, what are you? You do not exist'" (Unsworth 1991, p. 419). Nejib's stance can be read through a more recent investigation of communitarianism, which, for Andrew Vincent brings to light "this fairly elementary distinction between individual and communal ontologies", undoubtedly, "a neglected point that particularity *can* be viewed from widely different theoretical perspectives" (Vincent 2002, p. 4). Yet, in the tempestuous times of the clashes between an individual and a group, Markham's pain as much as his fiancée's death, are merely collateral damage.

Accentuating such a dictum, Unsworth weaves the story of the counter-revolution of April 1909 with Markham witnessing the assassination of Hasan Fehmi – and possibly being accused of it – with the historical events that surround the death and funeral of Hasan Fehmi.³⁶ Markham is later enlightened by Najib that

---

35 Wilson states that in 1915, Armenians were suspected of siding with the enemy, which prompted mass exterminations, frequently accompanied by tortures. 300, 000 perished, and 40, 000 disappeared during their flight to Russia.
36 Fehmi had no wife, only a cousin, but his funeral assembled quite a lot of people. A lot of them did not know him personally. "But it was among people who did not know him personally that anger at his murder grew most rapidly: among the poor and fanatical elements of the population, obliged to live in close proximity to Christian communities, and among the rank and file of the troops at the Tacsim Barracks […] This murder of a champion of Islam became a focal point for various discontents: and when it was learned that the police had made no arrest, the anger grew fiercer, it was rumoured that the authorities themselves had had a hand in Fehmi's killing" (Unsworth 1991, p. 409).
"Printed leaflets were distributed among the crowd, denouncing the Young Turk regime. The choir of priests chanted in fierce nasal descent. A dervish named Vahdeti, standing in the midst of the crowd, began preaching the wholesale massacre of Unionists and a return to the Holy Law" (Unsworth 1991, p. 410).

both sides, the British as well as the Ottomans, would have implicated him in the incident, using him for their own narrow-minded goals.[37] Fehmi, the editor of one of "the fiercest anti-Unionist papers, was killed, probably by a unionist agent" (Züricher 2021, p. 94).[38] Committed to the amelioration of the public life in Turkey, the Unionists nevertheless, managed to antagonize their co-nationals by suggesting "[...] European headgear compulsory for men. That was very wounding to Moslem sensibilities" (Unsworth 1991, p. 417).[39] Used to suppress the secularist forces, Hassan Fehmi's funeral and ensuing demonstration was, in Nejib's opinion, the work of the mollha and Abdul Hamid's agents (Unsworth 1991, p. 416). Whoever was behind it, at dawn, on April 13th, armed men gathered in the square, and some thirty officers were "sabred or shot to death" (Unsworth 1991, p. 411). The Sheikh-ul-Islam and other high-ranking ecclesiasts incited the crowd which continued to cry: "'*Yahassin, Sheriat, Peicamberi*' – 'Long live the Law of the Prophet!'" (Unsworth 1991, p. 411). The protest was followed by the dissolution of both the Parliament as well as the party of Union and Progress, the incident unleashing the chain of events that the Sultan could not have conjured up in his wildest nightmares. On the morning of 27 April, 1909, "Abdul Hamid was informed by a deputation consisting entirely of non-Turks that the Turkish nation had deposed him."[40] Although A. N. Wilson places his demise in 1909, in reality he died in 1918 (Wilson 2005, p. 132). Wilson sees the nation's brief exhilaration with the ideas of 'Young Turks' who professed a brotherhood of all peoples of the empire; but once the state was not described in terms "of imperial authority and territory controlled" the problem with the definition of the Turkish nation was shifted to "ethnicity and religious allegiance" (Wilson 2005, p. 133).

Related mostly through the eyes of a British Officer entangled in the momentous events in Constantinople, *The Rage of the Vulture* illustrates how the western mindset prevails in shaping the totalizing visions of the Orient at the end of one era and the beginning of another. Abdul Hamid II is unashamedly neg-

---

37 Nejib claimed that "[...] the *Henchak* wanted to involve Britain, mainly for propaganda purposes. They would have claimed responsibility, published the details of your involvement" (Unsworth 1991, p. 418).
38 The symbolic significance of clothes is highlighted by Orhan Pamuk when Fatma's husband, Selâhattin, did not pay attention to the war news from Palestine, Galicia, and Gallipoli. Fatma, whose voice is that of orthodoxy, is extremely pleased: "When I learned that the Unionists had been overthrown, I left the news like a beautiful ripe fruit on his plate." Her husband, however, claims that: "The Unionists have sunk the Ottoman Empire and run off, and we've lost the war, too!" (Pamuk 2012, p. 27).
39 The fez has been a part of Turkish culture and this necessary element of the Ottoman identity will also become a bone of contention between the main characters of Orhan Pamuk's *Silent House*.
40 He was exiled to a villa in Salonika, a property of a Jewish banker. Rassim Pasha, Chief of the Secret Police was to be executed by the Gypsies; it was not an easy hanging (Unsworth 1991, p. 438).

atively depicted, yet, by switching the perspective from Markham to Abdul Hamid, Unsworth manages to create a space in which constant surveillance is partaken by both characters. Their vigilance and loneliness together with the recognition of the clashes between the old and the new worldviews seem to highlight the early twentieth century dynamism of interactions between the Occident and the Orient. Still, the instability of the empire's colonial dominance suggests that ethnic identifications expose the disturbing features of nationalism, equated with violence. The fiasco of pan-Islamism, the disruption of the Ottoman model of the supremacy of Muslims over non-Muslims, impaired the existing order and compelled the ruler to reshape the idea of nationhood. In the words of one of the characters: "What would you call a Levantine yes? You know what they say of us: the language of six nations and the soul of none" (Unsworth 1991, p. 128). Such a taciturn maxim, in the long run, underwrote the ultimate and irrevocable fall of the Ottoman Empire, indirectly highlighting the tenets of one national language and the old-fashioned nationalism based on the shared culture.

Even though the counterrevolution of 1909 ostensibly restored the position of Islam in the empire, with the rise of Atatürk, it turned out to be a Pyrrhic victory. Used as a two-way mirror, the imperialistic and religious aims of Abdul Hamid II in Unsworth's novel foster the inevitable clash of the old Ottoman identity and its modern age version of the irreligious, enlightened and westernized Turkish one scrutinized in Orhan Pamuk's *Silent House*. Devoid of its Ottoman past – the very baggage, which one of the characters, Farouk, will try to save from perishing – Pamuk's novel unearths the struggles of the young Republic to create a modern Turkish character. The novel, set at the time of Atatürk's rise to power, is narrated by Fatma, an old woman who spends most of her days in bed, waiting for the arrival of her grandchildren – her son and his wife being already deceased – and recollecting her married life. The history of the Republic is given in the voice of Selâhattin, Fatma's husband, whose progressive views are in a stark conflict with Fatma's traditionalism. The fact that he is dead might serve as Pamuk's implied commentary on Kemalism,[41] but Fatma's age and her intensely personal point of view likewise make her an unreliable narrator. Incidentally, she is as intolerant of new ideas as her husband is prejudiced against the old ways of the world. His vehemence, verging on ludicrousness, manifesting the vicissitudes of being a (new) Turk.

Dr. Selâhattin Bey (1881–1942), a free thinker, born in the same year as Mustafa Kemal Atatürk, dared to express a negative opinion of the actions of the Committee of Union and Progress. This transgression warranted his exile in Gebze, to the house where Fatma Hanim lives at the time of the account. Reconciled with

---

41 The term referring to the visions and reforms instituted by Mustafa Kemal Atatürk.

his fate of mandatory banishment, he convinces himself and tries to persuade his wife that he is happy that they have left the "whole cursed thing called society" and are living "like Robinson Crusoe" on a "desert island" (Pamuk 2012, p. 268). Like in Defoe's novel, the image of isolation can also be read as a figurative rendering of the difficult relationship between the center and the periphery, the dominant forces and the subdued subjects. Selâhattin promises himself whilst assuring Fatma that "[…] we won't return until the day I can overturn the whole East with my encyclopedia" (Pamuk 2012, p. 268) Curiously, the mixture of acceptance and ferocity in Selâhattin's behavior plays into what Adolphus Slade associates with "Moslem resignation", which "is often the indifference to life generated by mental and physical languor, and sometimes the impatience of it" (Slade 2012, p. 7). Blinded by sanctimoniousness Selâhattin did not acknowledge similar traits in himself, seeing his co-nationals through oriental cum national stereotypes: "[…] in the languor of the East a person can accomplish nothing" (Pamuk 2012, p. 168). Using expressions comparable to Slade's, Selâhattin oscillated between despondency because "the East continued to slumber in the deep and despicable darkness of the Middle Ages", and euphoria communicated through "a great enthusiasm for work", with which he hoped to infect his nation. Logically, the inherent significance of the Ottoman and Muslim self-identification had to be contested with the new vision of secular Turkey. Selâhattin's perception of the past and the present through the apposition of dark and light, is akin to the philosophy of the Enlightenment announcing the departure of the dark ages and the emergence of the reign of reason. As a scholar, he comprehended that the Turks "were not obliged to take all this knowledge and transport it from there to here, but to discover it all over again, to close the gap of centuries between East and West in a shorter time" (Pamuk 2012, p. 29).

The stimulus of his lifelong endeavor to create a compendium of knowledge aimed to edify the nation, was an awe-inspiring mission. In one of his outbursts, rendered so as to reflect his agitation, Selâhattin expresses the qualms and joys of his undertaking:

> […] this encyclopedia is exhausting me, I don't want to be like some Eastern despot saying I don't have any time, I want to make my wife happy, let's at least walk a little in the garden, and we can talk, I'll tell you about what I read today, I think about the necessity of science and how we're so backward because we lack it, I truly understand now our need for a Renaissance, for a scientific awakening, there is an awesome job before me that must be done, and so I am actually grateful to Talat Pasha for exiling me to this lonely corner, where I can read and think about these things, because if it weren't for this emptiness and all the time in the world, I could never have come to these conclusions, would have never realized the importance of my historical task, Fatma, anyway, all of Rousseau's thoughts were the visions of a solitary wanderer in the countryside, surrounded by nature, but here the two of us are together (Pamuk 2012, p. 75).

Wrapped up in his work, Selâhattin did not want to go back to Istanbul without finishing his encyclopedia which was to "shake the foundation of everything, of the whole life of the East" (Pamuk 2012, p. 121). Analogously to Dr. Edward Casaubon in George Eliot's *Middlemarch* (1871), he felt defeated by his project, blaming his "damned country! All for nothing! If I had been able to finish those volumes" (Pamuk 2012, p. 142). He knew that he had lost fifteen years of his life and still "[...] everything's beyond the power of our speech and our words" (Pamuk 2012, p. 145). His long-term project remained unfinished, his wife, far from being converted to his, retained her beliefs, which, in Erdağ Göknar's view, suggests the dwarfing of the cultural revolution. Through the rift in their marriage, Selâhattin's implicit use of the western idea of modernization as a benchmark for Ottoman society to aspire towards is challenged in Pamuk's novel. The encyclopedia, modeled on "the positivist knowledge of the European Enlightenment", as Erdağ Göknar argues, "is a trope in Turkish literature, where it often functions as a textual space for the intersection of historical and literary or objective and subjective knowledge" (Göknar2013, p. 75). Intent on creating a new version of the Orient, Selâhattin pursued his fantasy of eradicating the sense of difference between East and West. By supporting the processes of a technological, and, above all, philosophical transformation of Turkey, he wanted to contribute to the creation of the new Turkish identity. While Fatma mourned the changes wrought by the Republic, her husband chased his dream of moving "beyond the foolishness of the East, the guilt and the sins [...] I am proud of the things that you are pleased to condemn and find revolting!" (Pamuk 2012, p. 267).

Away from Istanbul, and secure in his advocating of the Republic, Selâhattin fails to recognize his own precarious position. The mentioning of Mehmet Talât Pasha (1874–1921) in the above long quotation, testifies to his misreading of reality. Historically, Talât Pasha was a member of CUP and the founder of the Ottoman Freedom Society (Züricher 2021, p. 436). Abdul Hamid had him banished to Salonica in 1906. Having returned to Istanbul, between 1913 and 1917 he was minister of the interior, and grand vizier between 1917–1918. At the end of WWI, however, he had to escape to Germany and in 1921, he was assassinated by an Armenian in Berlin, as Züricher claims: "because of his involvement in the persecution of the Armenians." Talât's fate was not an isolated one. Erickson stresses that the representation of the former CUP leaders as war criminals as early as 1919, was precipitated by the Ottoman government, seeking "to appease the Allies regarding the Armenian massacres and the ill-treatment of prisoners of war" (Erickson 2013, p. 31).

As has been mentioned, Talât held significant influence following the deposition of the Sultan, but his power diminished after his departure from Turkey. His character and his political stance, in Selâhattin's view, undercuts the vision of

Turkey's nationalism based on occidental modernity. "Do you understand Fatma, these Unionists are going off the deep end, they can't stand freedom, how are they different from Abdülhamid?" (Pamuk 2012, p. 23f). To this effect, the narrative becomes a vent for criticism of both the Ottoman and Turkish nationalisms. Like Robert Markham in Unsworth's novel, Selâhattin also saw the rule of Abdul Hamid as a record of crimes, but unlike Unsworth, Pamuk stresses that such a thoroughly stereotypical behavior of an autocrat, prone to anger and violence, is continued by his successors. "All of the sultans were idiots [...] But Resat[42] the puppet of the Unionists was the biggest idiot of all" (Pamuk 2012, p. 261). Reşad was Abdul Hamid's brother, who, as Mehmet V, became a figurehead Sultan, his sovereignty curtailed by the Parliament and the Cabinet, the real sources of power.[43] Allowing Selâhattin to verbalize his dislike of the previous rulers, to contest both the Ottoman as well as the republican forms of government, Pamuk nonetheless refrains from letting his character express a straightforward denunciation of the Republic. Because of his exile, Selâhattin does not have a first-hand knowledge of the events; the information he receives is filtered through the stories of Avram, the Jewish jeweler from Istanbul. Avram never replies to Selâhattin's question – or conceivably Fatma does not remember or wants to remember the answer – whether the people were happy "with the proclamation of the republic" (Pamuk 2012, p. 116).[44]

In Pamuk's novel, the nation-state edifice of the Ottoman empire, a multiethnic polity, proved, in the end, to be a sandcastle. The Kemalist dream of the new Turkey, though still housing Armenians, Kurds and Jews, and geographically smaller, but perhaps easier to re-unite in the post-war mayhem, was never fully accomplished. Atatürk granted citizenship to Armenians, Kurds and Jews; they had the right to vote and serve in the army. Concurrently, in the case of the Kurds, he introduced the policy of denial, "according to which the Kurdish identity, language and culture were forbidden in Turkey" (Erickson 2013, p. 58f). Ilan Peleg reads Kemalist reforms as an example of mild democratization as the new Republic was "'engineered'" from the ruins of the empire "in a hegemonic fashion by [a] determined, cohesive political and military elite." The state instituted a newfangled idea of "nation-building" that called for "standardizing the citizenry to make them Turkish in language and nationality, secular in orientation, and obedient to the state" (Peleg 2007, p. 169). Anyone who rose to prominence could only do so as a 'Turk', though the Republic housed other Muslim non-Turkish groups of Albanians, Bosnians, Circassians and Georgians (Peleg 2007, p. 170).

---

42 Spelling original.
43 Finkel spells his name as Reşad. (For more, see Finkel 2006, p. 518f).
44 When her husband died, and her son took her last two pieces of solitaire diamonds, her jewelry box was empty (Pamuk 2012, p. 125).

Atatürk's aim was to create a relatively homogenous culture, whose tenets were defined by the state authorities rather than by religious ones. That kind of "cultural nationalism", as Margalit assumes, "considers the nation as an organic entity whose supreme expression is the national culture – particularly the national language" (Margalit 1997, p. 77). Modern societies have official languages, usually equated with the high, literate culture – an expression of the creative potential of its members, who used literature to sustain national distinctiveness – consigning the minority languages to the low, and sometimes forbidden culture.[45] In 1928, Atatürk decided to replace the Arabic based Ottoman script with Latin lettering, and this was followed by the introduction of the metric system, which further integrated Turkey with Europe (Kinross 2001, p. 441 ff, Erickson 2013, p. 60). The revolution in letters as Göknar terms it, was a violence against itself (Göknar 2013, p. 74). To soften the blow of the changes, and confirm the importance of the Turkish language, Atatürk endorsed a hypothesis that Turkish was the sun language, the original world language from which all others evolved.[46] The reformed language undoubtedly bridged the gap between the written and the spoken word in the long run; however, the change of the alphabet, resulted in the loss of the Ottoman past for the generations born in the Republic. In toto, the compulsory romanization, as Anderson argues, was instituted "[t]o heighten Turkish-Turkey's national consciousness at the expense of any wider Islamic identification" (Anderson 2006, p. 46).

Treated as a remedy to the political and social problems of post-First World War Turkey, the multifaceted nationalism of Kemal Mustafa Atatürk, was based on the substitution of the family with a grander idea, that of the nation. Atatürk's goal, to have the national allegiances surpass the family and the religious community[47] was attained when The Grand Assembly dissolved the Sultanate in November 1922 (Erickson 2013, p. 47). Although Abdul Hamid's cousin was elected caliph, in the end, Atatürk exiled Abdulmecid to Switzerland thereby

---

45 Harold Pinter in his play *Mountain Language* portrayed the conflict between the Kurds and the Turks. The story of his inspiration is offered by Antonia Fraser (2010, p. 149). Peleg outlines the Kurdish guerilla campaigns against the Turkish military, which was orchestrated to keep the Kurdish question on the agenda (Peleg 2007, p. 170).
46 Erickson (2013, p. 59) and Kinross (2001, p. 466f) show Atatürk's involvement with the sun language theory, with Turkish as the mother of all languages, stating that the president himself was engrossed in the search for "pure Turkish words." Atatürk searched for the philological links between Turkish and foreign words but was also intent on substituting the borrowings with Turkish equivalents. The whole nation was involved in the project and lists of words were published daily in the newspapers (Kinross 2001, p. 466).
47 McMahan, claims that an individual identification with one's nation "as the primary locus of collective self-identification [...] has become a fecund source of self-esteem" (McMahan 1997, p. 119).

abolishing the Caliphate (Kinross 2001, p. 384ff).[48] Accordingly, as an exponent of atheism, Pamuk's character argues that "atheism and secularism will do the whole country good" (Pamuk 2012, p. 259). This statement might be in agreement with Fukuyama's hypothesis, that countries undergoing economic modernization need to "unify nationality on the basis of a centralized state, urbanize, replace traditional forms of social organization like tribe, sect, and family with economically rational ones based on function and efficiency, and provide for the universal education of their citizens" (Fukuyama 1992, p. xv). The republican secularization of school curricula understandably lay emphasis on the importance of the new Turkish national identity, accompanied by the efforts to create an official culture, the products of which would be "poetry, prose fiction, music, [and] plastic arts" (Anderson 2006, p. 141). It made the inhabitants aware of their Turkishness, and in order to stress its significance, Atatürk encouraged the examination of the history of Turkey and of the Turks (Kinross 2001, p. 467). His belief in westernization prompted the reform of the calendar; the year was no longer 1345 but 1926. The day of rest was also altered from Friday to Sunday (Erickson 2013, p. 59). Erdağ Göknar in his analysis of *Silent House*, points to the presence of dual time, which affects the characters in the novel: the Muslim time, *din*, and the social revolutionary time of the secular *develet*. Selâhattin, forcing the authoritarian progressivism on his family, is desperate for all of them to embrace the *develet*, the transformation being the best testimonial to the cultural revolution and the republican literary modernity of *homo secularis* (Göknar 2013, p. 86). Regrettably, the widespread implantation of *develet*, corresponded with the decline of the Ottoman legacy of *din*. Two generations later, all historical documents would require a transcription from the Ottoman script into the Latin one and a conversion from the Muslim time into the Christian calendar; this, as has been noted by Fukuyama, is the price for advancement.

Whereas the inclusion of Turkey into the modern, European world was seen as an inevitable development, Farouk's determination to read and transliterate the forgotten histories discloses that the country was unalterably cut off from its Ottoman identity. His laborious efforts to delve into Gebze court records demonstrates his avidity in recreating the past and is comparable to his grandfather's eagerness to fashion the future, encapsulated in science. For Farouk, the stories of Ottoman merchants are inextricably bound with his life: "this is history and life" (Pamuk 2012, p. 197). That is why his accounts are intermingled with autobio-

---

48 With the proclamation of the Turkish Republic by the Grand National Assembly on October 29, 1923, as the new nation's first president, Atatürk moved the capital city from Constantinople to Ankara, the first one being the prized city of the Ottoman Empire and the second, a rural small town. (For a more detailed account, see Kinross 2001, p. 384ff).

graphical references and commentaries.[49] His attempts to re-validate the Ottoman past are analogous to Pamuk's efforts to restore versions of those bygone stories in his ensuing novels: *The White Castle* and *My Name is Red*, with both novels showing the trajectory of public history and individual memory from the past into the future. Sharing the same idealism of his grandfather, but choosing a different premise of his investigation, Farouk, struck with melancholy, an almost paralyzing sadness, and frequently drunk, dreams of re-writing and explaining the History through the (hi)stories of common people (Pamuk 2012, p. 203).[50] In an epiphanic moment he realizes that "[w]ith this story of the plague I could destroy a host of historical 'facts' just floating in the air without doubt as to their truth, like so many potted plants. In this way a whole crowd of credulous historians, realizing clearly that their work was actually storytelling, would find the scales falling from their eyes, as I did" (Pamuk 2012, p. 200). Farouk hopes that his recreation of the lives of ordinary individuals would endow the coming generations with a knowledge of their past, the history being "nothing more than a seamless picture of things" (Pamuk 2012, p. 276). Destabilizing leading orientalist and nationalist binaries, Farouk, another disgruntled member of the Darvinoğlu family, embarks on an idealistic project hoping to enlighten his peers. Collecting scraps of knowledge, his method resembles the form of narration employed in *Silent House*, where voice is given to the five main characters, their points of view, their versions of reality, as fragmentary as the stories that Farouk finds in the archives. The ramifications of his research undermine the Republican historical social realism. Invested in finding the truth about the past, Farouk is, therefore, blind to the new political forces, equally ferocious in their dislike of Kemalist reforms, as his grandfather was of the Ottoman models.

Freeing his country from an irrational belief in God was synonymous with progress; the profanity, which only seemingly reinforced the superiority of the west. Accepting Kemalist secularism prompted Selâhattin to repeatedly declare that since his existence could not be "proven by experiment" (Pamuk 2012, p. 355), God was dead, substituted by science (Pamuk 2012, p. 31). In Selâhattin's mind, the fact "[…] that things are made by other things and absolutely nothing exists by the hand of God" (Pamuk 2012, p. 169), a blasphemy Fatma had to

---

49 A good illustration of Farouk's narrative method is the chapter entitled 'Farouk Looks for Stories in the Archive' (Pamuk 2012, p. 146 ff).

50 He hopes that to find some remnants of that history in the ruins nearby Gebze (Pamuk 2012, p. 201). In *Istanbul. Memories and the City*, Pamuk offers the story of Ahmet Refik Altınay, a Turkish historian, academic, writer and poet, who was teaching at Istanbul University, then known as Darulfunum, and in his spare time he "was combing through the 'dirt and dust' of the disordered Ottoman archives (then known as 'the paper treasury') for the handwritten accounts of Ottoman Chroniclers; he scavenged whatever he could." He wanted to "make history something that could be ingested with ease" (Pamuk 2006, p. 142).

swallow, but could not forgive.[51] In his ramblings about religion he negated the existence not only of the afterlife, but also spirituality, thereby falling back onto the stereotype of the sleeping, inert East, lagging behind and failing to acknowledge "that nothingness" which reveals the truth about life. Ironically, in an almost medieval way, he admitted that in death there is no difference between the East and the West. Depicting himself as a more enlightened thinker, he reiterated: "I think of death, therefore I'm a Westerner!" (Pamuk 2012, p. 359). Selâhattin's statements seem to echo Marxist pronouncements that "the masses [are] stupefied by God" (Pamuk 2012, p. 29), yet he unarguably foregoes the communist idea of subjugating people with similar promises of a perfect future life. Trying to convince Fatma that all knowledge came from experimentation (Pamuk 2012, p. 258). Selâhattin found a wall of resistance, their conflicting worldviews aggrandizing the disagreements in their marriage. In Gebze, Selâhattin was not allowed to treat the female patients because the wives could not be examined and he refused to give the patient medicine without examining her. He understood that the government never gave them a chance to get a good education, but his behavior, nonetheless, drove all of his patients away (Pamuk 2012, p. 81f). Atatürk's reforms touched the core of family life: Polygamy was banned, civil marriages were made compulsory and a man could no longer divorce his wife in a Muslim way – saying it three times; they had to "go to a civil court now" (Pamuk 2012, p. 123). By giving women the right to vote in 1934,[52] and discouraging them from wearing the veil, the president strove to form an unprejudiced and progressive society, similar to those he observed in the west (Erickson 2013, p. 59). Muslims were required to wear a hat instead of the fez (Pamuk 2012, p. 122); the adoption of European style dress was aligned with Atatürk's outlawing of the Sufi orders (Göknar 213, p. 75f, 222ff). What is more, against Muslim fear of idolatry, the portraits of Atatürk began to appear and the practice of engraving religious phrases on public buildings was forbidden from 1927 onwards (Erickson 2013, p. 59). Within a short span of time, Turkey was to become an entirely different country, but the implementation of cultural changes aimed at de-orientalizing Ottoman Turkishness in real life proved not as straightforward as on paper.

Unmindful of the westernized freedoms granted to all inhabitants, Fatma obstinately shut her husband out of her life, even though Selâhattin tried to

---

51 "It follows that the heaven and hell they babble about also don't exist [...] If there is no life after death, the lives of those who die disappear altogether. There remains of them absolutely nothing" (Pamuk 2012, p. 355). The discussion concerning death is one of the corner stones of Selâhattin's philosophies, it is also a bone of contention between secular and religious viewpoints. Rewriting the famous Descartian assertion, he proclaimed: "I think of death, therefore I exist" (Pamuk 2012, p. 359).

52 Ironically, the early nationalisms of revolutions that "sought to liberate states consisted of free men, excluded women and slaves" (Taylor 1997, p. 52).

discuss the importance of his project and his belief in Darwin's theory, regarded by him as "a triumph of human thought" (Pamuk 2012, p. 261). Raised to be a traditional Muslim wife, Fatma could never agree with "gorillas being grandfathers of men;" nor with his claims that "[...] the incredible advances of the sciences in the West had now made God's existence a ridiculous question to be cast aside" (Pamuk 2012, pp. 28-29). Fatma kept clinging to the conviction that religious identification was synonymous with the Ottoman traditions. She rejected her husband's "sinful papers" (Pamuk 2012, p. 29);[53] while Selâhattin admittedly called his work his beloved sin (Pamuk 2012, p. 260); his enthusiasm evident in the choice of the family name, Darvinoğlu, the son of Darwin (Pamuk 2012, p. 124). Fatma disliked their family name, it was yet another alteration in her world that she had to live with. Mustafa Kemal himself had the parliament decree his last name: Atatürk, meaning 'father of the Turks' (Erickson 2013, p. 60, 5)[54] and subsequently forced the nation to assume European style names. The decree was passed by the parliament in 1928, five years after the proclamation of the Republic. This edict was followed by the abolition of the Ottoman titles: "Pasha" and "Bey" (Erickson 2013, p. 60). Failing to accept her husband's unwavering emulation of Kemalism, but discerning that they lived in auspicious times, she agreed to name her son Doğan, signifying 'Birth', "[...] so that he'll always remind us of the new world that is dawning." The name also resonated with Selâhattin's theories that their son should live in "security and prosperity and believes that his strength is a match for the world!" (Pamuk 2012, p. 112).[55] Presumptuous in his belief that all enlightened people should partake in his visions of the new Turkey, and continuing to be the incurable idealist, Selâhattin dreamt of a world unclouded by superstition: "The world is like the apple from that forbidden tree [...] it is only because you believe in lies and are afraid that

---

53 Fatma would have opted for a more traditional family model. Even though she knew about Selâhattin's trysts with the woman in the village, she did not confront her husband, but beat her husband's illegitimate sons so hard that one was permanently lame, and the other remained a dwarf.
54 Atatürk appeared on the cover of Time Magazine in 1923 as a general and in 1927 as a statesman (Erickson 2013, p. 5).
55 District Administrator Doğan Darvinoğlu (1915-1967) was buried in the cemetery in Gebze alongside his wife, Gül Darvinoğlu (1922-1964) (Pamuk 2012, p. 83). Fatma recalls being unhappy that her son, instead of becoming an engineer or a businessman so that he could use the education of the French school, decided to become a politician (Pamuk 2012, p. 84). Doğan, exhibiting idealism similar to his father's, retorted that "[...] this country can only be straightened out through politics," and then he could no longer be the district administrator because he hated the people (Pamuk 2012, p. 84). He gave up his position as a district administrator before he was eligible for a pension and settled in Cennethisar (Pamuk 2012, p. 153). Doğan is yet another character for whom the cultural revolution was incomplete, his disillusionment with the birth of the new Republic being in utter contrast with his father's aspirations.

you don't pick it and eat it; pick the fruit of the tree of knowledge and eat it, my son" (Pamuk 2012, p. 209).[56]

Considering the fascination with the West as aping rather than inspiring and eye-opening, the young generation discerns what Slade pinpointed more than a hundred years ago, that Turkey was a stepchild of Europe. They unabashedly identify "imperialist Europeans", as "treacherous [and] slanderous," spreading their old-time negative opinions of Turkey, such as: "Plants don't grow where the Turk has passed" (Pamuk 2012, p. 214). The old Ottoman pride resounds in an angry torrent by one of the characters who deems "[...] two sunpowers, America and the Soviets [...] want to divide up the world, and that Jew Marx lies when he says that what makes the world go around is what he called the class struggle, it's nationalism, and the most extreme nationalists are the Russians and the Europeans" (Pamuk 2012, p. 214). Interestingly, while renouncing Atatürk's vision of their country, they unwittingly follow his belief that Turkey was the center of the world, the key to the Middle East. Offering a well-known mixture of nationalism and religious fundamentalism, recapitulated in the question: "Are you a Muslim or a Turk?", the young men in Pamuk's novel want to recreate the myth of the Ottoman empire falsifying and idealizing the image of the past. As Taylor suggests, "[...] nationalism, proletarian internationalism, and religious fundamentalism in the same register may help us to understand their interaction, that they often fight for the same space" (Taylor 1991, p. 51). Eisenstadt disputes that contemporary fundamentalist movements are thoroughly modern movements, because of their anti-modern or anti-Enlightenment ideologies (Eisenstadt 1999, p. 1).[57] Instead, he sees the fundamentalism as a prevailing Jacobin anti-modern utopia and heterodoxy based on the totalizing reconstruction of tradition (Eisenstadt 1999, p. 82). Repressed by the Kemalist regime, these movements tried to "renovate utopian sectarianism" (Eisenstadt 1999, p. 3) offering another vision of salvation, resounding positively in countries with a strong religious past. Eisenstadt diagnosis is that "Islamic societies [...] with their sectarian tendencies was often connected with processes attendant on the expansion of Islam and especially with the continuous impingement on the core of Islamic politics by tribal elements who presented themselves as the carriers of the original Islamic vision of the pristine Islamic polity" (Eisenstadt 1999, p. 23). Atatürk's modernization shaped a new secular collectivity but for the young people born in the

---

56 Faruk's musings would be somewhat more positive than his father's wry estimates of his country. In his view: "The world is a place to be described and experienced as it is, usually with equanimity, occasionally with or as something bittersweet; but it's not a place for finding fault or cause for anger while you're in it" (Pamuk 2012, p. 275).

57 Eisenstadt reads the great revolutions through the transformation of sectarian utopianism in the cultural and political program of modernity (Eisenstadt 1999, p. 39).

Republic of Turkey cut off from their Ottoman Muslim roots, the immaculate pan-Islamic identity had more appeal.

As has been argued above, Kemalists promulgated and believed in progressive Turkey. Pamuk's novel, however, predicts the transformation of the modern *develet* in the form of military coups. The new nationality was forged at the cost of the refutation of its Muslim history and the repudiation of spirituality. The loss of this social anchor left the young generation unhinged, deprived of the sense of belonging.[58] For this reason, Farouk fantasizes that through reconstructing Ottoman lives, he can restore the threads that link his contemporaries with their disowned traditions. The young Turkish men living in 1980s Gebze, on the other hand, are certain their selfhood can only be reclaimed through the revival of the country's Muslim origins. The vision of the Islamic purity of their Turkey, drives them to attack Nilgün, Selâhattin's granddaughter, who buys a communist paper, for they "don't allow Communists around here" (Pamuk 2012, p. 225). The physical and verbal cruelty perpetrated on the innocent young woman is the most serious relapse against modern national humanism. In their pro-Muslim, against-the-West mercilessness, these young men punch Nilgün so hard that she later dies from a hemorrhage. Thus, the sins of the fathers – the grandfather in this case – are revisited in the third generation, because Nilgün's beating might be seen as the retribution for the maiming of Selâhattin's illegitimate sons by Fatma. The inherited brutality in the family history is subsumed in the call of the (new)nationalism and explained through the psychology of violence sustained by the previous forms of nationalism and, prophetically, upheld by the coming new military rulers in Turkey. Such an implied cycle of history, though not universal to all countries, as Fukuyama holds, is predictable in violent regimes substituting one for the other (Fukuyama 1992, p. 55). The final images of the novel are not those of hope, as neither the secular nor the religious forces are capable of restructuring the nation battling the stagnant atmosphere and struggling to revitalize its individuality while at the same time maintaining its position on the international arena.

In Joyce's *Ulysses*, Leopold Bloom, caught unawares by John Wyse, offers the definition of a nation as "the same people living in the same place." Correcting himself to account for diasporas, he then broadens the definition as including those "living in different places" (Joyce 1990, p. 331). The anxieties of Bloom, an Irish Jew, might not be shared by the inhabitants of the Ottoman Empire, or the succeeding Turkish Republic, but would point to the early twentieth century fluctuations in accounting for what a modern nation is. In the existing discourses

---

58 In a later novel, *Snow*, Pamuk shows the need for belief and belonging. The novel tracing the development of events leading up to a military coup, opens with a group of young female high-school students fighting for the right to wear hijabs to school (Pamuk 2004).

on nationalism, countries whose statehood is based on ethnicity and religion are bound to be perceived as regressive, their narrow-gauge nationalism treated as an impediment in their cultural development. Despite the globalizing tendencies of the contemporary world, there exists an observable tendency to assert one's own indigeneity. National identities and, for that matter, religious affinities, still mark the perception of oneself and others within international communities; even more so in times of on-going conflicts. Similar leanings are present in Barry Unsworth's *The Rage of the Vulture* and Orhan Pamuk's *Silent House*. In *The Rage of the Vulture*, the sultan, Abdul Hamid II, caters to the aspiration of the legendary founder of the Ottoman Empire, Osman, trying to maintain his rule over the grand Turkey, whose territories include the Balkan states and house the minorities that is Armenians and Kurds. Dedicated to the consolidation of hitherto subjugated lands, Abdul Hamid II nevertheless witnesses the gradual reduction of his domain, his iron fist politics signposting not the resurrection but the imminent demise of the empire. Failing to analyze the entirety of Abdul Hamid's reign, Unsworth puts the blame of its collapse on the Sultan's paralyzing anxieties concerning his personal safety and political security. He repeats the, all too obvious, allegations of Islamism and the resultant backwardness, besides disregarding the fact that the country, thrown at the mercy of the European powers at the beginning of the twentieth century, was conflicted internally, its self-image weakened by the economic crisis and nationalistic movements within its borders. For Unsworth, the anti-constitutional movements of Abdul Hamid II stand for the very image of the eastern autocrat, but are, in reality, repetitions of the stereotypical Western depictions of the Orient, already present in medieval Saracen Romances. Abdul Hamid's attempts at preserving the Ottoman rule and traditions were akin to the new leader's, Mustafa Kemal Atatürk's, efforts to institute the republic. In his pursuit of modernity Atatürk was dedicated to the proscription of the tyranny of religious leaders, whose orthodoxy, in his mind, hampered the progress and distorted Turkey's position on the global stage. Pamuk's *Silent House* unveils the impact of the rise of the modern irreligious state on average family life. For the main, albeit at the time of the novel's action already dead hero, the tensions between 'indigeneity' and 'tradition' are rooted in the interaction between the East and the West. Selâhattin's views validate the philosophy of the republic predicated on the destruction of the decayed Ottoman legacy. Concurrent with the inception of the new Turkish nationalism, his utter and total immersion in republicanism and Darwinism emphasizes the discursive hegemony of the west coexisting with his wife's reluctance to emulate Kemalist ideologies. Still, because of the juxtaposition of the western and eastern worldviews, his encyclopedia perpetuates an 'Orientalist' mode of thinking, reaffirming the separation of the Occident and the Orient. The fact that Selâhattin has never finished his life's work voices Pamuk's discomfited vision of Atatürk's reforms; their reiteration in the novel serving to contest their assumed success.

While *The Rage of the Vulture,* because of its negative attitude to Islam-based nationalism, points to the fundamental misunderstanding of the functioning of the Ottoman empire by the British, Pamuk's *Silent House* indicates the equally limiting domination of secularism at the cost of the loss of Muslim culture and spirituality. In the character of Selâhattin's grandson, Farouk, fascinated with the visual and written history of the Ottomans, Pamuk implies the possibility of salvaging their stories, and building a bridge between the past and the present. Yet Farouk's endeavor is marred by the presence of the new fundamentalist forces. Their anger, anchored in the current politics, erupts in the violence against his sister, Nilgün, thereby demonstrating that the mistakenly delineated 'imagined community' is bound to, yet again, vanquish the mirages of nationhood and cultural cohesion.

Bibliography

Anderson, Benedict: *Imagined Communities. Reflections on the Origin and Spread of Nationalism.* London and New York 2006 [1983].
Burton, Richard F.: *Personal Narrative of a Pilgrimage to Al-Madinah and Meccah.* Volumes I and II. New York 1964 [1893].
Byron, George Gordon: *Byron Poetical Works.* Edited by John Jump. Oxford 1970.
Cresy, Edward S.: *History of the Ottoman Turks. With a New Introduction by Zeine N. Zeine.* Beirut 1961.
Eisenstadt, S.N.: *Fundamentalism, Sectarianism, and Revolution.* Cambridge 1999.
Erickson, Edward J.: *Mustafa Kemal Atatürk. Leadership, Strategy, Conflict.* London 2013.
Finkel, Caroline: *Osman's Dream. The Story of the Ottoman Empire 1300–1923.* London 2006 [2005].
Fukuyama, Francis: *The End of History and the Last Man.* London 1992.
Glover, Jonathan: 'Nations, Identity, and Conflict', in: Robert McKim / McMahan, Jeff (eds.): *The Morality of Nationalism.* New York and Oxford 1997, p. 11–30.
Goodkin, Robert E: 'Conventions and Conversions, or Why Is Nationalism Something so nasty?' in: Robert McKim / McMahan, Jeff (eds.): *The Morality of Nationalism.* New York and Oxford 1997, p. 88–104.
Göknar, Erdağ: *Orhan Pamuk. Secularism and Blasphemy. The Politics of the Turkish Novel.* London 2013.
Grosby, Steven: *Nationalism. A Very Short Introduction.* Oxford 2005.
Hiro, Dilip: *The Essential Middle East. A Comprehensive Guide.* New York 2003 [1996].
Hoffman, Bruce: *Inside Terrorism.* New York 2006.
Horace: *The Complete Odes and Satires of Horace.* Translated by Sidney Alexander. Princeton, New Jersey 1999.
Joyce, James: *Ulysses. The Complete and Unabridged Text.* New York 1990 [1934].

Khair, Tabish: *The New Xenophobia*. Oxford 2016.
Kinross, Patrick: *Atatürk. The Rebirth of a Nation*. London 2001 [1993].
Kymlicka, Will: 'The Sources of Nationalism: Commentary on Taylor', in: Robert McKim / McMahan, Jeff (eds.): *The Morality of Nationalism*. New York and Oxford 1997, p. 56–65.
Lichtenberg, Judith: 'Nationalism, For and (Mainly) Against', in: Robert McKim / McMahan, Jeff (eds.): *The Morality of Nationalism*. New York and Oxford 1997, p. 158–175.
Mansfield, Peter: *A History of the Middle East*. London 2004 [1991].
Margalit, Avishai: 'The Moral Psychology of Nationalism', in: Robert McKim / McMahan, Jeff (eds.): *The Morality of Nationalism*. New York and Oxford 1997, p. 74–87.
Macfie, Alexander L.: *The End of the Ottoman Empire 1908–1923*. London 1998.
McMahan, Jeff: 'The Limits of National Partiality', in: McKim, Robert / McMahan, Jeff (eds.): *The Morality of Nationalism*. New York and Oxford 1997, p. 107–138.
McKim, Robert / McMahan, Jeff (eds.): *The Morality of Nationalism*. New York and Oxford: Oxford, 1997.
Owen, Wilfred: *The Collected Poems of Wilfred Owen*. Edited by C. Day Lewis. London 1963 [1920].
Pamuk, Orhan: *Silent House*. Translated by Robert Finn. London 2013 [1983].
Pamuk, Orhan: *The White Castle*. Translated by Victoria Holbrook. London 2001 [1983].
Pamuk, Orhan: *My Name is Red*. Translated by Erdağ Göknar. London 2001.
Pamuk, Orhan: *Snow*. Translated by Maureen Freely. London 2004.
Pamuk, Orhan: *Istanbul. Memories and the City*. Translated by Maureen Freely. London 2006 [2005].
Peleg, Ilan: *Democratizing the Hegemonic State*. Cambridge 2007.
Plato: *Republic*. Translated by Robin Waterfield. Oxford 1998 [1993].
Rogan, Eugene: *The Arabs, A History*. London 2010 [2009].
Slade, Adolphus: *Turkey and the Crimean War. A Narrative of Historical Events*. Cambridge 2012 [1867].
Sikorska, Liliana: *Nineteenth and Twentieth-Century Readings of the Medieval Orient. Other Encounters*. Michigan 2021.
Taylor, Charles: 'Nationalism and Modernity', in: Robert McKim / McMahan, Jeff (eds.): *The Morality of Nationalism*. New York, Oxford 1997, p. 31–55.
Todorov, Tzvetan: *The Fear of Barbarians. Beyond the Clash of Civilizations*. Translated by Andrew Brown. Chicago 2010.
Unsworth, Barry: *The Rage of the Vulture*. London 1991 [1982].
Vincent, Andrew: *Nationalism and Particularity*. Cambridge 2002.
Volkan, Vamik D.: *The Need to Have Enemies and Allies. From Clinical Practice to International Relationships*. Northvale 1988.
Wilson, Andrew N.: *After the Victorians. 1901–1953*. London 2005.
Zeine N. Zeine: 'Introduction', in: Cresy, Edward S.: *History of the Ottoman Turks. With a New Introduction by Zeine N. Zeine*. Beirut 1961 [1878].
Züricher, Erik J.: *Turkey. A Modern History*. London 2021 [1993].

Ryszard Bartnik

'A writer beyond borders on gross ethics-related negligence': J. M. Coetzee, life-writing and a moral railing against the modern world's maladies

At present, when writing about nationalism in its various guises, it is almost impossible to ignore the Russian context. In this country, in the name of defending the fundamental interests of 'the people', its leader/dictator has unleashed a war [special operation – sic!] in Ukraine. Of course, the purpose of this article by no means is to dissect the causes behind Putin's mad war, but we can think for a moment about the term nation/national, which seems to play a key role in the autocrat's narrative. His justification for starting the military action was not the declared defense of the Russians against Ukraine's purported aggression, but the vindication of "the imperial conception of the nation" (Cörüt 2021, p. 118). In other words, the aggressor justified his actions on behalf of an imaginary collectivity whose foundations nonetheless, as indicated by Benedict Anderson, are only apparently solid, homogeneous, and truly non-inclusive.[1] What seems disconcerting, in this regard, is the fact that even today, also among Western European democracies, many look favorably on such closed structures, construed in "nationalist terms", believing that they will ensure popular "support", "well-being" and "jobs for our people" (Clarke 2021, p. 98). The actual results of such polices, however, turn out to be less sanguine and are often fraught with unintended and rather adverse consequences.

Craig Calhoun writes about similar outcomes, concurrently pointing out that nationalism is both a "deceptive" and a powerful tool for 'manufacturing' a given community. Both through its overwhelming character, and also through its proclivity to employ language that is not geared towards presenting a nuanced view of the world, "nationalism does not resolve conflicts, [but] provokes and sustains them" [own translation] (Calhoun 2007, p. 23). Nationalist rhetoric

---

[1] Interestingly, Gözde Cörüt (2021, p. 118) points out the fabrication underlying Russian identity. Given that between the fourteenth and seventeenth century it was the "territory" which solely defined Russianness, then during the reign of Peter the Great the reference point was ethnicity, and in the nineteenth century, under the influence of Romanticism, it was determined by its roots in "folk culture". All this proves that fixed nation-ness is a myth, and the promotion of this kind of homogenous identity serves purely political purposes.

neither attains to the level of articulate ideas nor to that of a discourse able to pose universal questions about the human condition. In this sense, while it often is meant to be a response to chaos and confusion, such a strongly communicated need for clear cues as regards identity formations turns into an all-too-tempting-panacea for those who "demand recognition of [their] dignity". The problem is, as Francis Fukuyama indicates, that the remedy is dosed "in restrictive ways: not for all human beings, but members of a particular national group" (2019, p. 73). Under such circumstances, the universe of the individual is dominated by the imposed framework of nationalistic sentiment. Stefan Berger (2005, p. 655), considering contemporary European contexts, suggests that it is legitimate to say that today we are dealing with "a return to the national paradigm". In his opinion, we should even speak of "the heritage mania", within which the aforementioned national agenda reifies itself as representing the highest value.

Trying to place John Maxwell Coetzee in the above context, one might begin with the author's concern for the fate of Ivan Turgenev. This Russian writer, back in the day, wanted to leave a national context out of the backstories of his own characters; yet because he was not entirely consistent in that decision,[2] he was attacked from the left and right side of the political spectrum (Coetzee 2002, p. 274 ff). Coetzee acknowledges a noticeable sympathy for Turgenev, yet points to another writer who appears to have been on the same wavelength, namely André Brink, who lived and published during the apartheid era. Much space was devoted to him in Coetzee's *Essays on Censorship*, wherein Brink was displayed as a novelist reluctant to be circumscribed within national boundaries, who chose "the higher authority of his own conscience" to serve as his writerly and moral compass (Coetzee 1996, p. 205). According to Brink, it is not nationalism/nationalist policy/the national mindset that determines the role of a writer, but a "compelling duty […] to destroy simplistic polarities and open up complexities" (Coetzee 1996, p. 207). The writer, with all the tools at his disposal, must devote the greatest attention to language that squares off against the idea of "language [as] play[ing] a central role in constructing national identity"[3] (Stefanova 2020, p. 66). Its proper use and solemnity are supposed to reflect the author's moral integrity, the very trait that enables him go beyond the narrow scope of national/ist mentalities.

There can be no doubt that John Maxwell Coetzee is one of the most acclaimed contemporary writers, with his body of work having left an indelible imprint on

---

2 Coetzee writes about Turgenev's "various self-presentations [that] drew him […] into a political role" (2002, p. 275).
3 Svetlana Stefanova takes here as her point of reference Anderson's concept of imagined communities.

those focused on the act of universalist[4] writing and its tenuous correlation with reality. In the midst of the wealth of critical commentary regarding his literary legacy, a certain general conclusion seems to predominate, namely that that when one postulates *words* as a precise/adequate medium for representing the real, one instead discovers narrative uncertainties. Among the myriad scholars who have unquestionably endorsed Coetzee's approach to language and reality is David Attwell. In his understanding, the writer's literary production derives from a principled stance that undermines absolute trust in any all-embracing textual signification. At the same time, as Attwell emphasizes, he credibly and with conviction employs textual formats to "address the ethical and political" (1993, p. 1). Derek Attridge, likewise, emerges as a noteworthy voice. In a discussion on Coetzee's experimentation with the character of Elizabeth Costello, he underlines that the novelist, through his "fictional invention, [...] returns the living human being to language". In light of these observations, it would be a mistake to see Coetzee as merely interested in locating his characters and himself in a domain outside the real. As has been underscored, Coetzee acknowledges the ambiguous nature of his own voice, yet never has he implied that his attempts of "self-examination" (Attridge 2004, p. 199) are completely detached from the actuality of pressing socio-political contexts.

Coetzee has always been convinced that the actual can be touched upon obliquely, and 'truth' is obscured (to be individually discovered) behind a veil of (un)apparent textual signification.[5] As a result of this distrust in fatuously straightforward links between thought, language and the world's materiality, Coetzee distances himself from the characters or narrative voices that, by definition, are associated with him (consider Elizabeth Costello or Coetzee's use of a third-person pronoun 'he' instead of 'I' in *Youth* and *Boyhood*) or the confines of any specific nationality. Bearing in mind all this deliberate vagueness, the aim of this paper is, within or beyond mainstream criticism, to establish a framework for extrapolating the author's elusive stance on matters of public resonance,[6] which

---

4 The above-mentioned universalist perspective defies "the image of nation [implicating] a mentality [...] imbued with the desire to form totality through exclusionary procedures" (Teimouri 2019, p. 348).
5 Johan Geertsema's remarks about the novelist's perception of language, particularly its function in reflecting the real, are pertinent. Once again, we come across the notion that there is no direct, one-to-one correspondence between language and experience. Coetzee is presented as a man of letters who comprehends that "language enables communication of experience, [but] it does so at a high cost". As is further pointed out, this is so because language, as a "conceptualizing, metaphorizing force", shows the tendency to "reduce [...] the uniqueness of particular experience" (Geertsema 2014, p. 27). Experiences of the real, however, are not so much hidden within the text as they are seeded therein to be discovered.
6 In order to explain Coetzee's domain of expertise, I propose to consider Peter Scheingold's views on literary texts of political engagement. Contrary to what one might expect, that kind of

subsidiarily confirms his universalist doctrine and "post-national status."[7] In order to achieve that goal I will refer to two (semi) life-narratives by Coetzee, one of which – *Diary of a Bad Year* – could be regarded as a combination of fiction and non-fiction/chronicle formats, and the other of which – *Summertime* – as a fictionalized biography of the novelist's life. Before we embark on the analysis outlined in this manner, we shall take a moment, however, to look at the European episode in the formation of the writer's consciousness.

Reading Coetzee's early semi-autobiographies,[8] one might notice a striking resemblance between him and the character of Stephen Dedalus. Similarly to Stephen, Coetzee tended during his formative years to shake off the yoke of South African reality in order to gain intellectual and artistic independence. The actuality connoted with Worcester and Cape Town was too limiting, too suffocating and too raging. Hence, the novelist's desire to liberate himself from all possible constraints inflicted upon him by his motherland for, as Jean Sévry claims, "[...] Coetzee [did not see himself [...] as a member of a given socio-[cultural] community, but rather as a member of humanity [...] he look[ed] for universals" (Sévry 2000, p. 22).

A partly realization of Sévry's assumption can be observed in *Youth*, wherein Coetzee's narrative voice views his life initially from the perspective of Cape Town and eventually from that of London. He attempts to flee from all that constraining South African reality and find the 'Promised Land' in Europe. Before the departure, he reveals the fundamentals of his artistic manifesto, which is to "create art" that is as universal in its meaning as possible (Coetzee 2003, p. 30). He consciously, "[...] watching history being unmade" (2003, p. 38), chooses to distance himself from any direct involvement in recent conflicts, as he distrusts any literature with a national character. As Mike Marais claims, Coetzee is more inclined to express confidence in "[...] the ability of literature to recover what has previously been repressed by nationalist discourse" (Marais 2000: 160). Thus, what the writer demands of himself is to create as a universalist, with an im-

---

writing "shifts attention [...] to ordinary people", yet also to "regimes, bureaucratic institutions and professionals" whose objective remains to "colonize consciousness". The perspective provided by a writer differs from that practiced by "social scientists and historians who tend to gaze down from above". The former, according to Scheingold, characteristically delves into "the shattered lives, the moral dilemmas and the emotional chaos" of contemporary times. General attention, then, is directed towards "a collective catastrophe depicted through the lives of victims, victimizers, opportunists, true believers and those who simply avert their eyes" (2010, p. 2).

7 As Duncan Chesney claims, it is that "post-national status" that enables him "to reach a maximal audience and maximal success" (2022, p. 86).
8 The following two paragraphs are an excerpt from a larger discussion of Coetzee's autobiographical texts included in my book *Inscribed into past. A Comparative Study of South African and Northern Irish Literary Narratives After the Watersheds of the 1990s* (Bartnik 2017, p. 107 f.).

personal voice and emotional distance, especially towards issues which could anchor him to South Africa. Consequently, Coetzee begins to ponder over and adopt T. S. Eliot's stance on the nature of poetry, which states that "[p]oetry is not an expression of personality but an escape from personality" (Coetzee 2003, p. 61). The writer attempts to blot out memories of his personal past, which he associates with misery and views as ugly and dark.

Venturing into both poetry and prose, Coetzee develops a fascination with Henry James, whom the author asserts "[…] shows one how to rise above mere nationality" (Coetzee 2003, p. 64). James is perceived as an icon with regard to universality in fiction. Cutting the umbilical cord with his national background, Coetzee intentionally locates himself among such figures as Eliot or James. His insistence on artistic freedom of creation leads him to a new place of destination: London. Here, he can "[…] do what is impossible in South Africa: to explore the depths. Without descending into the depths one cannot be an artist" (Coetzee 2003, p. 131). As David Attwell indicates, Coetzee "is turning to the metropolis of Western culture for a better life and further development" (Attwell 1993, p. 4). Europe is believed to be the proper location for him to become a fully-fledged artist. Apparently, Coetzee presents himself as a writer who, like many before him, seeks artistic destiny abroad. At that moment, however, Coetzee's narrator appears as if he was still standing at a crossroads. One could say that the legacy of his past, of his culture, keeps hunting him down. Nevertheless, the author stresses a process of getting closer to a certain stage of acceptance, wondering whether "[i]t is true that art comes only out of misery" and whether "[h]e must become miserable in order to write" (Coetzee 2003, p. 160). The answer to that question, at least in relation to John Maxwell Coetzee, appears to be positive. Nevertheless, his grief, from then on, will have a more global character, and therefore the source of suffering and concern will become the wider world and humanity itself.

Given the considerable level of ambiguity generated and persistently maintained by Coetzee, particularly in texts of a referential character, another question arises, namely to what degree their premise allows one to draw conclusions regarding the author's *intellectual standpoint*. The elucidation of my use of this phrase will be provided in subsequent paragraphs. However, at this juncture, it seems crucial to invoke Mark Sanders's view on South African "complicities", with a particular emphasis on the accountability of intellectuals in responding to political peril. To define the role assigned to artists, academics, philosophers etc., Sanders has recourse to views formulated by Karl Jasper, specifically regarding the question of German collective guilt. He accepts the following: "There exists a solidarity among men as human beings that makes each co-responsible for every wrong and every injustice in the world, especially [when] committed in his presence or with his knowledge" (quoted in Sanders 2002, p. 6). I contend that Coetzee must be considered among the authors and figures who have not shirked this duty, but instead have stepped out onto the global arena intending to alarm the public about potential threats to universally cherished humanist values. Therefore, when speaking of his outlook upon and understanding of the world and human affairs, it becomes of importance to broach the topic of both Coetzee's sense of moral integrity and also the dispersed reflection thereof within a mosaic of textual material. Should an initial assumption be validated, specifically that (non-)fiction writing predominantly unveils the author's voice, then in the subsequent analysis, the novelist's ethical stance, albeit scattered, can still be discerned.[9] In light of both literary and non-literary critiques, filtered through Coetzee's made-up characters, there is a hopeful expectation that the sincere voice and values of a conscientious writer will take center stage throughout the entire spectrum of an interdisciplinary framework, as encapsulated in the following subchapters.

The form

A common observation regarding Coetzee's philosophy of writing is his predilection for challenging ready-made generic conventions.[10] Such willfully obfuscatory choice regarding form are evident in his (auto)biographical works, in which the fictionalization of personal histories play a crucial role. The question is whether, as many believe, Coetzee does so since he enjoys blending different modes of expression, simply reiterating well-known paradigms of postmodern meta-fictionality. Attridge underlines that consigning Coetzee within "the tradition of postmodern playfulness", with the ultimate goal to "tease the reader with fictional truths" is insufficient (2004, p. 199). The mere (re)creation of intertextual fabric is by no means how Coetzee envisions his role as a writer and intellectual. If the opposite were true, then formalities would prevail over textual substance, rendering the latter rather insignificant. Arguably, a more likely alternative is that Coetzee's coherent thought governs *the form*, notwithstanding a tendency to camouflage and avoid direct authorial self-communication. As is the case with narrative structure in the works of Virginia Woolf, in most of the texts written by Coetzee one finds miscellaneous characters that echo the author's

---

9 My line of argumentation in this article is to highlight discernible ethical agency on Coetzee's part, and for – as maintained by Wolfgang Hallet – "[i]t is impossible to identify values or (un-)ethical conduct in narrative texts unless one has a system of values" (2008, p. 198).

10 This approach is particularly visible, according to Jonathan Jacobs (2014, p. 265), in such (non-)fiction narratives as *Boyhood*, *Youth* and *Summertime*, where "a generic cross-over" resides in the foreground.

principled standpoint. In *Summertime*,[11] one of the female characters, when interviewed about her reminiscences of John Maxwell Coetzee, says the following: "[w]hat I am telling you may not be true to the letter, but it is true to the spirit" (Coetzee 2010, p. 32). This one sentence sheds light on the writer's creed, which rejects expectations of one-to-one correspondence between presented (hi)stories and Coetzee's real life and opinions. Nevertheless, there should be no doubt that within selected narratives one discovers essential tenets of the artist's normative beliefs.

Thomas Larson, referring to "the world of life-writing" sees it as "dominated by the personal tale of a public figure" (2008, p. 11). We might ask what the core of a personal tale is, and how one tends to define a public figure. As to the latter, I would argue that this format pertains to anyone who is eager to make use of his/her recognized grandeur to spread thought-out opinions for the betterment of a given community/society (on a smaller scale) or of humanity (a stature reserved to the greatest). Coetzee definitively falls into the latter category of highly esteemed personages. And even though his presence in the public domain is not deliberately projected, much less forced, his impact on people's/reader's mindsets, in different parts of the world, cannot be underestimated. As mentioned before, a public figure comes up with *a personal tale*, which – according to Larson – oscillates between "self-justifying" and "moral experience" (2008, p. 11). The first case is not pertinent for our analysis, but the second, which foregrounds ethics, moral principles, the notion of human decency and human rights etc. might be considered of pivotal resonance in Coetzee's works.

Both texts in question, regardless of their unorthodox/cross-generic convention,[12] can be associated with the tradition of life-writing, one of the objectives of which is to instruct. Ben Yagoda's claim, formulated in relation to such narratives, is that their "didactic" character "requires a certification of documentary truth" (2009, p. 239). Coetzee, whose literary output is stamped by constant validations of metafictional self-referentiality,[13] does not meet the standards of ex-

---

11 In this conceptually fascinating book Coetzee has created a narrative in which one scholar, along with his interlocutors, try to pen a biography of one John Maxwell Coetzee, a novelist and Nobel Prize winner.
12 Max Saunders points out that such "destabili[zation] of genres" serves a more salutary than disadvantageous purpose. In his opinion, even "novels, poems, short stories, travel writings", not to mention traditional sub-genres of life-writing, "can be used as routes into cultural memory" (2008, p. 322).
13 In *Diary of a Bad Year* one comes across Coetzee's anti-realistic approach. His idea of a meaningful text is at odds with *nomen omen* creating a mimetic image of the real. Bluntly put, Coetzee conveys skepticism towards the kind of writing based upon the sole premise of copying the tangible. Hence the following conclusion: "[t]he truth is, I have never taken much pleasure in the visible world, don't feel with much conviction the urge to recreate it in words" (2008, p. 192).

pressive/semantic transparency. Notwithstanding the 'shortcomings' of Coetzee's life-stories, various studies indicate that the writer's implied diffidence towards conclusive signification cannot be regarded as tantamount to undermining the serious weight of a given text. On the contrary, the author's reserve derives from Coetzee's inculcated humbleness, and from a lack of arrogance which ought not to be confused with any lack of intellectual reflection. Attridge, for that matter, analyzing the reasons for constructing the figure of Elizabeth Costello, strongly emphasized that such a "device" was not employed to "generate self-referential ironies". In other words, the figure of a distinguished female novelist had little to do with auto-thematic dialogue with postmodern literariness but was brought to life "as a means towards a profound self-examination on the part of Coetzee" (Attridge 2004, p. 200). This is not just a mode of testing, aimed at the writer's self-inhibitions, but also an address to the recipients/readers to actively take responsibility for any thoughts/concerns/warnings/alarms on extremely pressing issues, to be provided and pondered over within a given narrative framework orchestrated by John Maxwell Coetzee.

Paradoxically, a confirmation of the above can be found in *Summertime*, wherein Coetzee's 'biographer' refers to "letters and diaries" left by the novelist. As one is instructed, "[w]hat Coetzee writes there cannot be trusted, not as a factual record – not because he was a liar but because he was a fictioneer" (Coetzee 2010, p. 225). Is it the case that the author of *Summertime* disclaims all responsibility for meaningful content? Should readers conclude that his intention is to deprive the authorial figure of any seriousness? Quite the opposite, the quotation permits a positive interpretation. First, of ultimate importance is the closing remark that "he [Coetzee] is not a liar"; hence, it would be a mistake to see deception as one of the objectives. Second, the fact that he should not be trusted might be read in view of a postmodern dictum, according to which the writer is *no god of creation*.[14] His/her voice does matter, yet there are individual recipients of the thoughts and ideas conveyed within the texts. And *the others* are also held accountable for fostering and embracing the truth. In that sense, Coetzee could be classified as yet another writer who, as underlined by Larson, "adopt[s] a mask to tell a story" (2008, p. 127). It might be the case that, as Larson states, such a camouflage serves to imply a critical/moral stance behind the

---

14 In passing, I recommend John Fowles' assertion, included in chapter XIII of *The French Lieutenant's Woman*, that in contemporary literature there is not much room for any resurgence of "Victorian authority", but that instead the precept of "freedom" is welcome. A short passage from *Diary of a Bad Year* serves as an affirmation of that intent. Speaking on authority, Coetzee ponders over the presence of "some higher force" in the process of creation. As he indicates, "[t]he god can be invoked, but not necessarily come", and for this reason a prospective author must face the responsibility of "learn[ing] to speak without authority, says Kierkegaard" (Coetzee 2008, p. 151).

characters depicted. A similar conclusion, regarding Coetzee's approach, does not seem erroneous. In Katarzyna Rosner's view, his narratives function as epistemological excursions into the realm of morals. According to Rosner, "modern philosophy" sympathizes with the whole concept of "narrative" [e.g., (auto)biographical], seen as a specific construct which enables a living subject to "express certain crucial intuitions more precisely" [own translation], albeit less straightforwardly (Rosner 2005, p. 7). Anyone involved in practicing the formula of life-writing deploys "a structure of signification" that "evolves through time" to be constantly (re)formulated. Interestingly, any author of such narrative sequences facilitates "projections" or "interpretations" of his/her life-stories (2005, p. 13). This understanding of narrative cognitive capacity allows one to look upon Coetzee's storytelling as being imbued with resonance of the inner moral core, which haphazardly reflects the individual or collective unrest of a rapidly changing world. What seems crucial in this regard is that any explicitly or implicitly articulated "intuitions" and sentiments remain subject to both writerly self-introspection and readerly interpretations.[15]

By adopting a chosen narrative trajectory, which aspirationally culminates in a more comprehensive insight into the self and the world, Coetzee has tried to detach himself from any lines of thought that are attributable to any format of a fixed national identity. This claim aligns with Zygmunt Bauman's philosophy, which asserts that any solidified/fossilized form of identity becomes more of a burden than an asset, as it restricts one's formative perspective. Furthermore, to seek stability in identity formation is detrimental in the modern world. As Bauman indicates, "'identities' exist today solely in the process of continuous renegotiation. [...] 'identity' [...] re-formation turns into a lifelong task, never complete; [and] at no point [...] 'final'" (2016, p. 26). Bauman's viewpoint parallels Stephen Clingman's perspective on "transnational" writing. A writer or his/her work becomes recognizable as such when they "travel across national boundaries". In addition, classification under this category occurs when the "form" eschews any specific contextualization and "becomes content – a way of being and seeing" (quoted in Jacobs 2014, p. 261). In other words, formal universality orbits around the universality of content. Consequently, it should come as no surprise when the author indirectly informs us – through one of the female friends' reminiscence – that she and Coetzee "felt" as "opposite [to being] *native*

---

15 To shed light on Coetzee's perception of his own status as a text's author, I would refer to *Diary of a Bad Year*, where he declares the significance of being self-effacing, giving a telling advice to those interested in writing – "[n]ever try to impose yourself" (Coetzee 2008, p. 55). Speaking of the weight ascribed to "interpretations", it seems legitimate to claim that Coetzee "call[s] for reading [but] without being reduced to *neat interpretations* [emphasis added]" (Geertsema 2014, p. 33). Otherwise, the inferred understandings would be "put to rest once and for all", which would block any further circulation of ethical concerns.

or *rooted*". In fact, they were depicted as "sojourners, temporary residents, and to that extent without a homeland" (Coetzee 2010, p. 210). The lack of any nostalgic evocations of the bygone/lost proves that moving on to engage with and confront the outside world – literally and metaphorically construed – is not a tangential but a pre-defined objective.[16] Exposure to the (un)familiar, away from the coziness of a confined locality, enables Coetzee to continue his pursuit of ethical integrity[17] by probing socio-cultural or political conditionings throughout the world.[18]

Inasmuch as he adheres to a willfully convoluted mode of self-expression, one thing becomes clear to Coetzee; namely, that such expression must be achieved without regard for insular generic boundaries. Through the porte-parole of yet another female colleague, we come across one of the author's strongly-held opinions on the approach to "life-stories". As she informs, "[he] believed [they] are ours to construct as we wish, within or even against the constraints imposed by the real world" (Coetzee 2010, p. 227). *Summertime*, a self-conscious biography, seems to go beyond minute details or parochial sensibilities so as to better foreground Coetzee's own intellectual standpoint relating to global/universal socio-political issues. As Peter Rubie underlines, "the subject of a biography should also be a symbol of some sort for the spirit of the age" (2018, loc. 428). Some might find it difficult to recognize John Maxwell Coetzee as a representative of the zeitgeist; on the other hand, he is like that subject who has sharply observed the anxieties of the surrounding reality. In this sense, despite his literary self-awareness, Coetzee's referential textuality (at least some portions of it) seems closer to what can be encountered in New Journalism than, for instance, in works of mimetic realism. Its goal, according to Rubie, is far from reaching the most objective account of what actually occurred, which is elided, for the main issue is to "seek a larger truth than is possible through the mere compilation of the facts" (Rubie after Gay Talese 2018, loc. 119). Should one consider such conclusions legitimate, then embracing Coetzee's formal unorthodoxy in (non-) fiction becomes a prerequisite for empowering the viewpoint of *the subject*.

---

16 The best exemplification of this can be found in *Youth*, in which we learn about his wish to "rise above mere nationality" (2003, p. 64).
17 At the outset of *Summertime*, in a story about John Coetzee, a man from the 1970s, one learns about two "features of his character". One of them is "naivete", the other one – of greater significance – is "integrity" (Coetzee 2010, p. 12).
18 To outline Coetzee's general approach to his own (ethical) writing, I propose considering Brigit Naumann's reflection on "the process of [...] value-making", observable in referential literature. As she claims, an ethical stance in literary works is not tantamount to "teaching any particular lessons". Rather, what comes to the fore is "the ability to question established notions of value and initiating processes of change" (2008, p. 135).

Many share a common belief[19] that referential textuality is of assistance in providing mirror images of the real. Nonetheless, as Krystyna Stamirowska points out, the distrust towards the transparency of language, as noticeable in contemporary writings, translates into the "distortions" reflected in that "mirror". Irrespective of such distortions, however, she underscores that not many of us would challenge the validity of opinions/thoughts on current affairs as conveyed in only seemingly inaccurate/biased (non-)fiction accounts (Stamirowska 2007, p. 19). Coetzee, despite being aware of no fixed linguistic or generic formats which guarantee the filling in of gaps or resolution of the ambiguities in signification entailed, nevertheless remains adamant in communicating via *extended textuality*.

The content

For the above reasons one argues that Coetzee's ethical seriousness surpasses the aforementioned postmodern turn. Indeed, not only is he a renowned [avant-garde] novelist but also an authentic modern thinker and representative of the liberal intelligentsia. To gain further insight into his overall position, let us consider how Jacobs and Geertsema perceive Coetzee's critical mindset. Jacobs refers to the path taken by Coetzee as "dialogic", suggesting his eagerness to "awaken the counter-voices" (Jacobs 2014, p. 263). In other words, embracing free expression implies a certain attentiveness to other arguments and claims. This brings us to Geertsema's perspective that while Coetzee may not specifically pursue an "open confrontation" – construed, for instance, in political terms (2014, p. 23), he remains committed to addressing *injustice* and *wrongfulness* through his writing. Essentially, Coetzee, guided by a diverse range of concerns, viewpoints, and ethical principles, sees it as his destiny and obligation to uphold the moral dignity of man.

Noam Chomsky's conceptualization of *the intellectual* can offer additional clarity and complement in defining the writer's profile. While it may appear permissible to connect Coetzee with Chomsky, this association is not without a

---

19 Since the whole article concentrates on a writer of South African descent, I tend to refer to two distinguished representatives of the local literary realm who, to a degree, acknowledged the potential of language in grasping the real. Nadine Gordimer, rather categorically, said that "[t]he writer has no reason to be if [...] reality remains outside language. An accurate and vital correspondence between what is and the perception of the writer is what [he/she] has to seek, finding the real meaning of words to express 'the states of things'" (2000, p. 12). Less clear perhaps is Brink's stance, yet he also confirms the potential of language in terms of referentiality. According to him, "our very perception of the 'real' depends on language; language imposes on us the need to perceive, interpellate and interpret the 'real' [...] in a way language can handle" (1998, p. 14).

degree of reservation. As widely recognized, the latter is often identified as an individual with strong leftist inclinations; as someone who shows no hesitations in promulgating his own political sympathies (contrary to Coetzee); and finally, as someone who criticizes/treats his opponents in a rather uncompromising way. Although some ideological features of Chomsky's thinking may not be inherently contradictory to Coetzee's reasoning, a clear commitment to these by the novelist could present a significant obstacle when attempting to identify and write about universal truths. That said, there is no denial that Chomsky presents an interesting definition of the truth-seeker, dividing them into those who orient themselves toward "values" and those who are mindful of "the country's policies".[20] He sets forth this binary opposition, in a sort of ironic way, to ridicule the establishment that likes to see one party (the "value-oriented intellectuals") as an actual threat "to democratic [sic!] government". Unlike the other group (the "policy-oriented intellectuals"), that is thinkers/academics/scholars/writers who are into "the constructive work of shaping policy", the former were to "devote themselves [irresponsibly] to the derogation of leadership, the challenging of authority" (Chomsky 2016, p. 7–8). Given the above, Coetzee would probably agree with Chomsky that a *bona fide* intellectual, in fact, serves no government, for any involvement in formulating politicized agendas[21] makes him/her less capable of advocating core human values. In opting for basic human rights, it is of vital importance to position himself/herself outside a field of political interests: that is, to adopt a stance whereby questioning authorities, contradicting earlier assertions or received wisdom becomes the *sine qua non* of any intellectual endeavor.

In *Diary of a Bad Year*[22] Coetzee created a fictional equivalent of himself who, in a conversation with his female assistant/secretary, gives his reasons for being one of the co-authors of *Strong Opinions*. Theirs is the ambitious goal to "pronounce on what is wrong with today's world" (Coetzee 2008, p. 21). In such a framework, Coetzee writes from the position of an intellectual who is value-

---

20 In the background there is Chomsky in this context is referencing to a debate started by Michael Crozier, Samuel P. Huntington, and Joji Watanuke, *The Crisis of Democracy: Report on the Governability of Democracies to the Trilateral Commission*.
21 By no means can one regard Coetzee as a political writer (in the narrow sense of this term). There is a very telling passage in *Summertime* that shows defiance of narrative politicization. It derives from Coetzee's skeptical approach to raw politics: "human beings will never abandon [it] because politics is too convenient and too attractive as a theater [...] which play[s] to our baser emotions. Baser emotions meaning hatred and rancor and spite and jealousy and bloodlust and so forth" (Coetzee 2010, p. 229).
22 In terms of form, one should recall that *Diary of a Bad Year* is the composite of a fictional narrative about Coetzee, who is about to publish [together with five other authors] a book titled *Strong Opinions*, and his actual diary concerning a miscellany of *opinions* on current affairs.

minded, liberal and democratic.[23] Not driven by any form of economic rivalry or Darwinian philosophy, not motivated by any narrowly conceptualized political agendas, Coetzee shows no intention of escaping – *truly* – from the real. On the contrary, being vigilant about reiterating ideological slogans, he comes up with his own understanding of artistic responsibility. In order to counteract against the world that is operating like "a gladiatorial amphitheater, [...] the eyes of the artist are not on the competition but on the true [and] the good" (Coetzee 2008, p. 119). Coetzee's moral reasoning is encapsulated in Amy Gutmann's comment on the 1997–98 Tanner Lectures. According to her, Coetzee is no doubt determined to speak up publicly, and more importantly, succeeds in presenting "the kind of seriousness that unite[s] aesthetics and ethics" (2001, p. 3).

John Maxwell Coetzee has ruffled some feathers by being *politically incorrect*, yet never has he depicted himself as a moralizer,[24] which in turn does not mean he has ever abstained from eliciting debates over individual or collective transgressions. True, this very idiosyncratic mode of self-expression leads people like Peter Singer to raise doubts whether the "distance" Coetzee constantly keeps towards his own textual voice does not obstruct pertinent "responses" to the presented line of argumentation (2001, p. 91). Yet, the craftily designed aloofness, as I indicated before, does not negate the author's standpoint, be it exposed for further consideration on the part of the reader. Coetzee's exploration of ethical tensions/dilemmas/issues is always there, treated with utmost importance. With this perspective in mind, it is also up to *others* to map out any of those thematic areas in which Coetzee's voice recurs persistently and in the most resonant way. An interesting outline of the author's argumentative principle may be derived from one of the fictional characters of *Diary of a Bad Year*. What we learn about Coetzee's writing reads as follows: "[h]e wants to see cruelty. He wants to see greed and exploitation. It is all a morality play to him, good versus evil. What he fails to see or refuses to see is that individuals are players in a structure that transcends individual motives [...]" (Coetzee 2008, p. 97). Given Coetzee's assessment, however, filtered through my own interpretation, what he seems to be arguing for is the opposite. The writer's angle, as inscribed between the lines, not

---

23 Of course, Coetzee's liberalism has nothing to do with its economic variant. As one reads, liberalism can be easily mistaken with certain mechanisms of "the market economy", with "the moment when economic philosophy turns into religious faith", when people are "reward[ed] more or less in proportion to their contribution". This version of liberalism comes down to competition, to the "dog-eat-dog individualism, its narrow conception of self-advancement, and its ethics of hard work" (Coetzee 2008, p. 117).
24 This description is aptly used by Krzysztof Kowalczyk-Twarowski, who points out that Coetzee "is speaking to us in 'the middle voice'", being always mindful of "ethical responsibility" (2014, p. 301).

only hints at the individual's rights[25] vs. individual culpability, but also at discernible systemic failures/institutional actions that pressingly require profound discussions.

Central to such debates [transcribing the term used by the author himself] is Coetzee's fundamental conviction that "[t]he world is a jungle" (Coetzee 2008, p. 79). Overall, people are either compelled (institutionally) to behave indecently or inadvertently give vent (on their own) to primordial lust/frustrations. Some of us, of course, might infer from these words a subtext highlighting the policy of unavoidable "competition", by which we see and affirm ourselves as part of the *natural* order whereby only the strongest do survive. Afterall, life is "a race, a contest" (Coetzee 2008, p. 79). Yet others, and among them is Coetzee, shall consider such an understanding/portrayal of the human existence to be purely atavistic and wrongly thematized, due to the lack of moral and spiritual dimensionality in analyzing actual as well as paradigmatic behaviors. What *living in a jungle* denotes relates to the havoc unleashed upon the world not only by nature but also by various politicized institutions and their representatives for whom moral standards have faded into oblivion. This is a world that resembles the one described by Giorgio Agamben.[26] In his understanding, only a grim light adequately renders contemporary reality, for the world of today is merely driven by "modern biopolitics". One of its "essential characteristics" boils down to the "constant need to redefine the threshold in life that distinguishes and separates what is inside from what is outside" (Agamben 2010, p. 131). In light of the above, certain corrupt ideological agendas often lead to positing the "disposability" of individual existence – assessing one's life as (in)significant, thus on the margins of recognition, where universal values are being dismantled in order to turn into the foundation of public conduct.[27]

---

25 In *Diary of a Bad Year* we encounter an invented opinion on Coetzee, who is perceived as a person that "put[s] himself forward as a lone voice of conscience speaking up for human rights [...]". Concurrently, the same character criticizes the author for not being "out in the real world, fighting for them" (Coetzee 2008, p. 197). This quote is, however, not to be taken as an accusation against Coetzee for having retreated into the shadows, thereby avoiding a direct confrontation with tangible reality. Rather, it is a sign of the author's unpretentiousness, an indication that he understands the substantiality of his beliefs, yet has reservations as to the reachability of his textual arguments.
26 For a more extensive analysis of Agamben's theory, and its application to post-apartheid writing, see Bartnik (2014).
27 Agamben illustrates the problem by referencing the refugee crisis. Recapitulating his words, so long as the victimized/dispossessed/underprivileged fall into the category of *a political life*, their status remains deprived of any human dimension. Instead of a humanitarian approach, different organizations/national states/other people tend to construe this issue in a strictly politicized way, seeing "refugees [...] not as individual cases but [...] as a mass phenomenon" (Agamben 2010, p. 133). Their individual lives, in other terms, become of political insignif-

With regards to Agamben's assertions, the pressing question is whether individuals, subjected to such conditioning, can retain their status of sovereign authority. Whenever a state's policy endorses the elementary role of fundamental freedoms and human rights, whenever it is based on universally shared moral principles, the individual and his/her sovereignty are adequately protected. However, within globally observed biopolitics, the concept of sovereignty has been turned upside down and become tantamount to wielding politicized power over the dispossessed. Quite often, with that power being institutionalized, one's rights and life are simply endangered. As Agamben claims, "sovereign is he who decides on the value or the nonvalue of life", which paradoxically "becomes the place of 'sovereign' decisions" (2010, p. 142). By and large, this is Coetzee's field of interest and expertise. It is of no surprise, given the fact that we are talking about someone who was born in apartheid-era South Africa and lived long enough there to internalize similar mechanisms of exclusion/dispossession. Though, as it was mentioned in *Youth*, his life as an artist was projected outside the native country, still its grim legacy could not be forgotten.[28] It is no coincidence that in the fictional section of *Diary of a Bad Year* the place of Coetzee's descent is invoked as a crucial point of reference. Familiar with dynamics of oppressive systems, he underlines how vulnerable a person/citizen is when the collective power shows no scruples about instrumentalizing individual lives. As a broad-minded person, however, Coetzee expresses reservations towards the unintended naivete of liberals like himself. On the very first page of his 'diary', he passes a critical reflection on Thomas Hobbes' agenda. According to the author, "vis-à-vis the state, we are, precisely powerless [...]. [A]s set down by Hobbes, our descent into powerlessness [is] voluntary: in order to escape the violence of internecine warfare [...], we yield up to the state the right to use physical force [...]". By such [in]actions, we are "entering the realm of the law" (Coetzee 2008, p. 3), ceding decision-making to the state and its representatives (concrete people) who start proceeding in accordance with the logic of modern biopolitics. Eventually, those who benefit from wielding power *do mind* morality but only through verbal proclamations of intent.

Interestingly enough, Coetzee is not framing a discussion over wrongful conduct just within authoritarian regimes. It is a democratic realm that is of interest, for its constitutional framework presupposes the unquestionable validity of general declarations regarding the rights of men. When any legitimate authorities begin to abuse the legitimization of power for non-democratic purposes, the society begins treading on a slippery slope. In such cases, only by

---

icance, are thusly irrelevant to us, liable to being parenthesized without any pangs of conscience.
28 A fascinating intertext regarding the Coleridge's albatross hanging on the writer's neck.

"shame" can a given governmental or national agenda be defined. As Coetzee rightly notices, infamy dwells whenever "an administration [...], legal in the sense of being legally elected, is illegal or anti-legal in the sense of operating beyond the bounds of the law, evading the law" (Coetzee 2008, p. 39). By circumventing axiological premises,[29] the law becomes an instrument to implement coercive measures/force against *the other*. This "contempt" for legal standards, according to Coetzee, is observable in the United States or Australia. In both cases, the justifications to act harshly comes from various public figures, mostly politicians, who voice "the mantra [that] extraordinary times, [...] demand extraordinary measures". This is the moment when one feels obliged to sound the alarm bells because "people simply vanish or are vanished from society, and publicizing their disappearances qualifies as a crime in its own right" (Coetzee 2008, p. 43). These are signs attesting the detrimental effects, brought about by turning away from basic values. By opening up that void, the individual life, to use Agamben's terminology, becomes categorized as politically [ir]relevant. Apparently, much of the blame is institutional in character, yet the human factor, in this respect, cannot be ignored. A very telling illustration of the above is found in Coetzee's diary. Speaking of human capabilities, he draws a parallel between musical compositions and detention centers:

> A few years ago I heard a performance of the Sibelius fifth symphony. As the closing bars approached, I experienced exactly the large, swelling emotion that the music was written to elicit. What would it have been like, I wondered, to be a Finn in the audience at the first performance of the symphony in Helsinki nearly a century ago, and feel that swell overtake one? The answer: one would have felt proud, proud that *one of us* could put together such sounds, proud that out of nothing we human beings can make such stuff. Contrast with that one's feelings of shame that *we, our people*, have made Guantanamo. Musical creation on the one hand, a machine for inflicting pain and humiliation on the other: the best and the worst that human beings are capable of. (Coetzee 2008, p. 45)

In seeking correlations between collective and individual *sinfulness*, he seems to draw a similar conclusion to that presented by William Golding. The latter, in his essay "Fable" expressed an increasing disillusionment with humankind. In the aftermath of the WWII conflagration, Golding outlined bluntly the wrongfulness of human nature. According to him, war atrocities could materialize because "men were putting the cart before the horse. They were looking at the system rather than the people". Though in different words, Golding also recognized that

---

[29] In legal systems derived from the tradition of Roman Law, which is to say in all countries associated with/belonging to Western civilization, the question of human dignity/human rights is tightly woven into moral, axiological criteria that constitute "the rule of law" (Smolak 2011, p. 73).

behind such actions was a similar process of politicized dehumanization, for any form of mistreatment of other men and women "was being hidden behind a kind of pair of political pants". In that sense, "the condition of man was to be a morally diseased creation" (Golding 1965, p. 87); yet such decisions and the ensuing actions did (and still do) take place thanks to *convenient* systemic disorders. In today's world, in democratic societies, people can define certain undertakings as "inappropriate"; concurrently, they seem inert in "expressing a moral judgment" (Coetzee 2008, p. 143). It is so, for a genuine moral outrage would require proper responses. Unfortunately, various forms of politicized desensitization, as present in the surrounding reality we are creating, make man and even more fallen being. The results, as Coetzee highlights, are observable for instance in Australia, which so far has been regarded as a country rather immune to "setting [the] limits beyond which [one's] life" is of lesser value (Agamben 2010, p. 139). Nevertheless, even there a "system of [...] processing refugees" was created. It is "a system of deterrence, and indeed a spectacle of deterrence, [which] says: *This is the purgatory to which you will be subjected if you arrive in Australia without papers. Think again.* In this respect, [the] Center out in the South Australia desert is not dissimilar to Guantanamo Bay" (Coetzee 2008, p. 112).

Coetzee happens to be criticized for drawing excessive parallels, which are beyond what is generally acceptable. And of course, it is legitimate to ponder whether he has made an apt analogy juxtaposing, for instance, the Nazi *konzentrationslager* with slaughterhouses. Still, no matter how *blasphemous* such a comparison sounds, he seems to be striking the right note. There is no denial that *we* put the blindfold on to repress various acts of human indecency, most often carried out or executed on our behalf. Therefore, as underlined by Coetzee/Costello, the question that should be constantly posed is not whether "we have anything in common [...] with other animals"; whether the nature of death, suffering and violence is explicable by comparison to the sad fate of animals becoming fodder to another species. Rather, it is crucial to learn and internalize what happens after the demarcation line has been drawn, and *we* are ready to define *others* in terms of their relevancy [see Agamben]. Like towards *our* non-human brothers, by endorsing modern biopolitics, we feel "entitled to treat (the non-valuable) as we like, imprisoning them, killing them, dishonoring their corpses" (Coetzee 2001, p. 34). In the end, there is just the logic of disposability, and the human factor, thus compassion or sympathy for *the other*, is subdued. That was the reality of the camps, where *people* attributed themselves a privilege to do whatever they considered appropriate with *others*. Indeed, in that regard, Coetzee resembles all writers[30] who especially in times of crisis desire to underline the value of a single human life and the inherent dignity of every person.

---

30 As a Polish scholar, I would like to make a short digression on how often some WWII

On reading his *Diary of a Bad Year*, I conclude that the author sees the world as marked by moral disintegration, as standing on a precipice. Coetzee perfectly understands that on him – that is, on people of a certain intellectual status – lies the onus to take a swipe at the hypocritical silence, conformity and political violence which are more and more frequently becoming practice in Western democracies. For this very reason he goes back to the times of apartheid to highlight how certain mechanisms of oppression and belligerence, typical of authoritarian regimes, have become part and parcel of democratic governance. Wanting to maintain the clarity of Coetzee's argumentation, I present the quote at length:

> [...] my novel *Waiting for the Barbarians* 'emerged from the South Africa of the 1970s, where the security police could come in and out and [...] blindfold and handcuff you without explaining why, and take you away to an unspecified site and do what they wanted to you'. The police [...] 'could do what they wanted because there was no real recourse against them because special provisions of the legislation indemnified them in advance'. [...] 'All of this and much more, in apartheid South Africa, was done in the name of a struggle against terror. I used to think that the people who created these laws [...] were moral barbarians. Now I know they were just pioneers, ahead of their time'. (Coetzee 2008, p. 171)

This is the voice of someone who is deeply concerned about democratic procedures by means of which those in power uncompromisingly claim authority over basic human rights. Ethics, through this disposition, retreats into the shadows. The best way to illustrate a similar scenario is by discussing misfortunes of "[t]oday's refugees [who] find themselves in much the same boat as yesterday's transported. Someone, or more likely some committee, concocted a system of "processing" them. That system was approved and adopted, and now it is implemented impersonally [...], even if it dictates that people must be locked up in cells in camps" (Coetzee 2008, p. 113).

As for the final remark, I would like to reiterate that Coetzee is a writer who willingly disperses opinions by creating a mosaic across narratives. Some of those views, he explains in *Diary of a Bad Year*, are like "*Meinungen* – subject to fluctuations of mood"; but the other, which are "firmer" and "thought out", he terms as "*Ansichten*" (Coetzee 2008, p. 127 ff). Especially the latter, due to their

---

repatriates (from Poland to Siberia), when writing their diaries were transfixed upon the notion of human dignity and human benignity. As indicated by Małgorzata Stopikowska, theirs was a conviction that "[m]an must be recognized as the ultimate good, abiding everyone to affirm his/her subjectivity, dignity and (inalienable) rights". What is more, that one is a human being becomes the privileging "norm" and a point of reference for "evaluating [...] socio-economic systems as well as interpersonal relations". Hence, any actions taken "against humans" should be regarded as "unacceptable and wicked" [own translation] (Stopikowska 2006, p. 101).

moral weight, are traceable by delving deeply into Coetzee's narrative puzzle. This dispersal leaves room for meaningful participation on the reader's part; on the other hand, that disposition places the author – paradoxically – in the center of his own narrative at large. The essence of the seemingly disorganized narrative atomization has been captured by Grażyna Teusz, in an article about teleological writing. About various types of life-narratives, she singles out the subjects trying to find correlations between "haphazard sequences and fragmentary events" [own translation] that unfold on the scene of local or global mayhem. The idea is to construct a "personal understanding of the world" in order to find steadiness across variables (Teusz 2006, p. 406). Coetzee's outlook upon reality, following what has been analyzed so far, implies that the observable disorder, notwithstanding its chronic character, displays some traits of intensification over last decades. The objective, then, kept in view by Coetzee's narrative voice, is not to underestimate the magnitude of its ramifications. Art, instead of being playful, must solemnly attempt at restoring a sense of integrity and rectitude:

> In public life the role I play nowadays is that of distinguished figure [...] the kind of notable who is taken out of storage and dusted off to say a few words at a cultural event (the opening of a new hall in the art gallery; the prize-giving at an eisteddfod) and then put back in the cupboard. [...] The truth is, I was never a bohemian [...] At heart I have always been a sobrietarian, if such a word exists, and moreover a believer in order. (Coetzee 2008, p. 191)

Sadly, regardless of his sound diagnosis concerning various maladies of the world and humankind, Coetzee remains "skeptical about change" (Coetzee 2008, p. 203). Reminiscent of T.S. Eliot's punch line, he finds little or no antidote to his own pessimism concerning people's correctability or ability to respond to the warning sirens.

To recapitulate, this article intended to focus mainly on two texts, namely *Summertime* and *Diary of a Bad Year*, with the goal of highlighting Coetzee's intellectual and moral integrity, craftily blended into a (post-national) narrative mosaic. In both cases – though to a larger extent in the fictionalized biography of the author – readers are reminded to be wary of revering Coetzee for omniscience and omnipotence. His life-narratives are imbued with a considerable amount of fictionality, where authorial *truthfulness* remains subject to interpretation. Nevertheless, in between the lines Coetzee communicates not a set of seemingly miscellaneous/disconnected opinions but rather a thought-out ethical inquiry. From his perspective, the world might not be under the rule of warfare, yet – rephrasing W. B. Yeats – a form of anarchy is looming on the horizon. The observable policies of "democratic states" result in collateral casualties as well as in making people/citizens desensitized to individual suffering. In this world, it is the politicization of life that prevails. In consequence, along with the instrumentalization of law there is no room for nuancing reality ("down with the liberals" – one reads in *Diary of a Bad Year*). What we are left with are places like Guantanamo or other detention centers, which begin to resemble the former "camps" where some exercised arbitrary power over *others*. Coetzee, as a genuine intellectual and man of ethics, feels obliged to voice his concerns; concurrently, he shows no intention to position himself as a moralist. Instead, readers do have a chance to see a modest author, whose only aspiration is to be a whistleblower.

Bibliography

Agamben, Giorgio: *Homo Sacer. Sovereign Power and Bare Life*. Stanford 2010.
Attridge, Derek: *J. M. Coetzee and the Ethics of Reading*. Chicago and London 2004.
Attwell, David: *J. M. Coetzee. South Africa and the Politics of Writing*. Berkley and Los Angeles and Oxford 1993.
Bartnik, Ryszard: 'On South African Violence through Giorgio Agamben's Biopolitical Framework: A Comparative Study of J. M. Coetzee's *Disgrace* and Z. Mda's *Ways of Dying*', in: STUDIA ANGLICA POSNANIENSIA 2014/49, p. 21–36.
Bartnik, Ryszard: *Inscribed into the Past. A Comparative Study of South African and Northern Irish Literary Narratives after the Political Watersheds of the 1990s*. Poznań 2017.
Berger, Stefan: 'A Return to the National Paradigm? National History Writing in Germany, Italy, France, and Britain from 1945 to the Present', in: THE JOURNAL OF MODERN HISTORY 2005/77, p. 629–678.
Brink, André: *The Novel. Language and Narrative from Cervantes to Calvino*. New York 1998.
Calhoun, Craig: *Nacjonalizm*. Warszawa 2007.
Chesney, Duncan: 'Late Coetzee Revisited', in: INTERNATIONAL JOURNAL OF ENGLISH STUDIES 2022/22(2), p. 73–89.
Chomsky, Noam: *Who Rules the World?* London 2016.
Clarke, John: 'Which Nation Is This? Brexit and the Not-so-United Kingdom', in: Çörüt, Ilker / Jongerden, Joost (eds.) *Beyond Nationalism and the Nation-state. Radical Approaches to Nation*. London and New York 2021, p. 98–116.
Coetzee, John Maxwell: *Giving Offense. Essays on Censorship*. Chicago and London 1996.
Coetzee, John Maxwell: *The Lives of Animals*. Princeton 2001.
Coetzee, John Maxwell: *Stranger Shores. Essays 1986–1999*. London 2002.
Coetzee, John Maxwell *Youth*. London 2003.
Coetzee, John Maxwell: *Diary of a Bad Year*. London 2008.
Coetzee, John Maxwell: *Summertime*. London 2010.
Çörüt, Gözde Yazici: '*Narod* as a Radical Political Invention: The Outset of Intellectual Struggles over the Nation in Nineteenth Century Russia', in: Çörüt, Ilker / Jongerden, Joost (eds.) *Beyond Nationalism and the Nation-state. Radical Approaches to Nation*. London and New York 2021, p. 117–136.

Cörüt, Ilker / Jongerden, Joost (eds.): *Beyond Nationalism and the Nation-state. Radical Approaches to Nation.* New York and London 2021.
Dajczak, Wojciech / Szwarc, Andrzej / Wiliński, Paweł (eds): *Handbook of Polish Law.* Warszawa and Bielsko-Biała 2011.
Erll, Astrid / Grabes, Herbert / Nünning, Ansgar (eds.): *Ethics in Culture. The Dissemination of Values through Literature and Other Media.* Berlin and New York 2008.
Erll, Astrid / Nünning, Ansgar (eds.): *Cultural Memory Studies.* Berlin and New York 2008.
Fukuyama, Francis: *Identity. Contemporary Identity Politics and the Struggle for Recognition.* London 2019.
Geertsema, Johan: 'Hidden Literality: Coetzee, Beckett, Herbert, and the Attempt to 'Touch Reality'', in: Kucała, Bożena / Kusek, Robert (eds.): *Travelling Texts: J. M. Coetzee and Other Writers.* Frankfurt am Main 2014, p. 21-34.
Golding, William: *The Hot Gates and Other Occasional Pieces.* New York 1965.
Gordimer, Nadine: *Living in Hope and History.* London 2000.
Gutmann, Amy (ed.): *The Lives of Animals.* Princeton 2001.
Gutmann, Amy: 'Introduction', in: Gutmann, Amy (ed.): *The Lives of Animals.* Princeton 2001, p. 3-14.
Hallet, Wolfgang: 'Can Literary Figures Serve as Ethical Models?', in: Erll, Astrid / Grabes, Herbert / Nünning, Ansgar (eds.): *Ethics in Culture. The Dissemination of Values through Literature and Other Media.* Berlin and New York 2008, p. 195-215.
Jacobs, Jonathan: 'Writing from a Middle World: Perspectives on, and from, South Africa', in: Kucała, Bożena / Kusek, Robert (eds.): *Travelling Texts: J. M. Coetzee and Other Writers.* Frankfurt am Main 2014, p. 251-270.
Koczanowicz, Leszek / Nahirny, Rafał / Włodarczyk, Rafał (eds): *Narracje. (Auto)biografia, etyka* [*Narratives. (Auto)biography, ethics*]. Wrocław 2006.
Kowalczyk-Twarowski, Krzysztof: 'The Middle Voice: Positionality and Agency in J. M. Coetzee's Work', in: Kucała, Bożena / Kusek, Robert (eds.): *Travelling Texts: J. M. Coetzee and Other Writers.* Frankfurt am Main 2014, p. 295-318.
Kucała, Bożena / Kusek, Robert (eds): *Travelling Texts: J. M. Coetzee and Other Writers.* Frankfurt am Main 2014.
Marais, Michael: 'Little Enough, Less than Little: Nothing', in: MODERN FICTION STUDIES 2000/46(1), p. 159-182.
Neumann, Brigit: 'What Make Literature Valuable. Fictions of Meta-memory and Ethics of Remembering', in: Erll, Astrid / Grabes, Herbert / Nünning, Ansgar (eds.): *Ethics in Culture. The Dissemination of Values through Literature and Other Media.* Berlin and New York 2008, p. 131-152.
Rubie, Peter: *The Elements of Narrative Nonfiction. How to Write and Sell the Novel of True Events.* Kindle edition 2018.
Sanders, Mark: *Complicities. The Intellectual and Apartheid.* Durham and London 2002.
Saunders, Max: 'Life-writing, Cultural Memory, and Literary Studies', in: Erll, Astrid / Nünning, Ansgar (eds.): *Cultural Memory Studies.* Berlin and New York 2008, p. 321-331.
Scheingold, Stuart: *The Political Novel. Re-imagining the Twentieth Century.* New York 2010.
Sévry, Jean: 'Coetzee the Writer and the Writer of an Autobiography', in: COMMONWEALTH, ESSAYS AND STUDIES 2000/22(2), p. 13-24.

Singer, Peter: 'Reflections', in: Gutmann, Amy (ed.): *The Lives of Animals*. Princeton 2001, p. 85–94.

Smolak, Marek: 'Contemporary Polish Theory and Philosophy of Law', in: Dajczak, Wojciech / Szwarc, Andrzej / Wiliński, Paweł (eds): *Handbook of Polish Law*. Warszawa and Bielsko-Biała 2011, p. 59–82.

Stamirowska, Krystyna (ed.): *Historia, fikcja, (auto)biografia w powieści brytyjskiej XX wieku* [*History, Fiction, (Auto)biography in 20th-century British Novel*]. Kraków 2006.

Stamirowska, Krystyna: 'Preface', in: Stamirowska, Krystyna (ed.): *Historia, fikcja, (auto)biografia w powieści brytyjskiej XX wieku* [*History, Fiction, (Auto)biography in 20th-century British Novel*]. Kraków 2006, p. 7–20.

Stefanova, Svetlana: 'Cultivating Anti-oppressive Ethics: A Community-grounded Reading of Caryl Phillips and J.M. Coetzee', in: PAPERS ON LANGUAGE AND LITERATURE 2020 56(1), p. 60–82.

Stopikowska, Małgorzata: 'Dobro jako podstawowa kategoria interpretacyjna własnej biografii' ['The Good as a Basic Category of Interpretation for one's own Biography'], in: Koczanowicz, Leszek / Nahirny, Rafał / Włodarczyk, Rafał (eds): *Narracje. (Auto)biografia, etyka* [*Narratives. (Auto)biography, Ethics*]. Wrocław 2006, p. 99–114.

Teimouri, Mahdi: 'Nationhood and Justice in J.M. Coetzee's *Disgrace*', in: FORUM FOR WORLD LITERATURE STUDIES 2019/11(2), p. 345–362.

Bio Notes

Michael McAteer is Associate Professor (habil.) of English at the Institute of English and American Studies, Pázmány Péter Catholic University, Budapest. He has published extensively in the field of Irish Literary Studies. His most recent book is *Excess in Modern Irish Writing* (London: 2020) and his most recent edited volume is the *Ireland and Central/Eastern Europe* special issue of the journal, *Act Universitatis Sapientiae, Philologica* (2020). He is currently editing the Special Collection, *Local and Universal in Irish Literature and Culture*, for the *Open Library of Humanities* journal.

Paweł Meus is Assistant Professor in Humanities in the Institute of Literary Studies at the University of Silesia. He defended the dissertation *Between Silesia and Berlin. The narrative shaping of the world in Alfred Hein's work* in 2020. The area of his research includes German literature of Silesia, literary depictions of the First World War, as well as modern spatial and narrative theories.

Leszek Drong is Professor of Humanities in the Institute of Literary Studies at the University of Silesia. He is also Associate Dean for Research in the Faculty of Humanities as well as Vice-President of the Polish Association for Irish Studies. His most recent book was published in 2019: *Tropy konfliktu. Retoryka pamięci kulturowej we współczesnej powieści północnoirlandzkiej* [*Troping the Troubles: The Rhetoric of Cultural Memory in Recent Novels from Northern Ireland*]. His primary research interest is in the intersection of Irish studies, cultural memory studies and border studies. His current project explores parallels between regional and/or borderland cultures exemplified by writings from Northern Ireland and Upper Silesia.

Richard Jorge received his BA in English Studies at the University of the Basque Country (UPV/EHU) and later on proceeded to enhance his knowledge in the field of literature with an MA in Anglo-Irish Literature and Drama at University College Dublin, where his minor thesis on the relation of Joseph Sheridan Le

Fanu and the Gothic tradition was supervised by Declan Kiberd. He completed his PhD at the University of Santiago de Compostela researching the relationship between the short story and the Irish Gothic tradition in the writings of James Clarence Mangan, Joseph Sheridan Le Fanu and Bram Stoker. He is Junior Lecturer at the Department of Philology in the University of Cantabria.

Frank Ferguson is Research Director for English Language and Literature at Ulster University, Coleraine, Northern Ireland. He has managed a number Ulster-Scots and Irish literary projects. A researcher with over twenty-years' experience, he has authored many articles and was editor of the *Ulster-Scots Writing an Anthology*, and co-editor and contributor to *Revising Robert Burns and Ulster: Literature, Religion and Politics c. 1770–1920* (Four Courts Press). He is a Board member of the John Hewitt Society and a member of the Board of Governors of the Linen Hall Library Belfast.

Michaela Marková works as an Assistant Professor at the Department of English, Technical University of Liberec, Czechia. Her PhD research which she carried out at Trinity College, Dublin, dealt with narratives of difference in contemporary post-ceasefire Northern Irish fiction. This remains one of her main research interests, together with narratology, trauma studies, and children's/YA literature. Dr. Marková has co-edited several volumes on Irish writing, and is currently working on a monograph on o/Othering in NI writing for young readers.

Thierry Robin is a professor of anglophone studies at the University of Orléans. In addition to his work on media and translation studies, his research focuses on contemporary Irish studies and the connections between ideology, epistemology and the concept of reality, notably through the genres of satire and crime fiction. He has written numerous articles about Irish writers including Flann O'Brien, Samuel Beckett, Anne Enright, Dermot Healy and John Banville, amongst others. He has also published a book devoted to the study of Flann O'Brien's novels, entitled *Flann O'Brien, Un voyageur au bout du langage* (PUR, 2008) and coedited a collection of essays bearing on political ideology, *Political Ideology in Ireland from the Enlightenment to the Present*, (CSP, 2009). He is currently completing a monograph on Irish crime fiction, which should be published by Rennes University Press (PUR) in early 2024.

Liliana Sikorska – Head, Department of English and Irish Literature and Literary Linguistics, Faculty of English, Adam Mickiewicz University, Poznań. President, International Association of University Professors of English 2016–2019, President of the Poznań Chapter of the Agder Academy (2021–). Academic interests comprise medievalism and orientalism, Irish and English literature and culture.

Her publications include: *Ironies of Art/Tragedies of Life: Essays on Irish Literature* (ed. 2005), *A Universe of (hi)stories: Essays on J.M. Coetzee* (ed. 2006). She has also authored *An Short History of English Literature* (fourth edition 2011). She is the general editor of *An Outline History of English Literature in Texts.* Vol I–III (2007) and general editor of *An Outline History of Irish Literature in Texts* (2011). Her most recent publication is *Other Encounters: Reading the Medieval Orient in the Nineteenth and Twentieth Century Narratives* (2021).

Ryszard Bartnik is a tenured professor at Adam Mickiewicz University in Poznań [Department of English and Irish Literature and Literary Linguistics]. As an educator and scholar, he possesses expertise in contemporary British/English/Northern Irish fiction, with a focus on the interplay between novelistic writing and socio-political narratives. His research interests center around the exploration of themes such as trauma, memory, violence, reconciliation, divided societies, and fundamentalist thought/ideology within literary works. His very recent book, published in 2017, was devoted to post-apartheid South African and post-Troubles Northern Irish literary narratives, and the ways their authors tried to discuss/heal the wounds of the past. Currently, his scholarly interests have shifted slightly to analyze how literary (non-)fiction and socio-political discourse in the Isles grapple with the question of Brexit. This redirection of focus has drawn his attention again to the persistent divisions concealed behind Northern Ireland's 'peace walls'. Furthermore, an additional facet of his research involves exploring how literature engages with the subject of human rights.